Praise for *Labyrinth*

"Tony combines a deep wisdom of labyrinths and his personal experience to offer an opportunity to the reader to explore the labyrinth of their own sacred being. I love the mix of practice and theory. A truly enjoyable read."

—Abby Wynne, author of *How to Be Well*
and *AZ Spiritual Colouring Affirmations*

"This book is a confident statement of the limitless possibilities of the labyrinth on all levels of existence, material and immaterial. What Aquinas' *Summa Theologica* was to scholastics in the Middle Ages, this book will be to the modern labyrinth movement, a masterly encyclopedia of concepts and possibilities accompanied by detailed examples and instructions."

—Robert Ferré, master labyrinth builder
and author of *The Labyrinth Revival*

"This book by Tony Christie covers the entire spectrum of time—back to the big bang and into the future. If you are to read only one book on labyrinths this year, this is the one to read."

—Sig Longren, author of *Labyrinths: Ancient Myths and Modern Uses*

"This is an important book for anyone interested in working with labyrinths or who wishes to try to gain some understanding of the immense power of them. There are many books that give us the history of labyrinths, how to draw them, and how to walk them, but in this book, Tony Christie takes us deeper into the labyrinth and, in turn, offers us a way of moving deeper into our own selves."

—Yvonne Ryves, author of *Shaman Pathways: Web of Life*,
shamanic healer, Reiki master, and past life therapist

D1438453

"The often-powerful experience of walking the labyrinth is stirring the consciousness of people around the planet. It orders chaos, quiets the outer noise of civilization, and, as Tony Christie captures in this book, labyrinths have been the focus of esoteric knowledge and fascination for centuries. Well researched and written with a steady hand and heart, *Labyrinth* offers Tony Christie's unique understanding of this amazing tool."

—Lauren Artress, author of *Walking a Sacred Path: Rediscovering the Labyrinth as a Spiritual Practice*

LABYRINTH

About the Author

Tony Christie has been working with the labyrinth for over thirteen years. He is a labyrinth author, designer, artist, consultant, and workshop facilitator. Tony teaches about the labyrinth as a symbol of oneness, as a symbol of the interconnectedness of all of existence, and as a symbol of you. He also uses the labyrinth as a safe space to explore your journey in life. In 2005 Tony founded "Labyrinth Ireland" (see www.labyrinthireland.com) to raise awareness and use of the labyrinth as a tool for personal and spiritual growth. In 2012 Tony published his Labyrinth Wisdom Cards. Tony is an inspirational speaker and international presenter of labyrinth workshops. He is also an Advanced Veriditas certified labyrinth facilitator, a qualified reflexologist, and a Reiki Master. He developed Melchizedek Labyrinth Healing—a new healing modality based on the labyrinth that rebalances your energy centres and energy field and supports you to fulfil your life's purpose.

To contact Tony, or to learn more about his work, please visit his websites www.tonymchristie.com.

LABYRINTH

Your Path to Self Discovery

TONY CHRISTIE

Llewellyn Publications
Woodbury, Minnesota

FIRST EDITION
First Printing, 2018

Cover design by Shira Atakpu
Editing by Brian R. Erdrich
Interior art by the Llewellyn Art Department

Llewellyn Publications is a registered trademark of Llewellyn Worldwide Ltd.

Library of Congress Cataloging-in-Publication Data (Pending)
ISBN: 978-0-7387-5661-5

Llewellyn Publications
A Division of Llewellyn Worldwide Ltd.
2143 Wooddale Drive
Woodbury, MN 55125-2989
www.llewellyn.com

Printed in the United States of America

This book is dedicated to my wife, Fionnuala, whose presence in my life has been a source of love, support, and happiness. Without her encouragement, input, and overall presence, this book would not have been realised.

Contents

Foreword

I have waited for this book for a very long time.

It has been twenty-two years since I first discovered the labyrinth in Chartres Cathedral. Like many pilgrims, I was excited to visit the UNESCO World Heritage Site and take in the famous "Chartres Bleu" stained glass windows and flamboyant Gothic architecture. I was not disappointed. From the moment I entered the Western Portal in Chartres Cathedral, I was changed. Yet it was not the stupendous stonework and stunning glass that created this deep, cellular disturbance in my being. It was, instead, an enigmatic pattern that inlaid the floor of the nave—a sinuous labyrinth which stretched nearly forty-three feet in diameter across the cathedral.

I was unprepared for the Chartres labyrinth. It was not mentioned as a feature in the guidebooks that originally inspired my journey. This raised a series of questions for me that have driven my personal quest for over two decades: What is this magical form called a labyrinth and what are its origins? Why did the Gothic architects expend such time, care, and resources to create it? What is it used for and why isn't more known about it? How can we work with it in the modern world?

Over the years of my own labyrinthine journey, I have read just about every book on the labyrinth I can get my hands on. I have usually been unfulfilled by the offerings that are available. Of course, there are perfectly lovely labyrinth books out there. There are beautiful books about how to pray in the labyrinth and cerebral books that tell us what to think about them and even how to build them. Each of these efforts is worthy of its place in my library, but none of them satisfied the real desire of my heart: a more complete book about the labyrinth, which combined what we know, what we feel, and how we can experience this uniquely powerful tool in our lives.

When I first learned that Tony Christie was writing, I was thrilled. I knew I was finally closer to holding a book in my hands that would satisfy all of my labyrinth cravings.

I have known Tony personally now for a good few years and am proud to call him my dear friend and brother on the greater spiritual path. His wisdom is matched by his charm and his compassion, and he is the rare teacher who can slip back and forth to both sides of his brain: Tony can rattle off the appropriate measurements and geometric facts about labyrinths at the same time that he can give you advice on how to work through your more challenging personal issues in meditation and prayer. Tony Christie is a walking encyclopedia on not only the labyrinth, but on many and varied aspects of spiritual teachings and practices the world over. The fact that he was going to share some of that wisdom with the world was cause for celebration.

I first met Tony when he traveled from Ireland to Los Angeles to meet with me after I built my first labyrinth. He measured it both in terms of geometry and energy, and it was in that meeting when I first glimpsed his brilliance. I also understood that I was standing in the presence of real commitment. Tony "walks the talk"—he travels all over the world to both learn and teach and really lives this journey every day in a way that is both rare and inspiring.

I was honored to be one of the first to view Tony's completed manuscript, and I am thrilled by the finished product. Here, finally, was the book I have been waiting for these twenty-two years: a thorough, inspiring, entertaining volume on the magic that is the labyrinth, written by a master.

Solvitur ambulando!

Kathleen McGowan

Los Angeles, California

Acknowledgements

There are many people without whom this book would not have been written or appeared as it does now. First and foremost, my parents, Breeda and Peter Christie, for bringing me into this world. To my children—Cara, Eoghan, Cillian, and Aoibhinn—for their support and encouragement; and also to Fionnuala's children—Linda, Lisa, Rob, and Jack—and her granddaughter, Ella.

Thanks to everyone who has helped me along my labyrinth path of life, and in particular to those wonderful labyrinth friends who read and provided feedback on what I had written: Sig Lonegren, Lauren Artress, and Robert Ferré. Thanks to my friends Don Hogan and Ruadhan Hogan for their willingness to read the first draft of the manuscript.

Thanks to Andrew Smith for his astrological insights and feedback on the star section, and to Benebel Wen for her appraisal of the tarot section.

Thanks to Ozark Mountain Publishing for permission to use the extract from the Dolores Cannon book and to Robert Ferré for permission to use his Chartres labyrinth graphic.

A special thanks to my editors at Llewellyn, Amy Glaser and Brian Erdrich, whose enthusiasm, insights, and editing have brought this book to a more complete and accessible work.

A sincere thanks to Kathleen McGowan for kindly agreeing to write the foreword of this book.

Finally, thanks to my friends and followers whose enthusiasm for what I am doing with the labyrinth is a major driving force in getting this book to the world.

Go raibh míle maith agaibh go léir. (Thank you all very much.)

Introduction

In life you experience a series of doorways, gateways, and openings to love, light, and wisdom that, if taken, will bring you to a higher state of existence.

You are at a gate, a doorway, an entrance, an opening. Perhaps like me you got here via a circuitous route—the labyrinth of life. Rather than looking back to see how you got here, pausing briefly to consider where you are can bring you to realise that you are at the doorway to your future, the entrance to the integration of your inner and outer worlds, a gateway to self-discovery and to fulfilling your life's purpose.

The labyrinth has played a huge role in my life. This ancient symbol has been a source of wonder, wisdom, healing, fun, and enlightenment for me. Through the labyrinth, I have met some wonderful people and have had amazing experiences. In my work with the labyrinth, I have experienced a gradual and growing energy of transformation that is bringing me increased wisdom and understanding of my place in existence, as well as prompting me to share this with you and others.

I first became interested in the labyrinth in 2005. Since then I have designed and built labyrinths all over the world. I have given talks and presented workshops on the labyrinth to thousands of people, helping them to learn and experience the labyrinth as a tool for personal and spiritual growth.

The more I work with the labyrinth, the more it shows me new and more powerful ways to access its healing energy and wisdom. In 2012 I published a deck of guidance and inspirational cards based on the labyrinth, creating and painting all the labyrinth images myself. I have been featured on radio and TV shows, bringing the message of the labyrinth to a wider audience. In 2015 I developed a new healing modality based on the labyrinth that I call Melchizedek Labyrinth Healing. I have accessed previously hidden aspects of the labyrinth that I reveal in this book, and I continue to explore the labyrinth so that I can share my findings with the world.

Over the years, the labyrinth has helped me discover myself and learn about what was most important for me. I worked in the public service in Ireland for thirty-three years and rose to a senior management position. As my work with the labyrinth and the spiritual side of my life grew, it got to the stage where it was taking up all my spare time. So, in 2015, I left my job and embarked on the path of teaching and sharing the labyrinth, combined with the healing and energy work that are part of my soul's purpose. I have not looked back. Also in 2015 I got married to the wonderful Fionnuala. As part of the wedding ceremony, we walked a labyrinth together and took our vows at the centre of the labyrinth, an occasion that is indelibly marked in my memory and in my heart.

The labyrinth can help you positively influence areas of your life. Many people find that the labyrinth helps to quieten their mind, bringing a sense of calmness and peace. When walked with an intention or question, the labyrinth helps gain insights and answers to your life's issues. You can approach the labyrinth as a walking meditation to help you feel greater peace and find that quiet space within yourself. It is a safe container to let go of worries and troubles that are on your mind. You can use the labyrinth to gain greater understanding of all aspects of life and your place in the world, exploring your life's purpose and the next steps on your journey.

The labyrinth is an enigma, a seemingly ordinary symbol that holds within its coils and turns secrets and wisdom that are being revealed to our human family to be used for our advancement. There are layers and dimensions to the labyrinth that are still being revealed. The more I learn about the labyrinth, the more I realise how little I know, yet what I now know is so powerful that it must be shared.

One of my greatest learnings with the labyrinth is an awareness of the significance of every moment. To put that in context for you: it is significant that you are reading this book. It is not by chance that you are where you are as you read this. It is not an accident that the people who are in your life are in your life. Nothing happens by accident. There is a flow of energy between the earth and the heavens, between the human and the Divine, and you are in the centre of this flow. Everything happens in its own right timing. This is the time for you to read this book and to begin to take the next step on your journey.

Not only is the book significant, but the manner in which you came to have the book in your possession is also significant because that gives you a clue as to how things are interconnected. If you bought the book yourself, then you have an immediate connection with it. If it was a gift, then be open to receiving what you read. If you borrowed it, then you are being drawn to the labyrinth and how it relates to your life.

The relevance of focusing on this book at this time is that it immediately propels you into an awareness of the present moment. It gives you a glimpse of what can be in store for you when you begin to live your life in awareness and appreciation of the significance of every moment. When you fully live in the presence of every moment, you are tapping into the oneness of all of existence!

The labyrinth is also the best tool that I have found for showing me how everything is interconnected. Something that happened to me when I was on tour in Australia showed this clearly to me. We were in Byron

Bay with a seven-hour drive ahead of us the next morning. We planned to go out for a quick breakfast at a café near where we were staying to get an early start on the road. When we arrived at the café, there was a power outage so they weren't able to cook hot breakfasts. Wanting something warm and substantial for our long road trip, we decided to go into the town centre and find another café there. There are well over a hundred places to eat in Byron Bay, so we walked along the street, passing many, until we came to one that felt right. There was only one free table at this restaurant, so we sat down there.

We were sitting beside a wall that had posters for many events in the town. Immediately one caught my eye. It had a Chartres labyrinth on it and was advertising a temporary labyrinth event that was happening in the town at that time. I knew that this was significant as labyrinths on posters are not very common. I took a photo of this poster and shared it on social media as an interesting synchronicity. The lady who had put up the poster in that restaurant contacted me and said that it was the only restaurant in the town where she had put up a poster.

This was a wow moment for me. The labyrinth was showing me that everything is connected. It showed me that when I am in tune with what is happening around me, amazing things happen to give me messages that I am on the right path. Events like this always cause me to pause and consider what life is about and my place in it. The thought of a power outage happening in the first café that we visited to get me the message is astounding. Every time I think about it I feel uplifted.

We find ourselves in such times and places exactly when we do, so that we experience the opportunities that are presented to us. Some opportunities may not always appear as such, presenting as difficulties or problems. In situations where a blissful enjoyment of what is happening is not possible, you need to see the opportunity in adversity. Every event presents opportunities; it is up to you to take them.

One of the difficulties of appreciating the significance of every moment in today's world is that we are surrounded by distractions. Walking a labyrinth quietens the mind. Walking a labyrinth helps you feel more centred and balanced. When your mind is quiet, your awareness is heightened. When your awareness is heightened, you are more open to receiving signals, signs, insights, and answers to questions and issues that you are currently dealing with.

When you begin to examine your life and seek answers to questions and guidance on issues through the labyrinth, you are on the path of personal and spiritual growth. Every time you find a solution or receive guidance and implement it, you are addressing what is burdening you. You are metaphorically, and literally in some senses, lightening your load. When your load is lighter, you are lighter, and you begin to live your life in a new and lighter way. Living in this way, you progress from being weighed down by your worries and issues to being able to see beyond yourself. You can then begin to see how you are related to others. People who are at similar stages on their journey will come into your life. You resonate with different people, ones who are lighter and more vibrant.

The labyrinth brings you to a state where you feel more at one with yourself, and you begin doing things that you enjoy doing and make you feel alive. You begin to seek out and start living your life's purpose—the thing, or things, that you came to earth to do. You seek a meaning that is greater than accumulating material possessions, that is greater than just existing.

The labyrinth is a stepping-stone between earth and heaven. It contains symbolism, layers, and dimensions that make its path a wonderful path of self-discovery. Just as the labyrinth works as a stepping stone, so too is this book a stepping stone, or series of stepping stones, to show you a way across that great divide of separation from where you are now to where you want to be. This is a book that will enhance your use and experience of the labyrinth, and help make clearer for you the next steps in your journey of life.

This book has had several incarnations. Initially, it was primarily a knowledge-based book with information about the symbolism and associations of the labyrinth. But, as I worked more with the labyrinth, it became clear to me that something more than a book of knowledge was required. As my experiences with the labyrinth grew and the benefits of the labyrinth became clearer to me, I was more and more drawn to finding a way to present the labyrinth in new ways and share these experiences with others.

The first step on your journey may be reading this book. The book presents the steps on your journey in a logical, easy to understand, and easy to use approach, so that you can work through each step in your own time and your own way. For experienced labyrinth users, some of the content of the early chapters may be familiar to you. If you feel so inclined, you can move directly to the exercises at the end of chapters with familiar material.

You may consider that you have already taken a number of steps. And, while it may be appropriate for you to skip a few steps in this book, it can also be an empowering experience to retake these steps, to consider how far you have come in preparation for the next step that lies ahead. So, while it is possible to go straight to any of the chapters and exercises, more benefit can generally be gained by progressing in sequence through the information and exercises as they are arranged, each one building on the previous one.

Having said that, feel free to use this book in whatever way feels right to you. Just as there is no one right way to walk a labyrinth, there is no one right way to use this book. It is however laid out so that you can progress along the path. If you skip some parts and are finding it difficult to understand and take the next step, you will need to go back a little to where you feel comfortable and start again from there. If you do not feel ready to move on, then it is fine to reread a section and repeat an exercise until you feel you are ready to move to the next one.

My purpose, dream, and intention at all times was, and still is, to provide ways and methods of using the labyrinth that will help you advance on your own personal and spiritual journeys. This book is a guide for part of your journey, a source of information, a prompt for you to discover more about yourself, to find and live your life's purpose. It is my sincere wish that this book will be both a guide and companion to you on your path. I wish that it will lead you to wonderful revelations and experiences that enhance your life in many ways. I see this book as what William Blake would call the end of a golden string when he wrote: "I give you the end of a golden string, / Only wind it into a ball: / It will lead you in at Heaven's gate, / Built in Jerusalems wall" (Blake 1802–1820).

This book is composed of three main aspects that are found in many traditions and systems of self-discovery and growth. These are knowledge, experience, and reflection.

The knowledge contained in this book is designed to give you a greater understanding of the depth and breadth of the labyrinth as a symbol for self-discovery and growth. You will receive knowledge about the labyrinth, and about the symbolism and associations in the labyrinth. There is new information about how different systems of self-advancement are connected to the labyrinth and are even an integral part of the labyrinth. You will learn about the labyrinth connections with alchemy, the tarot, crop circles, the cosmos, Mithraism and more. The more you learn about the labyrinth the more you will see how the symbol of the labyrinth points to the sacred beyond the symbol.

I will be using both the classical and Chartres labyrinths to illustrate the many associations, the depth of symbolism, and the range of interconnections present in the labyrinth. And while some of the associations and symbolism are clearer in the classical labyrinth, there are others that are best illustrated and more apparent in the Chartres labyrinth.

The labyrinth helps you to fully experience yourself. Experiences are what make you feel alive. In the words of Gary Renard, "The only thing that will make you happy is the experience of what you really are. What will truly satisfy you is not a symbol of reality, but an *experience* of reality" (Renard 2006). The exercises in this book are designed to give you experiences of yourself—to discover yourself through the labyrinth. Taking the time to learn, focus, and practise these exercises will reward you with enhanced experiences. The exercises in this book can be done with any "active" labyrinth form, unless specifically stated otherwise. When I say "active," I mean one that has been tried and found to have a quietening effect on the mind and to bring the user into a place of centredness and balance. If you have a different type of labyrinth, I suggest that you use the classical or Chartres labyrinth for the exercises. Alternatively, there is a finger labyrinth for your use on page 259.

Time for reflection is equally as important as the knowledge gained and the experiential exercises. Progressing on your path can sometimes happen quicker when you stop and take time to absorb and integrate the learnings and experiences. Taking time to pause and explore what you have just passed through, what you have come through to reach this point, can give you a greater awareness of moving further ahead, and a greater understanding of where you are going. Keeping a journal and writing down your experiences and reflections on them fixes those experiences in your consciousness. Keeping a record of your learnings, answers to specific questions, and insights into issues will all be beneficial over time. Before you start any of the exercises, have a pen and paper handy so that you can write while still in the same state of awareness as you were during the exercise.

This threefold approach of knowledge, experience, and reflection has a cumulative effect greater than the sum of its parts, as each one not only complements the other, but enhances and amplifies the individual effects into a greater whole. Having knowledge about specific aspects of the labyrinth can enhance the experience of walking the labyrinth and vice versa, while reflecting on the experience and processing the knowledge combine to create an increasingly beneficial result.

Finally, while this book is laid out in a sequential and incremental way, please remember that this is a labyrinth-based book. So at any stage on your journey through this book you may feel that you are at your goal, your centre, or you may feel that your journey has taken a turn and you feel further away than ever. As in a labyrinth, particularly during times of uncertainty, just take another step!

1
The Labyrinth

The labyrinth is a symbol. It is a symbol of many things depending on how you look at it and how you approach it. It is a symbol of your journey in life with its twists and turns as you journey to your centre. If you are using it to seek an answer to a specific question or issue, then at that time the labyrinth symbolises all aspects of that issue. As a symbol of you, it enables you to journey into the labyrinth to explore who you are, where you are, and where you are going.

The labyrinth symbol can be viewed on several levels. It is a visible symbol, yet it holds a hidden meaning, particularly in the unseen and the intangible. At first glance, it looks like a design made from intersecting lines. Yet, on a deeper level, it represents a secret relationship between humanity, earth, and heaven. Just as the labyrinth symbolises that which is within you, it also symbolises that which is outside of you.

The labyrinth is usually circular in shape and consists of a series of interconnected lines that form a single path that you can walk or trace with your finger. The path leads from the outside to the centre and covers every part of the labyrinth. There are no dead ends and there are no choices to be made, apart from deciding that you are going to enter the labyrinth in the first place.

Something is prompting people all over the world to create this ancient symbol so they can interact with it. The appeal of and fascination with the labyrinth include the visual appeal of the symbol itself, and the wonderful experiences that people have on the labyrinth, the "deeper level" I just mentioned. Today, the labyrinth is primarily being used as a walking meditation where the user seeks peace of mind and a greater sense of centredness. Many people are also using the labyrinth to seek insights into their life issues. The deeper you delve into the labyrinth, the greater is the reward—the knowledge that you gain, and the experiences that uplift you. We will get into this later.

The most common way of walking the labyrinth is to walk the path to the centre, pause for a few moments in the centre, and then walk back out the same path that you walked in. There is much symbolism inherent in this approach of Release, Receive, Return, often referred to as the three Rs. The releasing happens on the way in as you let go of worries and what may be burdening you. At the centre you pause to receive guidance. The walk out is symbolic of returning to your everyday life with new insights.

Labyrinths vary in size from small ones engraved on jewellery, to large landscape designs that many people can walk at a time. Labyrinths are found in private gardens, public parks, hospitals, schools, holistic centres, churches, and in many more places. Portable labyrinths usually painted on sheets of canvas are being used in various locations where permanent labyrinths do not exist. Temporary labyrinths are being created for special events, festivals, and often just for short-term use on beaches and in parks.

Labyrinths can be made from almost any material that can be used to mark out a line on the ground. Cement, paving, paint, string, sticks, and stones are some of the more common materials used. Garden labyrinths are often made with flowers, hedging, and herbs. My current garden labyrinth is simply a path mown into the lawn with the lawnmower at a lower setting to create the path through the longer grass. Some quite creative labyrinths have been made using shoes, books, CDs, plastic spoons, and I have even seen a labyrinth in Ireland made from potatoes!

Types of Labyrinths

There are many types of labyrinths, and this book is about the labyrinth in all its active forms. There is a magic and mysticism about almost all labyrinths whether they are classical, medieval, Baltic, Roman, Chartres, or other form. Indeed, there are many similarities between the two main types of labyrinths: the classical and Chartres labyrinths. While less ancient, the Chartres labyrinth, which was created in 1201, holds the imprint of much of the same basic symbolism of the classical labyrinth: that of being on a journey, of getting to the centre, of releasing and receiving, and of having four distinct quadrants.

Figure 1: Classical labyrinth

The classical labyrinth is the oldest known form of labyrinth and its most common form has seven circuits and a centre (see Figure 1). The path, beginning at the outside, passes through all seven circuits and ends at the centre. It has appeared in many different cultures around the world at various times. Its presence in such a variety of cultures over the millennia illustrates that the classical labyrinth holds a unique attraction and contains an almost indescribable "something" that has appealed to so many over such a long period of time.

The classical labyrinth has been called by many different names since it first appeared. These names include the Cretan labyrinth, the Celtic labyrinth, Melchizedek's labyrinth, Luna's labyrinth, Ariadne's labyrinth. Each of these names illustrates a different aspect to the labyrinth and indicates some of the many ways that this labyrinth has influenced people since it first came into human consciousness.

Figure 2: Chartres labyrinth

The labyrinth in Chartres Cathedral in France has eleven circuits and a centre with six petals (see Figure 2). It measures approximately forty-two feet in diameter. Most of the turning points in the labyrinth happen at a labrys, the double-headed axe shape that cuts across the path. When viewed from above, the labryses help give the appearance of a cross and divide the labyrinth into four quadrants. This labyrinth is one of the most commonly reproduced labyrinth designs that people create in art and install, the other one being the classical labyrinth.

It is important to make a distinction at this point between labyrinths and mazes. In this book, the labyrinth that I am writing about is a unicursal labyrinth. It has one path leading from the outside to the centre. It is not a maze with choices and dead ends. This one path is symbolic of your journey; your journey to your own centre, your journey to self-discovery.

The Origin of the Labyrinth

People often ask about the origins of the labyrinth and the motives for creating it. Because the oldest known labyrinths are on rock carvings in Spain and Italy and are over four thousand years old, there is no recorded history of exactly where or how the labyrinth originated. We do not know if these ancient rock carving labyrinths in Galicia, Spain, and Valcamonica, Italy, were made by ordinary people, elders, or leading spiritual people of the time.

The large rock carving of a seven-circuit classical labyrinth almost half way around the world in Goa, India, also estimated to be over four thousand years old, adds further to the mystery. This labyrinth is nearly ten feet in diameter and is carved into a flat rock surface by a river along with hundreds of other rock carvings. In addition, it is the oldest known walkable labyrinth.

When you consider the labyrinth design or pattern, it is not a design that might happen by accident, or one that clearly appears in nature. In the words of Hermann Kern, "it is clear that the classical seven-circuit labyrinth is not the simplest of all conceivable configurations. It is neither a fluke nor an axiom. Instead, we have what was obviously a conscious choice from among numerous possibilities" (Kern 2000).

Yet, the fact that it was a conscious choice does not enlighten us as to why the labyrinth was first made or how it is found all over the world. Current academic thinking leans towards the origins of the labyrinth being in Northern Spain and Italy, from where it "travelled" around the world; being brought to India possibly by Alexander the Great and to the Americas by the Spanish. This thinking does not take any account of the phenomenon known in scientific circles as "multiple independent discovery," where two or even three people come up with the same discovery or invention independently of each other, often at opposite ends of the world. This could be what happened with the labyrinth and its simultaneous emergence in Europe, India, and America.

We are still left pondering what was the stimulus for the creation of the labyrinth. Because of its connection between heaven and earth, and because of the effect that the design of the labyrinth has on people interacting with it, there is a strong case to be made that the classical labyrinth design came from a higher consciousness. The first people who drew a labyrinth were, knowingly or unknowingly, tapping into a higher level of consciousness than previously accessed. Once accessed, the labyrinth design was then part of consciousness, contributing to its spread and evolution of the labyrinth as it resonated with people in many different traditions and societies on a symbolic and spiritual level.

Since these early creations, labyrinth builders and makers have left their mark on 2,500-year-old Cretan coins, on the 1,500-year-old Hollywood Stone (a rock carving in Ireland), and on rock carvings and baskets in the Hopi and Tohono O'odham Indian reservations respectively. Labyrinths have been found on older wooden Moslem mosques in Pakistan, Hindu temples in India, in Batak manuscripts from Indonesia, walkable stone labyrinths around the Baltic coast, turf labyrinths in English village greens, medieval manuscripts, and Gothic cathedrals. The most famous of these cathedral labyrinths is the one in the Cathedral of Notre Dame in Chartres, France.

While the ancient rock-carving classical labyrinths are surrounded in mystery, the Chartres labyrinth also generates speculation surrounding its origins and purpose. The progression of medieval labyrinth patterns can be traced through manuscripts, leading to the culmination that is the labyrinth at Chartres Cathedral. Yet, there remains a mystery and hidden knowledge in relation to the final design and purpose of one of the largest symbols installed in Chartres and other Gothic Catholic cathedrals from the thirteenth century onwards.

None of the ancient documents at Chartres detailing the activities in the cathedral mention the labyrinth. However, records from both Sens and Auxerre, which are just over one hundred miles from Chartres, give accounts of rituals at Easter Sunday of games played on the cathedral labyrinths by the clergy involving a large ball and accompanying round dance. The ball was passed or thrown between the dancers while they chanted and danced around the labyrinth. The ball most likely symbolised the Easter sun and the resurrection of Jesus. This is considered to be a Christian adaptation of a pre-Christian Norman tradition. Hermann Kern relates that the ball game and its accompanying round dance was "forbidden by legal decree in June 1538, although it continued to be performed at Auxerre until 1690 when the labyrinth was destroyed" (Kern 2000).

The relationship between the labyrinth and dance goes back much further to Greek mythology where there are accounts of Ariadne and Theseus performing dances related to the labyrinth, that we will explore further in the next section. The ancient Roman poet Virgil wrote in his account of the siege of Troy that after the fall of Troy Aeneas popularised a processional parade or dance that became known as the "Game of Troy." This Game of Troy involved participants, some of whom were mounted on horseback, engaging in a processional dance consisting of a series of steps in the form of a labyrinth that were most likely adopted by the Romans from the Etruscans. The participants were young men and the game was considered as a rite of passage into manhood, with the labyrinth being the catalyst for the transition from one form of existence to another.

Many of the later uses of the labyrinth appear to stem from the early labyrinth dances and games of Troy. In both Scandinavia and in England there are accounts of young men engaging in competitions racing to be first to reach a young maiden at the centre of the labyrinth. These events hark back to the times of goddess-centred religions. The safe and nurturing goddess energy in the labyrinth continues to resonate today with many labyrinth walkers expressing these feelings when walking a labyrinth.

Despite these ancient accounts of labyrinth use, we still do not have any complete answers to the questions surrounding the origin and purpose of the labyrinth. We are left to contemplate the possible origins while appreciating the benefits that the labyrinth brings. Lauren Artress, author of *Walking a Sacred Path,* summed up the origins and uses of the labyrinth when she wrote, "The labyrinth was designed by an intelligence we cannot fully understand. But this much I do know. The labyrinth is truly a tool for transformation. It is a crucible for change, a blueprint for the sacred meeting of psyche and soul, a field of light, a cosmic dance. It is a centre for empowering ritual. It is a container where we can meet angels and recover the great-grandmother's thread, the web of Mary, and the gracious, nurturing God" (Artress 1995).

Labyrinth Myths

We can gain further insights into the possible origin and meaning of the labyrinth through accounts related to the labyrinth that have appeared in mythology and stories from several cultures. The most well-known mythological story relating to the labyrinth is the myth of Theseus and the Minotaur. While there are several versions of the myth, in general, the story goes as follows:

The Minotaur was a creature with the body of a man and the head of a bull that ate human flesh. It was the offspring of a liaison between Pasiphae, wife of King Minos of Crete, and a magnificent bull sent to Minos by Poseidon to be sacrificed. King Minos had prayed to Poseidon, the sea god, to send him a snow-white bull as a sign of support and Minos was to kill the bull in honour of Poseidon. But Minos decided to keep the bull and sacrificed one of his own instead. Poseidon was not pleased, and to punish Minos he had his wife Pasiphae fall in love with the bull. Pasiphae got the Greek inventor Daedalus to make a hollow wooden cow and climbed inside so that she could mate with the white bull. As the Minotaur grew, its desire for human flesh became a serious threat that had to be resolved. King Minos, after getting advice from the oracle at Delphi, had Daedalus build a labyrinth within which to keep the Minotaur.

As Minos had defeated the Athenians in a war some years earlier, the Greeks had to send seven young maidens and seven youths as sacrifice to the Minotaur every nine years. Having heard about the tribute to be made, Theseus, who was the son of Aegeus, king of Athens, volunteered to be one of the sacrificial victims.

Ariadne, daughter of Minos, fell in love with Theseus. She asked Daedalus for the secret to the labyrinth. He told her to have Theseus unwind a ball of thread as he entered the labyrinth so that he could find his way out safely. Theseus found the Minotaur, killed it, and used the thread to find his way out of the labyrinth.

The Cretan labyrinth is almost always depicted as a unicursal classical labyrinth. It is unlikely that the actual labyrinth was so easy to get out of, and the labyrinth that Daedalus built is most likely to have been a maze with many paths from which it was almost impossible to escape. The single path of the classical labyrinth represents the one true path through the more complicated maze-type labyrinth that held the Minotaur.

Theseus escaped with Ariadne and the other youths and maidens and landed on the island of Delos, where according to Plutarch "he danced with his youths a dance which they say is still performed by the Delians, being an imitation of the circling passages in the labyrinth, and consisting of certain rhythmic involutions and evolutions" (Plutarch, n.d.). This dance is known as the geranos, or crane dance. The crane is known for its mesmeric and spectacular dances. As a totem animal it is frequently considered to be a messenger of the gods, with the ability to bring light into the darkness and take people to a higher level of spiritual awareness. The crane was a sacred bird to the ancient people of the eastern Mediterranean. On one of the ancient labyrinth rock carvings from the Valcamonica valley, there is a carving of a crane beside the labyrinth.

The crane and Ariadne are in many respects synonymous with each other, both showing the one true way.

In many traditions and cultures, dancing is used as a means of raising the energy of a location and the people present. Dancing in the pattern of a labyrinth has a double effect of drawing on both the labyrinth and dancing energies to raise the vibration and spiritual energy of the participants, creating a state of heightened awareness.

The goddess aspect of the labyrinth is also to be found in the story of Eurynome, who was one of the most important goddesses of the Pelasgians, people that arrived in Greece from the area of Palestine around 5,500 years ago. Eurynome was the creator, the Mother goddess born from chaos, who separated the waters from the sky. She was impregnated by the snake Ophion who wrapped himself around her seven times and created an egg.

According to Gardiner, the snake wrapping itself around Eurynome seven times indicated the "chakra points of the Hindu kundalini or coiled serpent" (Gardiner, 2007c). Gardiner goes on to write that this is the "creative force energised by the serpent fire. It is control, balance and power of the individual to bring about the new you." It also echoes the seven circuits of the classical labyrinth.

In a further labyrinth and snake connection, Gardiner writes that "In ancient Egypt, the labyrinth was synonymous with what was called the Amenti—the snakelike path taken by the dead to journey from death to resurrection. It was Isis, the serpent queen of heaven, who was to guide the souls through the twists of the Amenti. The path towards the centre leads towards treasure." A rock carving from Valcamonica can clearly be interpreted to be a combination of the goddess and snake forms in what is a possible precursor to the complete classical labyrinth. In it there is an intermingling of the human and serpentine forms from which a labyrinth-type pattern can be seen to emerge.

Using the Labyrinth

The essence of using the labyrinth is to develop a personal relationship with yourself and with the Divine. This is reminiscent of Gnosticism, which in the words of Kathleen McGowan involves "allowing the wisdom to come through you personally as a result of that relationship" (McGowan 2010).

The wisdom and insights therefore that come to you when you are working with the labyrinth are you accessing your inner wisdom. While the wisdom is always there, what is important to recognize is that wisdom and insights can come to you more easily when you are working with the labyrinth. These insights show you where you are in relation to certain events in your life. These insights bring clarity from confusion, love from fear, and hope from despair. What you receive on the labyrinth is exactly what you need at that time in your life. It may not always necessarily be what you think that you want, but it is beneficial and wonderful nevertheless.

You can benefit from the labyrinth without being fully aware of the many layers and dimensions that are inherent in it. The labyrinth is an active symbol that is continually working away quietly in the background. Yet, when you become consciously aware of the levels and dimensions on which the labyrinth is operating, you further empower yourself to tap into your inner wisdom through the labyrinth as a tool for the transformation of consciousness.

The labyrinth journey usually begins with physically walking the path, and progressing to the mental and emotional stages you pass through. When you start your labyrinth walk you are focused on the act of walking. During your labyrinth walk, your mind begins to quieten as you become familiar with walking the path. As your mind quietens, you become more aware of your thoughts and emotions, experiencing them on a deeper level because of the meditative effect of walking the labyrinth.

On your labyrinth walk, you are also moving on a journey concerning not only yourself, but also all others in your life; and then not only in your present life, but in past lives; and, not only in past lives, but future lives. Your journey moves you through your physical existence and progresses you on your spiritual journey. And you are not only moving on this earth, you are also moving on a universal, cosmic, and multiversal level; on as many dimensions as you are able to exist, and to comprehend. The labyrinth, as well as this book, is therefore about a journey, or journeys; your inner journey reflecting your outer journey, reflecting your spiritual journey.

And finally, remember that you are not alone. Just as Ariadne helped Theseus to negotiate his way in and out of the labyrinth, so too there is help available to you. As you become aware of your interconnectedness, and particularly when you are not aware of it, remind yourself that others are travelling the path with you. Remember that you have guides and helpers to support and prompt you; remember that you have this book to use as a guide. The essence of this book, and the labyrinth, is that you are always connected; you are always at one. You just need to tap into it, you just need to live it, you just need to be it.

EXERCISE: HOW TO DRAW
AND MAKE YOUR OWN LABYRINTH

When you know how to draw and make a labyrinth, you can always have one at hand. Whenever you wish to use a labyrinth, you can sketch one quickly on a piece of paper to trace with your finger, or if you have some basic labyrinth-making materials, you can mark one out in your garden, on the beach, or some other suitable place.

The basic way of drawing the labyrinth is to use what is known as the "seed pattern" (see Figure 3). This is a square shaped pattern with an equal-armed cross in the centre, dots on each corner, and L-shaped brackets in each of the four quadrants.

First draw the seed pattern on a page. As more of the labyrinth is created above the seed pattern than below it, start by making an equal-armed cross about one third of the way up from the bottom of the page. Then place a dot on the each of the four corners of the imaginary square that contains the cross. Finally draw an L-shaped bracket with the lines running parallel to the arms of the cross in each of the four quadrants. Your seed pattern should look like the one in Figure 3.

Figure 3: How to draw a classical labyrinth

To create the centre of the labyrinth, place your pen at the top of the vertical arm of the cross. Draw a semi-circle up from this point and around to the right to finish at the top of the L-bracket on the right. Next place your pen at the top of the bracket in the top left quadrant. To create the innermost circuit of the labyrinth, draw a semi-circle up and around to the right to finish at the dot in the top right quadrant.

The next circuit of the labyrinth is created by drawing a semi-circular line from the dot in the top left quadrant up and around the previous line to finish at the bottom of the L-bracket in the top right quadrant. The next line starts at the lower part of the L-bracket in the top left quadrant, goes up and around the top of the previous lines, and finishes at the end of the line at the right side of the arm of the cross. Notice at this stage that the method of creating the circuits consists of starting on the left side of the seed pattern and finishing at the right side of the seed pattern.

The next line starts at the left end of the arm of the cross, goes up and around the previously drawn lines, and finishes at the upper part of the bracket in the bottom right part of the seed pattern. You will need to draw this line out a little from the seed pattern to keep it equidistant from the previously drawn circuit lines.

Come back around to the bottom left of the seed pattern and place your pen at the top of the bracket. Draw a line out, up and around the previously drawn lines to finish at the dot in the bottom right of the seed pattern.

You will need to take care with the next line that you draw, as it is one of the most common mistakes made when drawing the labyrinth. First check that you have four points left to connect in the seed pattern: one dot in the bottom left and three lines made up of the bottom of the vertical arm of the cross and the bottom of the two brackets in the right and left quadrants. Place your pen on the dot in the bottom left of the seed pattern and draw a curved line out, up and around the top of the labyrinth to finish at the bottom part of the bracket in the bottom right quadrant. The most common mistake that the first-time drawer of a labyrinth makes is incorrectly attaching the line for the second-to-last circuit to the bottom of the vertical line of the cross rather than to the end of the bracket.

You should now have just two lines remaining to connect. Place your pen at the bottom part of the bracket in the bottom left quadrant of the seed pattern. Draw a line down and out, up and around the labyrinth to finish at the bottom of the vertical arm of the cross. Your labyrinth is now complete.

Making a Walkable Labyrinth

You can use the same method to make a walkable labyrinth, except the path width will need to accommodate a person walking it. If you are using raised material such as stones to mark the lines you will need to have the paths wide enough to comfortably accommodate the walkers without them tripping over the stones. If you are using a line that the walker can step on, then the path width can be relatively narrow.

Before making a permanent labyrinth, it is a good idea to practise with some temporary ones first. The easiest place to practise this is on a beach of wet sand where you use a stick to mark out the lines. That way, if you make a mistake, you can just rub it out and start again.

If you are making a labyrinth on grass or hard ground, you will need something to mark out the lines. Paint, chalk, cornmeal, flour, or string are commonly used. After you have made a labyrinth, always walk it to make sure that you have gotten it right.

2

The Parts of the Labyrinth

The labyrinth as a whole is a symbol of many things, and primarily it is a symbol of wholeness, oneness, your journey in life, and the interconnectedness of all of existence. When dissected, the labyrinth reveals many constituent parts, each of which symbolises an aspect of the wholeness that is contained within the labyrinth. When viewed as representing your life's journey, each part of the labyrinth is related to a part of you or a part of your journey.

The Path

The path, or journey, is central to many forms of personal and spiritual development. Writing about the tarot, Naomi Ozaniec says that "The path itself is a universal symbol of the spiritual life. Buddhism speaks of the Lam Rim, the graduated path towards enlightenment. Yoga speaks of the Marga, the Path or Way. In the Western Mysteries the Path is to be found in the twenty-two byways and the Sephiroth of the Tree of Life. In tarot trump 0, the Fool is clearly about to take the first step. We do not see the path. The path lies ahead somewhere in the future" (Ozaniec 2002).

The path of the labyrinth more clearly represents your journey. What is important to note about the path of the labyrinth is that to be on the path you first have to step onto it. This involves a clear decision and action on your part. Once on the path, to progress along the path you need to continue taking steps.

Ariadne's Thread

Synonymous with the path is the concept of Ariadne's thread that originated in the Greek myth of Theseus and the Minotaur. The term is now associated with any form of assistance through a difficult situation or problem. An Ariadne's Thread labyrinth is one where the path to be walked is indicated by a single line along which you walk. You are being guided along the path. Its significance for working with the labyrinth is the recognition that as you walk your own path you are not alone. There is help available to you, sometimes visible and sometimes invisible. But, as with everything associated with the labyrinth, you need to be aware enough to see the help, to recognize the assistance that is available and being offered to you, and to make the best use of this help.

The Circuits

The circuits of the labyrinth carry their own symbolism. There are seven circuits in the classical labyrinth. These are often shown as having the seven colours of the rainbow. They are commonly associated with the seven chakras or main energy centres in your body. The significance of the number seven is explored further in the section on sacred numbers.

The eleven circuits of the Chartres labyrinth have been considered to represent the seven chakras plus the elements of earth, air, fire, and water. Another interpretation of the Chartres labyrinth's eleven circuits is the seven planetary bodies, the stars of heaven as the eighth, and the veils of soul, mind, and God as the last three.

Turning Points

In the Tao Te Ching there is a phrase "Turning back is how the way moves" (Tzu 1963), indicating that life's twists and turns, even a turn in the opposite direction, are central to progressing. They are energizing and life enhancing. There are nine turning points in the classical labyrinth associated with key stages in your growth and development. When taken in a specific order, they illustrate a scheme of progression on your life's journey. The significance of these points is directly experienced when you become aware of a different sensation at any one of these turning points.

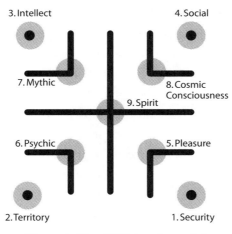

Figure 4: Nine DNA turning points

The associations of the turning points in the labyrinth (Figure 4) give you further guidance and insights into where you are in your life. These nine points are described by Vincent Bridges in his article "Notes on the Labyrinth, DNA and Planetary Alignment" (Bridges 2012) as DNA triggers, some of which trigger automatically (security, territory, intellect, social), some which we consciously trigger (pleasure, psychic, mythic, cosmic consciousness), and one (Spirit) that triggers randomly. The first four are related mainly to your physical development and trigger automatically at certain ages up to adolescence. Security is about feeling safe and triggers at birth. Territory is the definition of self versus others. It is a boundary imprint that is in place by the time you reach about three to five years old. Intellect is related to your environment and the world around you. The social trigger is about the groups that you engage with. It occurs at puberty, usually between the ages of thirteen and fifteen, drives us to seek out partners, and is essential for the continuation of the human species.

The second set of four turning points are ones that you consciously choose. When you are walking your path of personal and spiritual growth, you are seeking and developing these aspects. These inner trigger points are directly related to the lower outer ones. For example, the pleasure trigger is related to security, psychic, related to territory, and so on. The first main area of choice on the path of your spiritual life is pleasure. This is a tricky one and if not watched carefully can lead to excesses or pleasures that do not serve your path of growth. Next comes psychic, which appears to be prominent in some people more than others. If you are not yet fully aware of your psychic abilities, it is possible to fire this trigger by focusing on this aspect of you or even by contact with someone else who has it. The psychic connection to territory suggests that your ability in this area is related to how well your inner and outer boundaries are defined. The seventh point is mythic, which is about the truth that you find in myths and stories. Many gurus and teachers tell stories to their students to help them better learn life truths. For example, Jesus told parables so that his followers would better understand his message. Similarly, mythology holds many truths for you when you can see the layers and deeper meanings in the myths and stories. The eighth point is cosmic consciousness and is an awareness of the vastness of the cosmos and your connections to it.

The final turning point is at the centre of the cross of the labyrinth and is the spirit point. Spirit is the all-seeing, all-knowing, and all-loving presence that permeates all of existence. The labyrinth is a wonderful device for helping you become more aware of the presence of Spirit within you, and the actions of Spirit all around you. Spirit triggers in you at moments of gnostic grace. It is something that fires in you when you are ready and have travelled your path. It is not something that you can control, although you can ready yourself by working on all the previous points.

There are twenty-eight 180-degree turns in the Chartres labyrinth, while there are four 90-degree turns. Each of these turning points also has a meaning and significance that has yet to be identified. Most of the turning points in the Chartres labyrinth are created by a labrys, which is a double-headed axe shape that appears to cut across the path to create a turn.

labrys

The labrys turning points of the Chartres labyrinth (see Figure 5) carry their own symbolism. The labrys is a double-headed axe that has origins in Crete, where it was used by Minoan priestesses for ceremonial purposes. It was commonly associated with female power and female divinities. The labryses in the labyrinth have also been associated with butterflies, a symbol of transformation. In engaging with these when walking the labyrinth, you are being invited to step into your power and be transformed.

Most labyrinth walks entail walking into the labyrinth and walking back out the same path. Gothic cathedral labyrinths offer another approach. Almost all Gothic cathedrals in France are oriented eastwards. The entrance to the cathedrals is in the west and as you move up through the cathedral, you are moving in an eastward direction. This is the direction of the rising sun. The Christian belief in the second coming of Jesus saw the sunrise as a symbol of the resurrection and oriented their churches and cathedrals towards the east.

In Chartres Cathedral, the labyrinth is located approximately one-third of the way up the nave from the entrance in the west. When you walk into the centre of the labyrinth, you are facing towards the east, and have a choice depending on whether you feel the need to walk back out of the labyrinth the way you came in and revisit certain aspects of your experience and your life, or whether you feel ready to move on. Moving on from the centre of the labyrinth is done by using the labryses as stepping stones to exit the labyrinth and move further up the cathedral, stepping into your power and being transformed.

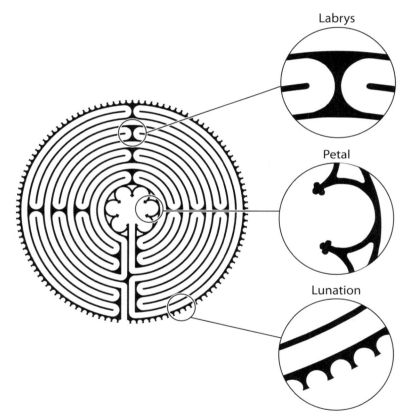

Figure 5: Parts of the Chartres labyrinth

This approach to exiting the labyrinth was further affirmed by my wife, Fionnuala, when she was walking a labyrinth at Seaton, Devon, England. As she stood in the centre looking across the labryses she heard the words "The doorway to Excalibur is open." Excalibur is Arthur's sword and is symbolic of stepping into your kingship and wielding your power. Through the labyrinth, you bring yourself to a stage where you are ready to step into your power and move on.

The Centre

The centre of the labyrinth is where the path appears to end. The centre of the labyrinth has been presented and represented as the ultimate goal that is to be achieved or attained following the journey. The centre is symbolic of the merging of heaven and earth where all is one. It is here that our sense of balance and equilibrium is re-established.

The centre is both a destination and a beginning. It is symbolic of the omega and the alpha, the journey's end and the gateway to the infinite self. Philip Gardiner writes that "we should also be looking for the idea of the centre being the true Gateway. This should be obvious to us now, as the true centre is the point between the brain's hemispheres, and the sacred location on earth where the earth energies cross … The key to the Gateway is through seven levels of consciousness, or alternatively through attaining the harmonious level with the frequency of the earth. But it is also gaining the centre, balancing our own minds" (Gardiner 2007a).

Chartres Centre

The centre of the Chartres labyrinth is one of the few ornate labyrinth centres. It is often called a "rose centre." Although there is some debate as to the correctness of this name, as a rose has five petals while there are six "petals" in the Chartres centre (see Figure 5). Staying with the rose for the moment, there is both apparent and hidden symbolism in this centre. The rose is a symbol of Our Lady (Mary), and as the cathedral is dedicated to

Notre Dame (translated to mean "Our Lady"), it appears to make sense to have a rose centre.

Yet, equally symbolic is the lily, with six petals. Or, more botanically correct, the lily has three petals and three sepals that are almost identical to the petals. The lily is a symbol of fertility and birth. The six petals represent the upward pointing triangle and the downward pointing triangle coming together into a six-pointed star. It is the coming together of the masculine and the feminine in a centre of wholeness.

The geometry of the centre is based on seven circles: the six petals and another circle in the middle. The six circles that make up the petals are slightly overlapped to create space for the entrance to the centre. Seven is also a number associated with Our Lady, the Virgin Mary.

Less well known are some of the associations of the centre petals. Kathleen McGowan in her book *The Source of Miracles* has associated the six petals with the qualities of faith, surrender, service, abundance, forgiveness, and strength contained in the Lord's Prayer, while the centre itself is love. The petals of the centre of the Chartres labyrinth can also represent the six realms or kingdoms of existence: mineral, plant, animal, human, angelic, and divine. In the centre of these six petals, you are in contact with each of them and in a space of enlightenment with knowledge and connectedness to all of existence.

When walking the Chartres labyrinth, you can stand for a few moments in each of the petals at the centre and contemplate your connection with the different realms. For example, when in the mineral realm, consider how your body is made up of compounds from the earth; in the plant petal consider how plants provide food for you and the oxygen in the air that you breathe. Having passed through all the petals, you can then step into the centremost point of the labyrinth centre and become aware of your connectedness to all of these realms at the same time.

The sevenfold centre can also be viewed on the deeper level of soul consciousness. The Rosicrucians considered that while there is only one soul, there are seven planes of consciousness to the soul: element, mineral, plant, animal, human, demi-god, and god consciousness. It is man's role to work through each of these to become fully self-aware. In *The Secret Doctrine of the Roscirucians* this is summarised as "The soul of man is sevenfold, yet but one in essence: Man's spiritual unfoldment has as its end the discovery of himself beneath the seven-fold veil" (Incognito 1918).

The Node, Cross, and Quadrants

The node of the classical labyrinth is the crossing point of the vertical and horizontal axes of the seed pattern. This cross is symbolic of the cross in many traditions; the intersection of the physical, or material, with the spiritual. The node is a powerful place in the labyrinth, and it is interesting to stand at the node of a labyrinth to see what you experience. While facilitating a labyrinth walk on a classical labyrinth, I had given the participants a brief introduction to walking in and out of the labyrinth. I noticed that one participant paused when passing the node and then stood directly over this point. She stood there for quite a while and then made her way out of the labyrinth. She told me afterwards that she felt a strong impulse to stand on this point. While standing there she first felt a deep sense of peace. Then she began to feel more powerful, almost as if she was being made to stand up taller while her legs felt solid and rooted to the spot. She said that this was a clear indication to her that she should stand up for herself in a situation that she was currently dealing with. It was only after being out of the labyrinth for a few minutes that she realised that she hadn't walked to the centre. She felt that she didn't need to and that she had gotten everything that she needed from that labyrinth walk.

While the node of the classical labyrinth is the centre of the cross in the seed pattern, there is also a cross in the Chartres labyrinth formed by the placing of the labrys and the entrance paths. Anthony Stevens in his book on symbols called *Ariadne's Clue* says that "the notion of wholeness seems to be satisfied by the representation of a quaternity, especially if the quaternity is integrated within a circle," just as it is in a labyrinth (Stevens 1998).

In the Chartres labyrinth, the labrys forms a cross shape so that when you stand at the centre you are at the centre of the cross. From here you can orientate yourself in all directions—you can be centred—and not only in the four traditional directions but in the seven with the inclusion of above, below, and within.

Lunations

The lunations of the labyrinth at Chartres are the part-circular type shapes around the outside edge of the labyrinth (see Figure 5 on page 32). They have also been called cusps, cogs, and several other names. The projections between the lunations are often referred to as foils. There are 112 cusps in total with 113 foils in between. If complete, the whole outside would contain 114 of each, but there are two cusps and one foil omitted to allow entrance to the labyrinth.

Semicircles amplify energy, and arcs of quartz crystals are found around several megalithic mounds in Ireland, although they are not always as visible as at Newgrange today. It is also interesting to look on the lunations in the context of the characteristics they give the labyrinth. The overall impression is of a radiant sun, or a large cog wheel. This could be a depiction or symbol of the great wheel of life or the turning of the cosmic cycle. Whatever their intended purpose, the lunations undoubtedly enhance the visual impact, while also contributing to creating a higher energetic vibration in labyrinths that have them.

Sacred Numbers

No exploration of the labyrinth would be complete without looking at the significance of the numbers contained within the structure of the labyrinth. In much of today's society numbers represent quantity. Historically numbers were associated with certain qualities, which we will explore. Each number represented an aspect of creation, or of our existence, or of the Divine. The numbers three and four appear repeatedly in both the classical and Chartres labyrinth. Their derivatives, seven, eleven, and twelve, are also to be found, while other multiples and combinations are also present.

There are seven (three plus four) circuits in the classical labyrinth. The seed pattern for the classical labyrinth is in effect a square with four sides; while there are four ends to the lines as marked by the dots in the seed pattern. In the Chartres labyrinth, there are twelve (three times four) circles required to make the labyrinth, creating eleven (3 + 4 + 4) circuits. There are twenty-eight 180-degree turns; the centre is one quarter the diameter of the whole; the diameter of the petals is one third the diameter of the centre; and the width of the path is one third the diameter of the petal.

Three

The number three, as the triad or trinity, has been considered sacred from ancient times. Hinduism has its triad of gods of Vishnu, Brahma, and Shiva; Buddhism has the three jewels of Buddha, Dharma, and Sangha; while the Christian Father, Son, and Holy Spirit constitute the three gods in one. In goddess wisdom, the number three represented the virgin, mother, and crone, while the triangle was an emblem of a holy triad. The properties of the number three include completion, divine energy, harmony, and unity.

One of the simplest forms of the labyrinth is the three-circuit labyrinth, which in its most popular form is drawn from a simple seed pattern with an equal-armed cross at the centre and one single dot in each quadrant (unlike the classic labyrinth, which has the brackets as well). Anyone interacting with a labyrinth, whether a three, seven, or eleven-circuit labyrinth in which three is an integral and hidden aspect, is also interacting with the qualities and characteristics of this number.

Four

Four is often used to represent the physical world; that which is tangible and visible. There are some well-known groups of four such as the four directions and the four elements. Martin Lings in his book *Symbol & Archetype: A Study of the Meaning of Existence* describes four as the traditional number of "earth" or "the world of time and space" (Lings 2005). History is understood by the ancients and by some modern traditionalists as being a cycle of four ages (we live now in the last age, or "age of lead"). Matter was generally understood in terms of four qualities (hot, cold, wet, and dry) that combine in what are called the four elements: earth, air, fire, and water. Human beings had four humours (blood, yellow bile, black bile, and phlegm), the balance or imbalance of which is the substance of our temperament, health, and vitality. These four humours gave rise to the four temperaments of being sanguine, choleric, melancholic, and phlegmatic. Four is also a significant number in alchemy, and later in the book we will explore how the four elements can combine to create the fifth, the quintessence.

The relevance of four to those working with the labyrinth is firstly seen in the four quadrants of both the classical and Chartres labyrinths. Such fourfold aspects permeate the whole labyrinth form and imbue the labyrinth with the associations and qualities of the number four, as well as direct associations with groups of four parts, such as the four elements, the four directions, and others.

The four quadrants in the Chartres and classical labyrinths have other associations. When seen as earth, air, fire, and water they also symbolise the four categories of zodiac signs. A further association is with the four evangelists, Matthew, Mark, Luke, and John, who are often depicted as winged creatures. The young man Matthew represents the element air and is Aquarius. Mark, as a lion, is Leo the fire element. Luke, the bull, represents Taurus and the earth element, while John, the eagle, is an adapted form of Scorpio and the water element. Many illustrations containing Jesus and the four evangelists show Jesus at the centre with the four evangelists at each of the four corners of the image.

Seven

Seven was always my favorite number. When I was younger, I had no logical reason for this being the case; I just liked the number seven. When I began investigating the meaning and symbolism of numbers, my relationship with the number seven became even stronger. I discovered that in numerology, the date of my birth (which determines your life path number) comes to seven. I wonder how much of my passion for the labyrinth is because of having seven as my life path number.

There is a saying that "information is power." When I apply this to my life, it leads me to find out as much as I can about my life and my soul purpose. It is surprising how much esoteric information is available out there for you to access. I have sought out people who gave me specific information about myself through numerology, astrology, tarot, and several other systems that I felt would be of help to me. I have learned much about myself and receive invaluable guidance on my path of discovery and growth. I also carry a healthy scepticism about the information that I receive. I trust firstly in myself and my own feelings about what I am hearing, while remaining open to considering new insights, even if they are ones that I might not necessarily consider complimentary.

The number seven holds special significance for many societies and cultures, and its appearance in a wide range of areas imbues it with an even greater importance. Four is the number for earth, and three is the number representing heaven, therefore seven is the first number containing both the spiritual and the temporal. The labyrinth holds the energy of many of the divisions of seven that are to be found in the physical, esoteric, and spiritual worlds.

It is difficult to identify a beginning for the significance of the number seven, although cosmic, or nonearthly, connections are an interesting starting point. The Bible mentions the seven days of creation and that the Elohim created earth. In his book *Genesis, Secrets of the Bible Story of Creation,* Rudolf Steiner writes that there were seven Elohim who were lofty, sublime spiritual beings (Steiner 1910). The seven visible heavenly bodies and their association with the names of deities (Luna, Mercury, Venus, the Sun, Mars, Jupiter, Saturn) are also one of the strongest cases for the beginning of the importance of the number seven.

The Romans divided the week into seven days and held the seventh day, the Sol or Sunday of Jupiter, as the most sacred; to this day it is the principal day of worship for Christians. To the Pythagoreans, seven represented the divine order and harmony in nature. Seven was twice the sacred number, the triad (three), to which the divine monad (the one) was added.

As regards the actual practice of interacting with the number seven, there are many records throughout the ages of sacred sites being circled seven times, some of which have lasted or evolved into current practices. The Ka'bah at Mecca is circled seven times in an anti-clockwise direction. In pagan times, seven naked priestesses circled the black stone at Mecca seven times. This older practise is a symbolic re-enactment of the descent of the Sumerian goddess, Inanna (Ishtar), through the seven gates of the underworld.

In Ireland at many holy wells and sacred sites there is a tradition of walking in prayer seven times around the well or site. In Ashkenazi Jewish wedding ceremonies, there is a custom of the bride circling the husband seven times. Some Indian wedding ceremonies involve the bride and groom walking around a sacred fire seven times. These practices are full of symbolism. They mimic the biblical seven days of creation, and the ancient sacredness attributed to the number seven.

The strong presence of the number seven in the labyrinth associates it with many of the lists, qualities, and characteristics of things that come in groups of seven. John Mitchell, in his book *The Dimensions of Paradise,* offers a succinct and thought-provoking interpretation of the number seven when he writes, "Seven is unique among the numbers of the decad because, as the Pythagoreans said, 'it neither generates nor is generated,' meaning that it cannot be multiplied to produce another number within the first ten, nor is it a product of any other numbers. For that reason the heptad was called the Virgin and was a symbol of eternal rather than created things" (Mitchell 1988).

Philip Gardiner considers that the number seven is "a characteristic feature of the entrance or Gateway to the celestial Otherworld…The number is also closely associated in the same way with the ascent to heaven or Otherworld on a tree, ladder, stairway or mountain." Gardiner goes on to say that seven is "always important in relation to the world of the esoteric and 'Gateway' travel" (Gardiner 2007a). Thus, the seven-circuit labyrinth resonates on an otherworldly level as a gateway to another dimension, or as a rung on the ladder to heaven.

Seven holds a significance in many more religions and belief systems. In Buddhism, seven is the number of ascent and of ascending to the highest level. The seven steps of Buddha symbolise the ascent of the seven cosmic stages transcending time and space. There are seven branches to the Tree of Life, each having seven leaves. Leaves are symbols of fertility, renewal, and growth. The seven branches represent a union of all that is, supported by the trunk. As a symbol of unity, it is like the labyrinth; the seventh branch of the Tree of Life, associated with the crown chakra, is the gateway to the Divine. Angela McGerr writes that "the Sacred Seven angel rulers of the weekdays and seven major planets of our solar system are also the angel rulers of each of the Heavens, although the ruler of the seventh (Cassiel) is actually classified as the Gatekeeper for God/The Creator who dwells in Seventh heaven. Melchizedek, father to the Sacred Seven, rules the seventh ray (violet)" (McGerr 2008).

The mystical number seven is also important in the world of intellect and philosophy. Greece had seven sages. The Christian Middle Ages had seven liberal arts (grammar, rhetoric, dialectics, arithmetic, geometry, music, astronomy). In some western societies, the healing gift is said to be associated with the seventh son of a seventh son. We order our lives around the seven-day week whatever our specific "religious" beliefs, because we have an innate resonance with the number seven.

Seven is the number of transcendence, and by being inherent in the labyrinth it imbues the labyrinth with all its associated qualities. The labyrinth therefore is both a symbolic and physical gateway to achieving a transcendent state of being. The presence of the number seven in the labyrinth is not a coincidence. The earth on which we live resonates with the number seven. So also does our representation of the heavens to which we aspire, and to which we will return as spirit energy when we leave this physical earth plane. The labyrinth, by holding the number seven within its folds, is not only symbolic and representative of all that resonates with the energy of the number seven; it also is a sevenfold tool for attaining higher spiritual awareness and existence.

Eleven

Eleven is a master number in numerology, in that it is a double-digit number with identical digits. It is a powerful number as the meaning and attributes of the prime number is doubled. As the number one has associations of new beginnings and purity, these attributes are doubled in strength with eleven. According to Pythagoras, the number eleven carries the frequency of balance. This is the balance that many experience in an eleven-circuit labyrinth. It prompts us to look at areas of balance in our lives such as between work and play, dreams and reality, and action and contemplation.

When eleven is viewed visually, it looks like a doorway between two pillars: a gateway between the dualities of the number two. It is calling us to enter the gateway presented by the labyrinth into a world where we occupy a place of balance. Physically focusing on the space between the two digits in the number eleven is a meditative practice that can help concentrate the mind and come more into the present moment and a space of conscious awareness.

The spiritual meaning of the number eleven is associated with light, awakening, and intuitive insight. It is related to spiritual unfoldment in a person, can be seen as a call to initiation and advancement, and is linked with our involvement with the progression of life. The number eleven is often called "the Illuminator," "the Messenger," or "the Teacher." This is significant in the context of the eleven-circuit labyrinth that can help illuminate, bringing messages and teachings.

Twelve

Twelve is a number that represents a complete cycle and cosmic order. There are twelve months of the year, and twelve signs of the zodiac. Twelve, composed of 3 x 4, represents both the spiritual and physical; the esoteric and exoteric. Twelve was considered to be an ancient number of completion as it indicated the end of childhood at age twelve and signalled the beginning of adulthood.

Twelve is a symbolic number in Christianity as it represents the twelve apostles, and in the Old Testament the twelve tribes of Israel, while there are twelve gates in the walls of the new Jerusalem. The labyrinth at Chartres, with its twelve circles, is sometimes known as "Chemin de Jérusalem," or the Road to Jerusalem. Also at Chartres Cathedral, the twelve labours of the month and the signs of the zodiac are found in several places, including over the entrance porch to the cathedral.

Spirals

Spirals are often described as the patterns of nature and creation. According to Geoff Ward, "the spiral is the sign of the eternal, creative, unifying and organising force or principle at work in the universe, and especially of the ongoing creation of consciousness" (Ward 2006). From the awe-inspiring great spirals of galaxies to the spiralling vortices of whirlpools, the spiral is found in a myriad of situations on this earth and beyond. Indeed, Colin Wilson in his introduction to Geoff Ward's *Spirals: The*

Patterns of Existence states that the spiral is "a glimpse into the mind of God" (Ward 2006).

There is an association between labyrinths and spirals that is not always apparent. In the common method of drawing the labyrinth using the seed pattern, a veiled spiralling motion is used to make the labyrinth. If you do not lift your pen from the page when drawing the circuits of the labyrinth, but instead continue from where you have finished each circuit and bring your pen back in a loop around to the next starting point, you will see the spiral pattern.

There are two aspects to the spiral: the expanding spiral and the contracting spiral. Just as in walking the labyrinth, you can experience going to the centre as contracting and concentrating, while emerging from the labyrinth is expanding yourself back out into the world.

The spiral pattern has several labyrinth-like associations. The Stone Age spiral carvings represent the soul's journey into the womb-like underworld, and its subsequent return towards rebirth. It can also represent creation, as something emerges from the point of nothing. Knud Mariboe, when talking of the relationship between the spiral and the labyrinth, says, "Although often intricate in form, the labyrinth is a spiral, and one which returns. It is a representation of the cosmos and all cosmoses, and hence of all ordered entities which correspond on the descending scale of analogy. It is therefore, at once the cosmos, the world, the individual life, the temple, the town, man, the womb—or intestines of the Mother (Earth), the convolutions of the brain, the consciousness, the heart, the pilgrimage, the journey, and the Way" (Mariboe 1994). Such a descent into the underworld (the kingdom of Pluto) is the theme of many initiation rituals and is comparable to the passage through the wilderness, or the "dark night of the soul," which is experienced by mystics on their path and is often symbolised by the spiral.

Mandalas

Mandalas are symbols found in Buddhism and Hinduism that represent the universe. Mandala is Sanskrit for "circle that contains the essence." Labyrinths and mandalas are archetypal collective symbols that transcend all cultures because they are grounded in consciousness itself. Mandalas, like labyrinths, are often circular in shape with the centre seen as its strongest point. The centre of both the labyrinth and the mandala represents what is central to us, what is core to us—either now, or on the higher levels of our soul journey. Working with labyrinths and mandalas engages the right side of our brain, enhancing our creativity and leading us to our centre.

Circles

The circle is often used to represent heaven. The circle, in the words of John James, "is the perfect geometric figure, being the same at the beginning as at the end, as with alpha and omega" (James 1977). Most labyrinth are circular, or almost circular, in shape. It is no coincidence that this is the case, as the circle on its own is a symbol of completeness. Contained within the boundaries of the circle are all the other elements and qualities found in the labyrinth.

Squaring the Circle

"Squaring the circle" has several meanings and interpretations. The origin of this conundrum was a mathematical problem proposed by ancient geometers of constructing a square with the same area as a given circle. Many tried and failed to solve this problem. It wasn't until 1882 that the task was proven to be mathematically impossible, when it was proven that pi (π) is a transcendental number, meaning that it is non-algebraic and uncountable.

Squaring the circle has several other meanings. The term is often used to describe an impossible task. The other meanings are best understood when we recall the esoteric meanings given to the square and the circle. The square represents earth, with its four sides representing the four elements, the four directions, and the encompassment of matter itself. The circle, having no beginning and no end, represents infinity, or God, or heaven. The circle from ancient times was used as a symbol of the sun, which was the most powerful object that came within sight and understanding of man from earliest times.

Therefore, from an esoteric viewpoint, "squaring the circle" is a metaphor for the integration of earth and heaven, and for finding your heaven here on earth. Jung wrote, "the squaring of the circle is one of the many archetypal motifs which form the basic patterns of our dreams and fantasies … it could even be called the archetype of wholeness" (Jung 1967). Similarly, Hermann Kern considers that the labyrinth "represents a sort of reconciliation, a union of both" (Kern 2000).

The square of earth and the circle of heaven are also to be seen in the drawing of the classical labyrinth from the seed pattern. Starting with the square seed pattern representing earth as you create the labyrinth, the shape is becoming increasingly circular, resulting in almost a complete circle. The opening in this circular shape provides the entranceway to a single path to the centre; the labyrinth is providing a path to heaven (circle) from the square of earth. The labyrinth can also represent and symbolise the coming together of earth and heaven. On another level, the squaring of the circle signifies that God has attained form and manifested in the square of man, the human soul.

Putting It All Together

In this chapter, I have given you information about many aspects of the labyrinth. You know more about the history of labyrinths, the types of labyrinths, the parts of labyrinths, and some of the associations of the labyrinth, including the importance of both the apparent and hidden numbers in the labyrinth.

Yet I feel that I have not described what a labyrinth is. Indeed, the more I learn about the labyrinth, the more difficult it is for me to describe it. In attempting to describe the labyrinth, I am drawn to the first few lines of the Tao Te Ching that say, "The way that can be spoken of is not the constant way" (Tzu 1963); in other words, the Tao that can be described is not the Tao. The labyrinth is very much like this. A labyrinth that can be described is not a labyrinth. Any attempt to define the labyrinth is lacking in something because the labyrinth is knowledge, experience, reflection, wisdom, enlightenment, and more all rolled into one. When you create a labyrinth with deep meaning and intention, you tune in to the parts and wholeness of the labyrinth on a deeper level, creating a labyrinth that is vibrant, alive, and unique to you: you create a labyrinth temple of you.

EXERCISE: HOW TO CREATE A LABYRINTH IMBUED WITH YOUR ENERGY (CREATING THE LABYRINTH TEMPLE OF YOU)

In the previous exercise, you learned how to draw and make a labyrinth. There is much more to the practice of drawing and creating a labyrinth. The practice of creating a labyrinth has a positive effect on the maker. In making a labyrinth you are actively engaging with the symbolism of the labyrinth. You are creating a sacred space with which you will be interacting to quieten the mind, seek answers to questions, and explore your life's issues. You will be using the finger labyrinth that you draw in this exercise in some of the other exercises in the book. So, the more focused you are doing this exercise, the greater benefits you will gain when using the labyrinth later, as your mindset and general disposition at the time of creating the labyrinth will be reflected in the completed labyrinth.

Many people who make labyrinths are aware of the special and empowering nature of drawing and building labyrinths. That's one reason that they keep making labyrinths. Making labyrinths is both energizing and meditative. It brings the maker into the positive energy field of the labyrinth.

There are also reports of increased intuition coming to people when drawing a series of labyrinths. In his book *Labyrinths: Ancient Myths and Modern Uses,* Sig Lonegren considers that there is "something very special about making a labyrinth yourself." He says that it happens the fifth or sixth time you make one; that it is quite easy to understand how to make one intellectually, but after you draw it half a dozen times "the labyrinth offers another way of knowing" (Lonegren 2015).

This exercise is not only about how to draw or make a labyrinth, it is also an exercise in actively creating and engaging with the symbolism and energy of the labyrinth. It has been recounted that if you draw a labyrinth ten times in succession that you will enter a deeper state of awareness. So, for full effect and benefit from this exercise, do it ten times in succession.

Any activity done with intention and focus is enhanced by such an approach. A typical example is the creation of icons, where the icon is made and used in an atmosphere of prayer. Monks creating icons often prepare by fasting and praying with the intention of being in a spiritually high place when creating the icon. When painting the icon, they typically pray over each brush stroke. This intense and attentive approach gives us a snapshot into the supersensitive world that is the goal of the spiritual path. It also illustrates that the creation of symbols and tools to assist us in progressing on our personal and spiritual growth paths becomes more powerful and experiential when done with concentration, heartfelt energy, and intention.

Applying this focused approach to the creation of the labyrinth, each aspect of the labyrinth and each line drawn to create it carries the energy that you imbue it with. Everything in the labyrinth is significant. Therefore, to enhance this labyrinth creation exercise, I have associated each action in the nineteen stages of creating the labyrinth with a quality or element to be contemplated and invoked. The seed pattern contains elements that are associated with the symbolism of the cross and the four quadrants, while the eight lines to complete the circuits are invocations related to the qualities associated with each circuit and with completeness. Saying the words out loud further enhances the effect of the exercise.

The words "I AM" are powerful words, and using them consciously is a creative force that generates the intention expressed. Anything said immediately after the words I AM is a statement to the world, the Universe, and beyond that this is what you are. The book of Exodus in the Bible reads that when Moses asked God what is his name, "God said unto Moses, I AM THAT I AM" (Exodus 3:14 KJV). Placing the name of God, the creator, in a sentence and saying the name of the creator is a dynamic statement that empowers whatever follows it.

In effect, what you are doing in this exercise is creating a symbol of you. The labyrinth, as you are drawing it in this exercise, represents you. Each line that you draw and each statement you speak out loud is creating and empowering the symbol of you that you are creating. You are creating a plan of the sacred temple that is you. It is one of the first steps in this book to realizing your true self.

Follow the instructions below in the order described to create your own labyrinth. When finished, trace the path to the centre, and leave your finger there as you rest in the centre of your being. When ready, trace the path back out of the labyrinth.

To make this exercise even more powerful, keep repeating this exercise until you have ten labyrinths made.

Creating the Sacred Space of the Labyrinth
—The Temple of You

Step	Action	Design	Invocation
1	Dot		I AM
2	Horizontal line through dot		I AM Present
3	Vertical Line through dot		I AM Divine
4	Bottom left dot		I AM Direction
5	Top left dot		I AM Dimension
6	Top right dot		I AM Space
7	Bottom right dot		I AM Time
8	Bottom left bracket		I AM Earth

Step	Action	Design	Invocation
9	Top left bracket		I AM Air
10	Top right bracket		I AM Fire
11	Bottom right bracket		I AM Water
12	Loop 1		I AM One
13	Loop 2		I AM Aware
14	Loop 3		I AM Insight
15	Loop 4		I AM Truth
16	Loop 5		I AM Love

Step	Action	Design	Invocation
17	Loop 6		I AM Power
18	Loop 7		I AM Creation
19	Loop 8		I AM ALL

Reflection

After you have created your labyrinth (or your ten labyrinths), take some time to sit quietly with your thoughts and feelings. What kind of space are you in now? What is different from when you started this exercise? Write down, draw, or paint what comes into your head. These reflections might not seem immediately relevant. But, when you look back at them after other exercises in later chapters, their relevance can become more apparent.

3
The Labyrinth Effect

The labyrinth is an archetype; it universally has both a conscious and subconscious effect on anyone interacting with it. Many people who see the labyrinth for the first time feel that they have seen it before. There is a recognition of something familiar. There is a sense of connection to this symbol that is greater than its visible appearance. For some, the labyrinth holds a presence that invites them to interact with it.

How Does the Labyrinth Work?

Many have asked the question "How does the labyrinth work?" Few can provide the unequivocal answer. In some ways, it doesn't matter how it works, only that it does. On another level, knowing some of what causes the "labyrinth effect" can help to understand what is happening when you interact with it. If you are seeking information about how the labyrinth works, then using the labyrinth will ultimately bring about the knowledge and understanding of its functions and benefits. Key areas to consider are what makes the experience of walking the labyrinth such a moving one for so many people, and what causes people to have insights and increased intuition as they walk the labyrinth.

The early labyrinth makers, and the later medieval labyrinth builders, did not leave us any information as to how the labyrinth works. We are left to draw insights and conclusions from a wide range of disciplines and beliefs including neurology, psychology, eastern mysticism, psychics, and our own experiences. The theories of how the labyrinth work include the integration of the brain's hemispheres, the generation of energy vortices, aligning the chakras while walking, and rebalancing your energy field.

Balancing the Brain

The classical labyrinth looks like a brain. It also has a positive effect on your brain and your disposition. Walking the labyrinth quietens the mind, and brings the walker into a more balanced and centred state. Tracing a finger labyrinth has a similar effect.

One explanation of how the labyrinth works is understood when we consider the theory of the right and left sides of the brain. The left side of the brain is responsible for the masculine qualities of rational and logical thinking, dynamic action, and doing. The right side of the brain is associated with the feminine qualities of receptivity, intuition, creativity, and nurturing. In today's world, your brain can easily be out of balance as the right brain is often overworked from too many tasks to do, things to think about, and other stimuli.

When you walk the labyrinth, you must focus on the narrow path ahead, or you may stray from the path. This act of focusing on the path fully engages the left brain, and has a quietening effect similar to meditating on a single point such as a candle flame or a rose. In its quietened state, where there is less thinking activity, there is now space for the right brain to come more to the fore and into balance with the left side. When in balance, you are in a state known as "whole-brained." In this state, you draw equally on the logical rational thinking qualities of the left brain and on the intuitive, creative qualities of the right brain. In this whole-brained state, you are more open to receiving insights, answers to questions, and seeking solutions to problems.

A further brain-related labyrinth effect happens when a person passes through the 180-degree turns in the labyrinth. The sharp change of direction is thought to shift the awareness of the walker from one side of the brain to the other. This induces a deeper connection between the sides of the brain, resulting in a more integrated brain functioning and a more receptive state of consciousness.

Philip Gardiner, in his book *Gateways to the Otherworld*, states, "All of the emotional problems people have stem from having a divided perception, because we perceive, or receive the world through either one brain hemisphere or the other, and so we can only understand it from one side or the other—logical or emotional." He goes on to describe how each hemisphere acts as a filter through which the images and meaning of our reality is received and interpreted. He also considers that we create our reality through either one or the other of these hemispheres or filters; whereas some of us create a "logical and ordered universe world," others create a "wondrous imaginative world" (Gardiner 2007a). The key aspect of Gardiner's theory is that because we are divided within ourselves, the world that we create is a world of division, fighting, and war. He concludes that "If we were all 'balanced' in left and right brain waves, then we might be able to see the other person's side of the argument" (Gardiner 2007a).

Therefore, in using the labyrinth to bring ourselves into balance, we are also leading to a situation where the world that we create is also coming into balance. Your outer world is a reflection of your inner world. If you want to change the world around you, you must first change within yourself.

Turn Around

The turns in the labyrinth have another positive effect. In making a 180-degree turn, you are shifting your energy field in a dramatic way. It is rare to make such a dramatic about-turn in everyday life. You might do so at eventful times when you have forgotten something and need to go back to get it urgently or when you turn and run in times of danger. Turns at such times are often taken in a rushed or panic state, and they lead you inevitably from one state of being to another.

In the labyrinth these 180-degree turns are made in a measured and predictable way, as the path you are walking prescribes the turns for you. In the Chartres labyrinth, for example, there are twenty-eight such turns on the way in and twenty-eight such turns on the way out, a total of fifty-six turns. There is no such situation in our everyday lives where you make so many deliberate energy shifting movements in such a short space of time.

The effect of such turns on your body's energy field is similar to some Tai Chi movements where the practitioner is deliberately making 180-degree turns from their core, followed by accompanying hand movements, often with the intention of moving the energy in such a way as to focus on it and to manipulate and concentrate it. Moving through the labyrinth has a similar effect on your body's energy field, shifting and realigning your energy field. As a result, you feel more centred after a labyrinth walk.

It is also thought that the many turns experienced while walking the labyrinth cause the brain fluid to move back and forth across the middle line of the brain. This contributes to a balancing of the brain function and an integration of the right and left sides of the brain. So, the combined effects of the turns in the labyrinth can be summarized by the expression that the labyrinth "turns you on"!

Your Chakras and the Labyrinth

One of the most powerful associations of the labyrinth is the correlation of the seven circuits of the labyrinth with your seven main chakras. Your chakras are energy centres that are located along the centre of your body, from the base of your spine to the top of your head. *Chakra* is a Sanskrit word meaning "wheel." If you could see your chakras they would look like spinning wheels of light emanating in a conical shape from points along the centre of your body. Your chakras feed and nourish your physical body with life force energy and are associated with certain qualities and colours. The colours of your seven chakras are the colours of the rainbow. When you know the associations of each chakra, it not only makes your labyrinth walk more interesting, it also helps you to understand many aspects of your life. From bottom to top, your chakras are as follows:

First chakra (in Sanskrit, muladhara), also known as the base chakra or root chakra. This chakra is located in the perineum area and spirals downwards into the earth. It connects you to the earth and is associated with security and safety issues as well as being here on earth. Its colour is red.

Second chakra (swadhistana), also known as the sacral chakra, is located at the sacrum in the pelvic area. It represents creativity and sexuality and is associated with your emotions, and the colour is orange.

Third chakra (manipura) is located at the solar plexus / stomach area. It is associated with your will and power, and the colour is yellow. It is related to your identity and how you see yourself in the world.

Fourth chakra (anahata), also known as the heart chakra, is in the centre of the chest. It is related to how you connect with others in relationships. Its colour is green.

Fifth chakra (vishuddha) is in the centre of the throat area. It is the energetic communication centre in your body and represents how you connect with speaking your truth. Its colour is blue.

Sixth chakra (ajna), or third eye, is in the centre of your head, between the eyebrows. It is connected to how you see beyond the physical—your psychic abilities. Its colour is indigo.

Seventh chakra (sahasrara) is located at the top of the head, spiralling upwards. It connects you to the source of all—Universal Energy, God, Great Spirit, Oneness. Its colour is violet.

The chakras are associated with the circuits of the classical labyrinth starting with the root chakra on the outer circuit and moving inwards to the crown chakra. The centre of the labyrinth is associated with your higher self, or soul star, sometimes called your "eighth chakra," and is located about twelve inches above your head. In walking through the labyrinth, you pass through each circuit and its associations with the chakras bringing them into balance and aligning your energy body. This aligning contributes to the feeling of being more relaxed and peaceful after walking the labyrinth. In a study by John Rhodes, PhD, into the effects of the labyrinth, 81 percent of the respondents reported that they felt "much more" or "more" centred following a labyrinth walk than before a labyrinth walk. In the same study, 87 percent of the respondents reported that they felt "much more" or "more" peaceful following a labyrinth walk than before a labyrinth walk (Rhodes 2008).

As well as representing your chakras, the seven circuits carry other associations with the chakras, such as the endocrine glands, planets, metals, and more (see Appendix 1). There are other connections between the labyrinth and your chakras that are not initially apparent. The number seven is mentioned many times in the Bible, and several of these have been interpreted to mean the seven chakras. The number seven is the number of biblical perfection and completion, so when all your chakras are in alignment and shining bright and clear then you are close to spiritual purity. In the book of Revelation in the Bible we read: "And I turned to see the voice that spake with me. And being turned, I saw seven golden candlesticks … And he had in his right hand seven stars: and out of his mouth went a sharp two-edged sword: and his countenance was as the sun shineth in his strength … The mystery of the seven stars which thou sawest in my right hand, and the seven golden candlesticks. The seven stars are the angels of the seven churches: and the seven candlesticks which thou sawest are the seven churches" (Revelation 1:12-20 KJV).

While many interpret this passage literally, there are other meanings that can be attributed to it. According to Edgar Cayce, the sleeping prophet, the seven endocrine glands are depicted in Revelations as seven stars. Connecting the seven chakras to the seven endocrine glands subsequently connects the body to the soul. Spirit manifests in the body through these spiritual gland centres.

Further on in the book of Revelation there is a passage about a book "written within and on the backside, sealed with seven seals," which no one has the ability to open on his own (5:3). However, one of the elders spoke that the "Lion of the tribe of Juda, the root of David" had prevailed and opened the book. This book symbolises the body and its seven spiritual centres, or chakras. Jesus, in bringing the Christ consciousness to humanity, opened our spiritual centres.

The message of the whole passage is that through the development of a Christlike state of existence, the spiritual centres are opened, and through the attainment of the experience and presence of Christ consciousness, all seven centres are opened. There are many ways to attain this level of consciousness, meditation being the most often used. The labyrinth as a walking meditation conducted in an ancient sacred symbol is also a powerful way to do this work. The connections between the chakras, endocrine glands, and the seven circuits mean that in working with the labyrinth you are also working with your spiritual centres—working to clear them, to fill them with light, and to bring them to a pure state of existence. Furthermore, in clearing, enlightening, and aligning your energy centres, you are bringing your physical, energetic, and spiritual centres into alignment, creating the tree of life of your body and standing as a link between heaven and earth.

Nonlinear

It's time to get off the straight and narrow! The "straight and narrow," while sometimes used to describe what is right and proper, can also carry with it a sense of restriction and absence of adventure. While the labyrinth path is sometimes narrow, it is rarely straight. Most labyrinths are nonlinear, as the path does not follow a numerical sequence through the circuits. This nonlinear movement through a labyrinth contributes to you losing your sense of where you are in the pattern, and can result in a sense of timelessness, or feeling lost, although "lost" is probably not the best word to describe the feeling and sensation in a labyrinth. The famous frontiersman Daniel Boone best described this sensation in the labyrinth when he said, "I can't say as ever I was lost, but I was bewildered once for three days." So, an occasional sense of bewilderment is quite possible in a labyrinth, especially when one walks one for the first time.

This sense of detachment from the logical mind, and the outside world, can be quite relaxing and refreshing for the labyrinth walker, as it involves a form of surrendering to the labyrinth and a letting go of a sense of having to control everything. Hermann Kern, in describing how a walker moves through a seven-circuit classical labyrinth, writes, "The deeper the wanderer moves into the labyrinth, the further diminished the active radius (the number of quadrants entered) and the walker's grip on the world and his bearings within it become" (Kern 2000).

Edgar Cayce has said through his written work that information helping us to grow spiritually comes to us in two ways: through our experiences and through archetypes from the collective / cosmic consciousness. The labyrinth involves both of these ways: it is a practice through which we have an experience of walking, and turning, and of entering a different state of being. It is also an archetype, a symbol grounded in the collective consciousness.

Circling Towards the Centre

The practice of labyrinth walking is a form of circling towards the centre. The power and energy of the inherent spiral as a creative energy is imbued in the walker as they interact with the labyrinth. This brings out the person's creative forces while creating a positive energy vortex where negative energetic patterns are transformed, allowing the walker to experience insights and heightened awareness. This energy vortex can also have the effect of transporting the walker to another dimension. Having traversed the spiral to the centre, to the point of oblivion, where else could it lead, but to beyond the nothingness and into another dimension.

Effect of Labyrinth Walking on Your Energy Field

You have an energy field, sometimes referred to as your aura. Some people can see this energy field. It is possible to measure the size of a person's energy field using the practice of divining (more commonly called dowsing, but I prefer the term divining as it is rooted in the "Divine"). I usually measure a person's energy field by asking the person to stand in one spot and then measuring the edge of their energy field with divining rods as I walk backwards away from them.

In all cases where I measured people's energy fields before and after walking the labyrinth, the person's energy field was much larger after the labyrinth walk. The radius of most people's energy field is doubled in size, and some people have expanded even more.

The human energy field expands in many different situations. The expansion of the energy field is due to a rise in vibration of the energy field. As your vibration rises, your energy field expands. Meditation, including labyrinth walking, is one of the best ways to raise your vibration and expand your energy field. When you disconnect from the worries, concerns, and fears of everyday life, and enter a space of peace, calm, and love, your energy field responds accordingly and expands. When your aura is expanded, you are more aware and able to pick up subtle signals. This may partially explain how some people receive insights and answers to questions on the labyrinth.

The Consciousness Field of the Labyrinth

The Consciousness Field of the Labyrinth (CFL) is the repository of all labyrinth knowledge and wisdom that has accumulated over the millennia. From the time man first carved the labyrinth pattern into the rocks in Spain, Italy, and India over four thousand years ago to today's labyrinth activities, the consciousness field has been expanding.

The labyrinth entered humanity's consciousness from the greater unified field, the field of oneness. Man accessed and tapped into this consciousness field and drew the first labyrinth pattern. From there, the labyrinth took on a significance that is still resonating with people today. The labyrinth pattern carries within it the vibration of Source, the divine essence. When interacting with the labyrinth you are accessing the unified field of all knowledge and wisdom.

A field in this context is similar to how physicists describe a field; it not only has duration, but also extension in space. Somewhere, the sum of all knowledge, information, and labyrinth related activity is stored and accessible. In keeping with many field theories in physics, the consciousness field of the labyrinth exists on many dimensions and levels.

The consciousness field of the labyrinth is similar to Jung's collective unconscious, within which a mode of transmission of archetypes and shared symbols and patterns exist. Jacques Attali in his book *The Labyrinth in Culture and Society* contends that "The labyrinth is a material manifestation of a collective unconscious, of a message sent forth into the beyond. It represents the first abstraction of a sense of human destiny, of an ordering of the world. It describes the universe in both its visible and invisible aspects—a universe whose traversal, like that of life, is both sought after (because it leads to the discovery of eternity) and feared (because nothingness waits there). It is like a place of precarious and dangerous passage, a breach between two worlds" (Attali 1999).

The Labyrinth of Opposites

On initial observation, the labyrinth appears static and immobile. Standing outside the labyrinth, you can see the whole pattern. Once you enter the labyrinth and start walking, your attention is mostly limited to a short part of the path ahead of you. When walking the labyrinth, it assumes a dynamic characteristic where you, as the walker, are now interacting with the labyrinth, engaging with the path and manoeuvring the turns to reach your goal—the labyrinth's centre.

The path is the connection between opposites: the static and the dynamic, the seen and unseen, confusion and clarity, between the outside and the inside. Walking the path brings the outer and inner worlds into balance. You start your walk in awareness of the world around you, bringing this awareness into the labyrinth. As you walk further into the labyrinth you become more aware of what you are doing and how you are feeling. Your eyes are focused on the narrow path ahead of you, your feet settle into a rhythm as you walk, and your breathing deepens. You become immersed in the act of walking, freeing your thoughts and feelings, and bringing an increased awareness of them, effectively merging your outer and inner worlds. Zara Renander expressed this beautifully when she wrote, "Two sides of a coin are revealed at the same time: The external, physical journey step by step illuminates our inner life, making the implicit explicit, creating a powerful resonance and revelation between inner and outer realities" (Renander 2011).

The aspects that began as opposites are united into an integrated whole in the labyrinth. The outer and inner worlds are merged. The labyrinth brings together matter and spirit, head and heart, the masculine and the feminine, leading to a sense of wholeness and unity.

Putting It All Together

The cumulative impact of all these labyrinth effects is both powerful and subtle. Once aware of even some of these effects, you begin to realise that you are interacting with a powerful and restorative symbol as well as a tool for transformation. Awareness of the known with the presence of unknown effects can contribute to your experience with the labyrinth. While the labyrinth heightens your awareness, the more you approach it in a conscious, attentive, and mindful state, the more enhanced your experience is likely to be. Awareness of yourself is achieved through being aware of your thoughts, feelings, physical responses, and all other signals received. So, let's experience yourself in the labyrinth.

EXERCISE: HOW TO TUNE IN TO HEIGHTENED AWARENESS IN THE LABYRINTH

We have seen in this chapter some of the possible effects that a labyrinth has on the walker. When walking a labyrinth, either knowingly or unknowingly, you are experiencing some or all of these effects. These effects can help to bring you to a different state of awareness, a state of awareness brought about by the labyrinth effect and by how you approach the labyrinth walk.

One of the keys to walking the labyrinth, and to life itself, is to be aware of the importance of every moment. The more aware you are, the more you are open to receiving insights into your life, and the more you will see your existence in the context of a greater existence.

This exercise, then, is to walk the labyrinth in an as open and aware state as possible—to become aware of yourself on as many levels as you can experience at the time. It helps, therefore, not to rush straight into the labyrinth but to first prepare for the walk.

Before the walk, bring yourself into as quiet a state as possible. Give your body and mind permission to slow down, and give your mind permission to become aware and remember what is significant for you. Take a few deep breaths, relax your body as best you can, and become aware of your feet on the ground, your heart beating in your chest, and your hands by your side. As soon as you are aware of your presence in your body and in your surroundings, you then are ready to walk with awareness.

While walking, be aware of everything. Use all your senses: sight, hearing, smell, taste, and touch, and even your extra-sensory perception. Messages and signals can come to you often from unexpected quarters. If outside, be aware of nature, the wind, birds, and animals. Apparent intrusive sounds can have deeper meaning, so be open to seeing beyond the immediate and your reaction to it. What can you see as you are walking? Take note of what you are noticing as you walk the labyrinth. What sounds are coming to your ears? Are these external sounds or internal sounds? What about smells? What do you smell? Taste the air. What does it taste like?

Become the watcher. Watch yourself walking the labyrinth, and see what you observe about yourself. Take a mental note of everything that comes to mind. See if you can sense slight changes in temperature and bodily senses. Do you feel colder or warmer at any stage? Is your body sending you a signal through giving you goose bumps, stiffness, energy jerks, slowing you down or speeding up, or reacting in some other way? Any change is significant, so take note of it for writing down later.

Beyond your bodily senses there are many other senses that send you signals. You are becoming conscious of the energy within you and around you, so tune in to this energy also and in to what it can tell you. Thoughts or images may come into your mind or vision. You may hear something coming from deep within you, or from somewhere outside of yourself. And it is okay if at first you do not experience any of these things. This is your walk and what happens to you is what happens to you. Have no expectations, and do not expect any specific experience, even if you had such an experience before. Every walk is different because you are different on every walk. Remember, this is about you, not the labyrinth.

Do not dismiss anything. I remember doing a walk before giving a workshop and asked if I needed to consider anything else, or if there was anything more I needed to do. I was a little nervous as the group that I was to facilitate were experienced labyrinth users, and some of the material that I was going to present to them was new and being used for the first time.

During the walk, I was distracted by a song going around and around in my head. I couldn't focus on the question I asked, and no answers or insights were forthcoming. I was so distracted by the song that I was beginning to get a little annoyed. Then, I stopped. I focused on what was happening and where I was. I listened to the words of the song in my head. It was the song "Don't Worry, Be Happy" by Bobby McFerrin! I smiled, got the message, and learned not to dismiss anything!

So, walk with awareness: awareness of everything. Be open to receiving insights, answers, and messages from everywhere and anything.

Reflection

When finished with your walk, take time to reflect on the walk and what it was like. Write down your experience of what happened during the walk. What caught your attention? What distracted you during your walk? Did you notice anything unusual or different? What sounds did you hear, or what smells did you notice? If you think that you had no experience, write that down, and write about how the walk felt for you.

4
Life's Turns in the Labyrinth

The turns that you meet on your labyrinth path are crucial elements that are easily overlooked. For many people, the drive to reach the centre is all encompassing, and, apart from the path that gets you there, everything else along the way is a distraction. Yet, the turns in the labyrinth are powerful points both symbolically and energetically. They are pivotal points on your journey to higher states of existence. They are sometimes known as doors or gates. These doors have been recognized in many ancient traditions and esoteric schools as central to the paths of personal and spiritual advancement.

Two of these ancient mystical traditions, Mithraism and alchemy, both involve seven stages of initiation and development. The transitions between these stages are located at the turns in the classical labyrinth. These turns into the individual circuits not only carry their own energy, they also replicate energetically and symbolically the stages of progression of interrelated paths to enlightenment. There is a transformation happening at the turns of the labyrinth that requires your focus and attention to fully access the knowledge and experience that they bring. To get a greater appreciation of these connections and the power of the turns in the labyrinth, it helps to have an understanding of Mithraism and alchemy as well as the stages of advancement that they contain.

The Mithraic Journey

Mithraism revolved around the worship of the ancient Persian god Mithras in subterranean caverns and caves. It involved initiation through seven stages of an astrologically themed hierarchy. It is thought that the ascent through the seven stages represents the seven stages of the descent of man, which man is now progressing back through.

When I was in Rome several years ago, I came across the Basilica San Clemente, which is one of the oldest in Rome. It commemorates St. Clement, who was the fourth pope and lived in the first century AD. The church that you see today was built in 1108. Beneath the present basilica is a fourth-century basilica that was converted from the house of a Roman nobleman, part of which served briefly as an early church in the first century. In the basement of this house and church is a mithraeum: the cave or underground chamber in which Mithraic ceremonies took place. I descended through the layers of history into the basement. The walls were of rough stone and the ceiling was quite low, although I could stand upright comfortably. Water was flowing along a channel in the ground, giving the whole place a cave-like effect.

As I walked through the underground passages, I came to the mithraeum itself, the entrance of which was blocked off by a metal barred gate. I looked in through the gate and saw a rectangular space with stone benches along each side of the room. Initiates, who were men only, would have sat on these stone benches to celebrate a ritual meal. At the far end of the room, a niche was carved out of the doorway, in which was placed a statue of Mithras at his birth emerging from a large bumpy rock. Between the two benches was a stone slab, or altar. On one side of this altar was an image of Mithras shown as a young man killing a bull. Apollo commanded Mithras, a god born of rock, to slay the bull to ensure fertility and renew life. Each of the other sides had carvings of the twin torchbearers Cautes and Cautopates, symbolizing the waxing and waning of the seasons, and a snake, a symbol of regeneration. On the top of the altar were carvings of the sun god Helios on the left and Selene the moon goddess on the right.

As I stood looking into the mithraeum, I felt a sensation come over me, and I was transfixed. It was the feeling that I get whenever I am somewhere I believe I had been in a past life. I stood gazing through the gate into the inner sanctum of the mithraeum. I just wanted to stay there. My wife, Fionnuala, came over to me and asked me if I was coming along, and all I could say was "I just want to stay here." So, I stayed on that spot for some time. I don't know how long I stayed there; I didn't want to leave!

It is difficult to describe this feeling of knowing that you have been somewhere before—in a past life. It is a sense of connection, of belonging, and of almost expecting something to happen. On this occasion, as happened on some other similar occasions, I was in a half haze between this world and the past. In almost all my other past life experiences, I know the significance of the memory for me in this lifetime. With the mithraeum, it was to reactivate and reveal some of the wisdom of Mithraism, including its connection with the labyrinth and its relevance for today.

The cave of Mithras had seven doors, seven altars, and a ladder with seven rungs depicting the seven grades of initiation into the mystery schools. The seven grades of initiate were progressed through, with the first three being mainly of the physical body while four to seven were spiritual. The cave, subterranean world of darkness, representing death and rebirth, is also echoed in the form of the labyrinth. Mithra emerged from a rock in a cave. The cave/labyrinth is also symbolic of the universe into which the soul descends for mortal existence, and then ascends through the levels to reach immortality and union with the Divine.

The key teaching from Mithraism on your path to self-discovery is that the turns that your life takes are opportunities for greater awakening and awareness. Mithraism mapped and described seven significant stages of transformation, or grades of initiation. The seven grades of initiation of Mithraism and their associated planets corresponding to the turns into the seven circuits of the classical labyrinth are: Corax/Raven (Mercury), Nymphus/Bridegroom (Venus), Miles/Soldier (Mars), Leo/ Lion (Jupiter), Perses/Persian (Moon), Heliodromus/Sun-courier (Sun) and Pater/Father (Saturn).

Followers of Mithraism believed that the heavens were divided into seven spheres, each with one planet that was endowed with certain qualities and associated with one of the grades of initiation. In descending from the empyrean to the earth, the souls successively received from them their qualities and passions. On its ascent back to the highest heaven, the soul rids itself of the qualities it received on its descent by traversing the different spheres. The initiations into each stage represent symbolically, and spiritually, the advancement of the individual. On its symbolic journey through the planetary zones, the soul "abandoned to the Moon its vital and nutritive energy, to Mercury its desires, to Venus its wicked appetites, to the Sun its intellectual capacities, to Mars its love of war, to Jupiter its ambitious dreams, to Saturn its inclinations. It was naked, stripped of every vice and every sensibility, when it penetrated the eighth heaven to enjoy there, as an essence supreme, and in the eternal light that bathed the gods, beatitude without end" (Cumont 1903).

The Mithraic ladder, with seven gates, had an eighth gate at the top, similar to the labyrinth with seven circuits and the centre. In walking the classical labyrinth, the walker has to turn in to each of the seven circuits and make a final eighth turn into the centre. As previously mentioned, the seven circuits also represent our seven chakras, with the centre representing our connection to our higher self, or a reunification of the soul with God. On another level, if we view the seven circuits as representing the seven visible heavenly bodies, then the centre again represents our going beyond the visible world of earth and entering a higher state of awareness, the soul's reunification with Source.

The *Mithras Liturgy* is a text from the Great Magical Papyrus of Paris, held in the Bibliothèque Nationale. It was given its modern name by its first translator, Albrecht Dieterich, in 1903. It is based on the invocation of Helios Mithras as the god who will provide the initiate with a revelation of immortality. The liturgy is a mix of astrology and magic whose main focus is the mystical journey of the ascent of the soul in seven stages. On this journey, the soul encounters the four elements: Aion (the god of unbounded time), the seven Fates, the seven Pole Lords, and finally the highest god, Mithras. The Mithraic journey resembles the path through the labyrinth having seven stages with a gateway at each, and the four elements in the quadrants. We can also see the labyrinth as being a map of the cosmos, and even as our journey into and out of this reality, representing your soul's journey in all its stages.

The Alchemical Labyrinth Path

Alchemy is an ancient practice where the alchemist outwardly sought to change lead into gold. It is shrouded in secrecy and mystery, and secretly the alchemists were seeking to transform their base nature into the gold of enlightened beings. Their manuscripts appeared to describe chemical processes relating to the transmutation of matter. However, their experiments were also representative of the processes and stages that they themselves went through on their journey to enlightenment.

Alchemy is concerned with the transmutation of the personality and self-realization. It is about the transformation of you. You begin to transform yourself when you discover and learn to understand your true nature—that you are a divine immortal being. You are on a journey of transformation moving through different stages by transmuting your everyday earthly nature into your true divine presence. The labyrinth provides a roadmap for the stages of the alchemical processes that you undergo. On the labyrinth path, you progressively realise the infinite potential of your true being, taking steps and turns on your path, where you increasingly get out of your own way and allow your higher self to reveal itself.

Many alchemical texts are difficult to understand. There was a two-fold reason for the alchemists taking the approach of keeping their knowledge hidden. Firstly, as the knowledge was being transferred from master to initiate, writing in ambiguous and oftentimes difficult to understand language helped prevent the knowledge being taken up and used by someone less ready or able to use it in a correct or worthwhile manner. Secondly, at a time when it was quite easy for one to be accused of heresy, expressing personal and spiritual growth in terms of chemical interactions and experiments was a clever disguise for keeping esoteric knowledge safely hidden.

Alchemical texts were written to reveal their teachings only to the initiated. Therefore, much of what is written should not be taken literally, and needs to be understood in a greater context. This hiding in plain sight of alchemical and labyrinth knowledge is summed up perfectly by Titus Burckhardt in his book *Alchemy: Science of the Cosmos, Science of the Soul* when referencing the alchemist Artephius: "'I assure you in good faith (for I am not so jealous as other philosophers), that whoever would take literally what other philosophers (that is, the other alchemists) have written, will lose himself in the recesses of a labyrinth from which he will never escape, for want of Ariadne's thread to keep him on the right path and bring him safely out.'" (Burckhardt 1997).

The reference to the labyrinth in this extract is just one of several labyrinth references found in alchemy. There are many similarities between the paths of the labyrinth and alchemy. The main correlation between these paths of self-discovery is that what initially appears confusing eventually leads you to a state of greater clarity and understanding. The similarities and connections between the labyrinth and alchemy are an indication of the increasing connections between all of existence that you will realise as you move through the stages of your journey to self-discovery.

Alchemy and Labyrinth Associations

The alchemical transformation involves a process with stages that have a clear beginning and a clear point of achievement. Other correspondences with the labyrinth include the seven stages in the alchemical process, as well as the previously noted four elements in the quadrants of the labyrinth. Fulcanelli, an unidentified master who wrote the book *Le Mystère des Cathédrales*, makes a number of alchemical connections with the labyrinth being "emblematic" of the whole labour of the work. He considered that the cathedral labyrinth was part of the magic tradition associated with Solomon, and had two major difficulties: "one path which must be taken in order to reach the centre—where the combat of the two natures takes place—the other the way which the artist must follow in order to emerge" (Fulcanelli 1971).

Central to the alchemists' processes is the vessel within which the reactions and transformations took place. As well as the physical work with substances, the alchemist's vessel can be equated with your physical and energetic bodies within which the interior work that you do on your soul takes place. The labyrinth is not only a metaphor for the alchemical vessel, but also serves as a physical and energetic container within which the walker conducts the purifying practices on himself and undertakes the transformation of his own being. Indeed, the power of the labyrinth as a transformative alchemical-type vessel is evidenced by the transformational effect of the labyrinth on many people, sometimes without their clear conscious knowledge of what they were undertaking.

Another interesting connection is the use of the word "vitriol" by alchemists. Vitriol was what we know as sulphuric acid, but it also had another meaning, especially when capitalized. VITRIOL stood in Latin for *visita interiora terrae rectificando invenies occultum lapidem*. This can be translated as "visit the interior of the earth, through purification (rectification) you will find the hidden stone." In a labyrinth context, this is a reference to the journey to the centre of the labyrinth through which you become purified. Your labyrinth path to self-discovery is your journey inwards to find your true essence—your own philosopher's stone. In a subtler connection, the symbol for vitriol is a seven with a sickle through it (see Figure 6). This is a clear connection with the seven-circuit labyrinth, where the sickle is a symbol of death and purification.

Figure 6: Seven with sickle strike-through

Alchemical Metals, Planets, and the Circuits of the Labyrinth

The alchemists treasured seven metals, each with an increasingly higher vibration and associated with a heavenly body or planet. A knowledge of these associations brings greater understanding of what aspects of your life are being influenced at different stages of your progression through the labyrinth.

The associations of metals with the planets are: lead with Saturn, tin with Jupiter, iron with Mars, copper with Venus, quicksilver (mercury) with Mercury, silver with the Moon, and gold with the Sun. The planets and their metals create an association between alchemy and astrology; while astrology interprets the meanings of the planets and the zodiac, alchemy relates the planets with earthly metals. Combined they create a fusion between heaven and earth. The qualities briefly associated with the planets are: goddess with the Moon, communication with

Mercury, feminine qualities with Venus, king with the Sun, masculinity with Mars, theorizer with Jupiter, and death with Saturn.

When you walk the labyrinth with an understanding of the planetary qualities assigned to the seven circuits you embark on a revealing journey of insight and growth. From Earth at the centre the planetary bodies are arranged by circuit as follows: Moon, Mercury, Venus, Sun, Mars, Jupiter and Saturn. Walking the labyrinth as a symbol of your life and soul's journey, you begin on the third circuit associated with Mars, as you enter the labyrinth at the third circuit. This is the masculine quality of drive and initiative needed to commence your journey. You next move into Jupiter where you begin theorizing about your journey and trying to figure out exactly what is happening. Moving into Saturn you realise that you need to let go fully of your need to make sense of what is happening, to bring death to the ego, and to free yourself from mental and earthly concerns. As you move into the fourth circuit of the Sun you become a king and ruler of your own life and path, not by anything you do but by having let go of everything that was driving you on in the first three circuits. You are now comfortable within yourself, with who you are, and with the path that you are walking.

The next circuit that you enter is the seventh associated with the Moon. This is the goddess circuit where you begin to integrate your feminine aspects so that you are now becoming full, complete, and balanced in all your aspects. Moving into Mercury's sixth circuit you are receiving communications on a nonphysical level that is further prompting and guiding you on your soul's path. The final circuit that you enter is the fifth associated with Venus, which not only represents all your feminine aspects, but is a representation of the Divine Mother. This is the precursor to the short section of path leading to the centre, the "birth" canal, before you are born into the light of the centre and endowed with an understanding of your true origin, nature, and purpose.

The layers and dimensions to the labyrinth become even more apparent when you place the Sun at the centre. The planets, including Earth, are then assigned to the circuits of the labyrinth according to their distance from the Sun as follows: Mercury, Venus, Moon, Earth, Mars, Jupiter, and Saturn. You pass through the three outer circuits and planets as before. The fourth circuit now represents Earth, where you assume your rightly and "kingly" entitlement to be on earth. The next and seventh circuit is now Mercury and communication, where you tap into your intuition and become aware of receiving guidance from without and within. You then move into the sixth circuit associated with Venus and your feminine qualities of creativity, nurturing, and receptiveness. You are now nurturing yourself on your path and receptive to the meaning of all events happening in your life. The final circuit is the Moon Goddess circuit, where you step into your divine feminine aspect in preparation for approaching and merging with your divine masculine aspect of the Sun at the centre.

These approaches to seeing the seven planetary and metallic stages as increasingly refining and progressing on your path to enlightenment are just some of the ways that your path to self-discovery in the labyrinth is an alchemical process. When considered within the container of the labyrinth, the alchemical approach illustrates how your outer characteristics reflect your inner qualities, and how these qualities and characteristics can be explored, discovered, and refined in the labyrinth.

Seven Circuits and the Seven Stages of the Alchemical Process

The seven stages in the alchemical process that aim to restore the alchemist to a state of perfection are reflected in the laboratory purification process involving seven stages or turnings during which all the imperfections and imbalances in the substance (soul) are resolved. Exploring each of these seven stages in more detail gives you an understanding of the stages that you pass through on your own journey to enlightenment. The seven stages of transformation, which are found at the turning points into the next circuit of the labyrinth, are calcination, dissolution, separation, conjunction, fermentation, distillation, and coagulation. These stages can be more easily understood when put in the context of your journey of personal and spiritual growth.

Calcination is the burning off by fire. It is a purifying process that gets rid of what does not serve you. It can be seen as the breaking down of the ego and the destruction of your attachment to material possessions, as you grow in maturity. It can be identified by your willingness to be wrong about key issues, and no longer clinging to hard held positions. Calcination is the beginning of the demise of your stubbornness, arrogance, and pride. It is the deliberate speeding up of the process of not being attached to the outer personality, and giving you time to experience your deeper inner nature. It is the first turn you take just after entering the labyrinth, and symbolises that you are now on an inner journey of growth that is more important than outer appearances and what people think. In deciding to walk your path to self-discovery you have already taken a step to change from who you were to what you are going to become.

Dissolution is the process that involves dissolving the ashes from the fire of calcination in water. It occurs at the turn into the second circuit of the labyrinth. In your own self-development, it is a further letting go of the ego so the true self can be revealed. It is often experienced by an immersion in the unconscious, feminine, and nonrational parts of your mind where the conscious mind lets go of control. At this stage, you move away from seeing the cause of your life's events as external, and begin to realise that everything is a reflection of yourself. You also begin to see in others what you most dislike about yourself. This stage may involve grieving for painful past incidents, allowing the pain to dissolve so that you truly experience the event with awareness. Dissolution also involves the awakening of your creativity and passion, where you redirect the energy previously tied up in holding together the memories of past experiences into authentic and constructive aims.

Separation involves extracting material from the solution by heating, filtration, or other process. It is a further refinement where you separate your emotions and thoughts so that you can clearly see each individual emotion and thought as you are experiencing it. The separation stage enables you to take a clearer look at life, where you can admit and learn from past errors. It is where you separate out your thoughts and decide what to discard and what to reintegrate into your refined personality. This stage equates with the turn into the outer circuit of the classical labyrinth. It is at this stage also that you face your shadow side, allowing all thoughts and feelings within you to surface. You are now separating out what really matters in life, both in your inner self and in your outer life, stemming from a place of complete honesty with yourself and owning everything that is happening in your life.

Conjunction is the recombination of the saved elements from separation into a new substance. It can involve an amalgamation of metals, or the mixing of the saved elements in a new chemical process by adding a catalyst. On a personal level it is the joining together of the true essences of your being following the purification and refinement of the first three stages. It creates an inner space where you can be fully honest, open, and accepting of all states of mind and heart within yourself. You are creating a space where a connection is clearly recognized between your individual soul and Spirit. It is a sacred marriage in which your masculine and feminine energies come into balance, bringing a deeper personal and spiritual awareness and empowering your true self. On the labyrinth, conjunction occurs at the long turn from the outer circuit into the fourth circuit. It is an awareness of the importance of balance on your path of self-discovery, and includes an awareness of those parts of you that remain out of balance. The conjunction labyrinth turn brings you into the heart chakra, which is a space where differences and conflicts are held unconditionally so they can safely work themselves out and come together in union, bringing an increased balance to relationships in your life.

Chemically, fermentation involves the adding of new life into the product of conjunction to completely change its characteristics, like adding a ferment such as yeast in beer making. On a spiritual level, fermentation is a stage in your spiritual development where further processing takes place to bring about a more refined essence. It starts with the inspiration of spiritual power from above that energizes and enlightens. It involves an element of putrefaction, or breaking down, and creation of a more refined, and almost new, substance from what already existed. It is the death of old parts of the personality or ego that are no longer needed, and the tapping into higher energies. Fermentation can be achieved through deep meditation, intense prayer, desire for union with Spirit, transpersonal therapies, and other practices that lead to enlightenment. Sometimes it is seen as "the dark night of the soul" where what initially appears as a dark, smelly, and a not-so-pleasant process is a necessary part of the purification process. In the midst of what seems like darkness and rotting, a new substance is being created that is the basis of your higher and advanced state of being. It is a type of rebirth resulting from the willingness to let go of all elements that no longer serve your spiritual evolution.

Distillation is a refining process that on a physical level involves heating a substance and condensing the essences driven off into a more purified form. On a spiritual level distillation represents further purification processes of integrating your ongoing spiritual realizations into your daily life. This can mean being as impeccable in your life as you can be, dealing with mundane tasks with integrity, and not using your inner spiritual work to escape from the everyday world. Your actions become more compassionate and impeccable because that is your true nature. As you deal with everything in your life with integrity and honesty, all impurities are removed and you can feel an immense transformation in yourself. You also become more concerned with the greater good and begin to know yourself as part of the collective consciousness, yet you are not negatively affected by what you find there. You now know and understand that your soul is primarily guiding your life. Repeated practise of this stage leads to a profound inner transformation that can be equated to the enlightenment of eastern philosophy.

Coagulation is the precipitation of the purified ferment from distillation. It represents the final balancing of opposites where you can negotiate all levels of existence. It is the fully transformed person, the illuminated person who is fully spiritualized and living in spirit with earth and heaven, seen as one. The soul and Spirit have merged into the oneness that you are, and now know and understand.

While it is easy to describe each of the stages in the personal alchemical process, in reality it can be somewhat difficult to progress through them in real life. It can also be difficult to identify at times exactly which of the processes you are currently working through. One way of gaining insight into what stage you might be experiencing is to pay attention to the turn on the labyrinth that feels most significant to you. The beginning of each of the stages of alchemy equates with the turn into one of the seven circuits of the classical labyrinth. When doing the exercise at the end of this chapter, take note of the turn that feels the most important to you.

The Four Elements in the Labyrinth

The four elements of earth, air, fire, and water that are a significant part of the alchemist's work are also to be found in the labyrinth. Each of the four quadrants in the classical labyrinth is associated with one of the elements. In the Chartres labyrinth, the cross of the four elements is created by the positioning of the labrys and 180-degree turning points. The cross, rather than being in the seed pattern, is placed firmly within the overall labyrinth with the centre point of the cross at the centre point of the labyrinth. In another alchemical connection, the circle with a cross inside it is the alchemical symbol for planet Earth. The Chartres labyrinth is not only a container within which our transformation takes place but also a symbolic representation of this earth on which our soul's transformation happens.

When walking the labyrinth, you pass through each of the four quadrants and their associated element several times in different sequences. You are having the effect of rotating the elements not only in the space in which you are walking, but also in yourself. This rotation of the elements can bring you into contact with the quintessence, the ultimate philosopher's stone that the alchemists were seeking. Therefore, the labyrinth is not only a symbol of the alchemical journey through the elements to the ultimate destination but a tool that you can use to reach your own philosopher's stone.

Titus Burckhardt describes the quintessence as the hub of a four-spoked wheel, the spokes being one of the four elements, and the quadrants of the wheel being their respective natural qualities. He explains the "fifth essence" at the centre this way: "Alchemically speaking, the hub of the wheel is the quinta essentia. By this is meant either the spiritual pole of all four elements or their common substantial ground, ether, in which they are all indivisibly contained. In order once again to attain to this centre, the disequilibrium of the differentiated elements must be repaired, water must become fiery, fire liquid, earth weightless, and air solid. Here, however, one leaves the plane of physical appearances and enters the realm of spiritual alchemy" (Burckhardt 1997). So, in walking the labyrinth of the four elements, the walker serves as the catalyst that brings about the rotation of the elements.

When you place the elements in the order of earth, air, fire, and water starting in the bottom left quadrant of a left-handed classical labyrinth, then your labyrinth walk takes on further meaning. In walking the labyrinth, you start in the earth element, move through the elements in a variety of orders, and finish in the centre in the fire quadrant. You are walking symbolically, commencing on the earth plane, and progressing to the fire of an enlightened being at the centre.

Rotation of the Elements

In alchemy, the four elements are often represented by an equal-armed cross. Earth, water, air, and fire can be represented either by the points of this cross or by the quadrants it creates. Most significant about the symbolism of the four elements is their point of interaction, the node of the seed pattern, or the hub of the wheel.

The path of transformation involves a separation of the elements, rotation of the elements, and then a reconfiguring of the elements into the fifth element, the quintessence. If the seed pattern, with brackets in the shape of arcs, is first separated into its individual four elements of earth air, fire, and water, then each quadrant is rotated 180 degrees, and then reassembled, a symbol of a circle within a square with a dot at the centre is produced (see Figure 7). This symbol is the alchemical symbol for gold! The separation and rotation of the elements results in the gold of an enlightened being.

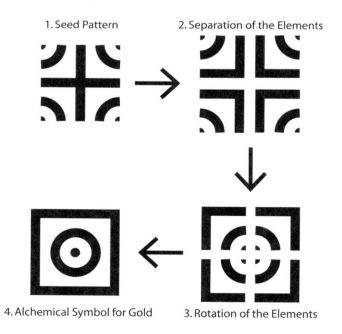

Figure 7: Separation and rotation of elements

Lesser Work & Greater Work

Alchemy is often divided into two main parts: the lesser work and the greater work. The first three stages (calcination, dissolution, and separation) are considered as the spiritualization of the body, and the last three (fermentation, distillation, and coagulation) as the embodiment of the Spirit, sometimes known as the fixing of the volatile. The goals of these works are summed up by Burckhardt when he writes "Whereas the 'lesser work' has as its goal the regaining of the original purity and receptivity of the soul, the goal of the 'greater work' is the illumination of the soul by the revelation of the Spirit within it. This sequence of six stages can be transposed to all kinds of spiritual realization, but nevertheless it remains no more than a schema, for neither of the two movements (the ascent of the soul, the descent of the Spirit) can be entirely separated from the other" (Burckhardt 1997).

The labyrinth epitomizes and illustrates effectively these two stages in the alchemical process. Just as the stages in the alchemical process cannot be separated and must be seen as a whole, so also must the labyrinth be viewed in its entirety as a symbol of wholeness. These two stages are seen further in the sequence that you walk the circuits in the seven-circuit classical labyrinth. You first walk the three outer circuits corresponding to the three lower chakras and your physical existence here on earth—the spiritualization of the body. After moving through the fourth and heart circuit, you then walk the inner three circuits in the order of the chakras seven, six, five, which in effect is bringing down the Divine into the body, the embodiment of the Spirit.

In summary, alchemy illustrates how there are many different elements and aspects working together at one time to bring about transformation. In alchemy, just as in the labyrinth, the seven stages return to rest as one, the beginning of creation, and the four elements are resolved in a single point where their qualities come to rest, the quintessence.

Putting It All Together

The labyrinth journey is one among many esoteric journeys that you can take. What is significant about the labyrinth is that it incorporates many of the elements of the other paths and journeys. These ancient teachings become clearer through their relationship with the labyrinth, although interpretation of one's place within the framework is not always so clear.

In walking the labyrinth, you are not only encountering the labyrinth as an isolated symbol, you are interacting with a multi-dimensional tool that carries the energies of several other symbolic systems of understanding and growth. The following exercise is one in which you as the labyrinth walker take a somewhat different approach than usual, focusing on the turns, the entry into each circuit, the refinement of your nature into a more purified state, and your passage through the gateways to a higher state of existence.

EXERCISE: HOW TO EXPERIENCE LIFE'S TURNS ON THE LABYRINTH

This exercise is about walking the labyrinth to seek new experiences of how you become aware of subtle changes in yourself, and the relevance of these insights to your personal and spiritual growth. Some of life's greatest teachings come from the significant turns and events in your life. These can be revealed in the labyrinth, where each turn can hold the energy of change through which you are moving. As discussed in the third chapter, moving your energy field through a turn of 180 degrees can have a significant effect on that field.

The alchemical aspect to this walk is associated with the seven alchemical stages of transformation, and in particular with the seven turning points, through which you transit on the labyrinth into another level of being. These are the points where you shift from one level of being to another. You can often miss these turns and shifts in life because you are too busy looking ahead on the path. Turning points are some of the most powerful and significant moments and stages that you can experience on your journey. Be aware of your turns and you are aware of your journey.

It is not necessary to remember each of the seven alchemical stages, or what they represent. What is important is that you walk with the intention of focusing on being aware of all sensations that you experience as you take the turns. Take each turn in as high a state of focus and awareness as you can. See if you can feel your body and energy body moving through the energy field of the labyrinth as you take each turn.

Once you have experienced the turn, proceed on the circuit with an awareness of being in a more elevated state. As each circuit brings you to a higher state of being, you arrive in the centre haven taken your seven turns to transformation. Stay in the centre for as long as feels comfortable, then walk out of the labyrinth holding as best as possible the state you are in. On the walk out of the labyrinth, be also aware of each of the seven turns that you are taking, of your heightened state on each circuit, to emerge from the labyrinth with an understanding of being the gold of an enlightened being.

Reflection

You have walked the labyrinth in awareness of yourself, and of what you were moving through. What thoughts, ideas, and memories came to mind? What did you notice on the turns in the labyrinth? Which part of the labyrinth was most prominent for you during the walk? Write down everything that comes to mind. When you have finished writing, read back over what you have written and consider what is new to you in what you have written and experienced. Underline or highlight what seems significant to you. What is significant is what is relevant to your path at this time.

5

The Fool and the Hero in the Labyrinth

Taking the path of the labyrinth is a journey. It is a journey towards something greater, better, and more beautiful. It is not always an easy journey, and the end is not always clear. Yet, when you embark on this journey, you are entering into a new relationship with yourself where you are externally interacting with the labyrinth, and internally getting to know yourself better. Dag Hammerskjold, former secretary general of the UN and deeply spiritual person, wrote, "The longest journey of any person is the journey inward." The labyrinth journey, in representing your inner journey, leads you to insights of some of life's fundamental questions about who you are, where you came from, where are you going, and what is your purpose.

The labyrinth journey contains symbolism and associated metaphors unique to the labyrinth. It also shares many characteristics with other great journeys that you can learn from. Strong similarities exist between the labyrinth journey and the Fool's journey of the tarot, and the hero's journey as represented by the myth of Theseus and the Minotaur. While each of these journeys or paths can be looked on as an external undertaking, they primarily illustrate the greatest journey of all—the journey inwards. Hidden within these paths are the keys to self-realization and enlightenment. When you walk the labyrinth path you are accessing and interacting with these teachings in a new and insightful way.

Your Journey Through Life

The way of the labyrinth is a single path on which you are always moving forward, where the centre represents what you are moving towards. On this journey, you experience many twists and turns, some that appear to take you away from your centre and some that bring you closer to it. At times, your life is progressing well, you feel in control and everything is "rosy in the garden." Then, something happens and your life takes a turn. It is no longer obvious where you are going. You cannot see clearly where the next step will take you, and you feel further away from what you thought was your life's purpose and destination. Stopping is not an option, as you will just stay stuck if you don't move. So, you keep going, and take another step. Then, your life takes another turn, this time one for the better. You feel like everything is back on track and once again you have a strong sense of what you are doing and where you are going. The labyrinth turns reflect your life; some turns take you away from your centre, and others bring you nearer. Your life must be lived going forwards, but can often only be understood when you look back at it. This is also the case with the labyrinth, when it is often just before you enter the centre that you realise where you are.

The labyrinth can represent more than one journey at a time. In exploring your life through the labyrinth, your labyrinth walk may represent a single issue in your life that you are moving through seeking clarity and resolution. It can also be the whole journey of your current life from birth to death. And, it can be the journey of your soul through many lifetimes. You do not need to choose which one it is; the labyrinth can accommodate them all. The labyrinth is multidimensional and represents all facets of your journey within a journey, and more.

You may not be aware of all aspects of your current journey, and may not be able to identify clearly the current stage of your journey. However, the more aware you are, the greater will be your understanding of the stage you are at, and the greater benefit you will gain from the combination of the knowledge and the experience. In considering where you are on your journey, and at what stage you are now at, looking at some of the other journeys that the labyrinth reflects will give you some insights your own.

The Labyrinth and the Tarot

Just as the labyrinth is the path of your progress through life, the tarot is also a progression from one way of being to another. The tarot is comprised of seventy-eight cards divided into major and minor arcana. The major arcana consists of twenty-two cards, each one experienced on the path of the labyrinth and representing some aspect of your personal and spiritual journeys. The minor arcana cards are the equivalent of the four suits in the standard deck of playing cards. The suits of tarot cards, pentacles, swords, wands, and cups, which are associated with the elements of earth, air, fire, and water respectively, are represented by the quadrants of the labyrinth.

The Fool's Journey in the Labyrinth

The Fool's journey is a metaphor for your journey through life, where your life events present different situations for your personal and spiritual growth. Each major arcana card represents a stage or aspect of your labyrinth journey of life. At times, there are pleasant and enjoyable experiences, while at other times you need to face adverse situations. Like the fool starting out on your journey, you feel like you know very little. Yet there is something driving you forward. Your step into the labyrinth of your life is a journey of faith, one that culminates in greater wisdom and understanding. The major arcana enhances your understanding and experience of your labyrinth path of self-discovery, giving you greater understanding of what is happening in your life and where you are going.

Major Arcana Cards and Their Labyrinth-Related Symbolism

The Fool's journey begins with you about to step off the cliff and into the labyrinth of your new life. The Fool card is initially outside the labyrinth as you contemplate setting out on your journey. The first group of seven cards in the major arcana is made up of those forces that prepare the fool for his journey, and are found on the three outer circuits of the labyrinth (see Figure 8). These three outer circuits correspond to your three lower chakras, the physical chakras representing power, creativity, and safety that you must master to advance on your spiritual path. The walking of these three outer circuits is grounding—preparation for the remainder of your journey.

The first two cards that you meet almost immediately as you enter the labyrinth are the Magician and the High Priestess, representing your spiritual parents at the beginning of your spiritual journey. The Emperor and Empress, which are on the first path and turn into the second circuit respectively, are your physical parents. You then turn full into the second circuit, leave home, and receive education from the Hierophant. The turn into the third circuit holds the Lovers card, representing passions and motivation. While the outer circuit, equating to the Chariot, is the actual setting off on the quest. This is the longest circuit on the labyrinth and is symbolic of how long your journey appears at the outset.

You are now prepared for your inner journey. On the labyrinth, you move almost immediately on to the short section between the outer and fourth circuits where the Strength card represents the Fool's mastery of himself and the world. Having mastered the material world, you are now leaving it behind. However, at the turn, the Hermit indicates to you that you need to go further inwards and shines a light to show the way to enlightenment. You are about to enter the fourth circuit that equates to your heart chakra and you can feel the energy in your heart expanding in anticipation. The fourth circuit is the Wheel of Fortune and shows that things are in motion. Which brings you to the next turn and understanding in the Justice card.

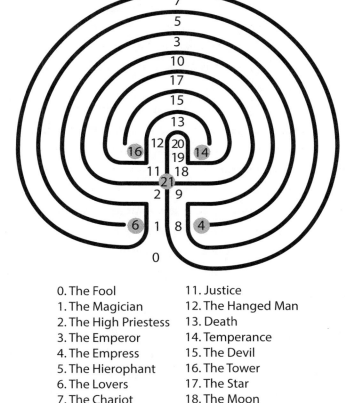

0. The Fool
1. The Magician
2. The High Priestess
3. The Emperor
4. The Empress
5. The Hierophant
6. The Lovers
7. The Chariot
8. Strength
9. The Hermit
10. Wheel of Fortune

11. Justice
12. The Hanged Man
13. Death
14. Temperance
15. The Devil
16. The Tower
17. The Star
18. The Moon
19. The Sun
20. Judgement
21. The World

Figure 8: The Fool's journey in the classical labyrinth

The next short section of the path represents the trials and challenges of the Hanged Man, leading to a defeat of sorts in the Death card. You are now on the shortest circuit of the labyrinth and rather than be defeated, you are transformed and reborn into a deeper spiritual life, as shown in more detail in the Temperance card at the turn into the next circuit.

This turn and the next circuit equating with the Devil card appear to be taking you away from your centre, where it seems that things can't get any worse. But the Tower card, in seeming to destroy your world and turning you further away from the centre of the labyrinth, saves you by shaking you free of attachments. As the dark despair is blasted away, the Star shows a glimmer of hope as you walk the final circuit in the light of truth.

The final turn of the Moon illuminates the way, and the final narrow path before the centre Sun is indicating that you are a shining light. You then enter the centre of the labyrinth where the Judgement card represents your triumphant victory.

The final major arcana card the World is found at the centre point of the cross in the labyrinth. This is the point from which you create the labyrinth and from which all aspects of the labyrinth emanate. It is the spirit point; it represents order restored and understanding of your place in the world when you see the labyrinth as representing your whole life.

The Labyrinth and the Tree of Life

The labyrinth is also connected to the Kabbalah Tree of Life, another path to spiritual illumination. Eliphas Levi published a book in 1856 which was the first book of the modern era to associate the twenty-two cards of the major arcana with the twenty-two letters of the Hebrew alphabet. He also associated the four letters of the name of God (the Tetragrammaton: YHWH) with the four suits of the minor arcana.

On the Tree of Life in the Kabbalah, the major arcana represent the lines, or flow of energy, between the ten sephirot in the Tree of Life. The sephirot are states of being, while the twenty-two paths between them are states of becoming. So, representing the twenty-two paths in the circuits, turns, and paths of the labyrinth make the labyrinth a tool for "becoming," a tool for realizing your true self.

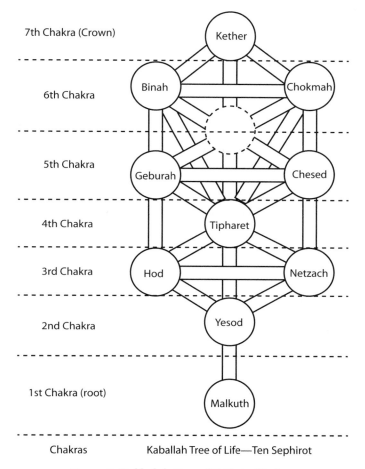

| Chakras | Kaballah Tree of Life—Ten Sephirot |

Figure 9: Kabbalah Tree of Life & Chakras

The labyrinth and the Kabbalah are also connected through their associations with the seven chakras. While some sources associate the seven lower sephirot with the chakras, a more complete association is to map the chakras onto the Tree of Life in its seven distinct levels, as in Figure 9. In this approach, Kether at the top is the crown chakra. Chokmah and Binah representing wisdom and understanding are the third eye. Chesed and Geburah representing love and might are at the throat chakra. Tipharet, beauty, is at the heart chakra. Netzach and Hod, eternity and majesty, are at the solar plexus centre. Yesod, the foundation, is at the sacral chakra. And Malkuth, the kingdom, is the root chakra.

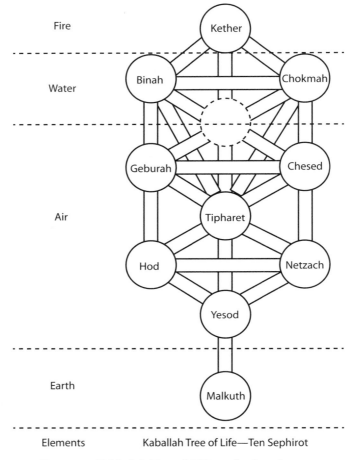

Figure 10: Kabbalah Tree of Life & the four elements

The ten sephirot also correspond to the four elements: earth, air, fire, and water (Figure 10). The four elements represented by the four quadrants of the labyrinth are found in the Tree of Life as follows (The Tree of Life, n.d.):

Fire (world of Atziluth)—Kether

Water (world of Briah)—Chokmah and Binah

Air (world of Yetzirah)—Chesed, Geburah, Tiphareth, Netzach, Hod, and Yesod

Earth (world of Assiah)—Malkuth

As the energy can flow both ways on the paths between the sephirot on the Tree of Life, walking into and out of the labyrinth can have significantly different meanings and impacts. So, just as you can ascend and descend the Tree of Life learning and experiencing new aspects of yourself each time, you can also walk the labyrinth in and out as many times as you wish learning something new each time.

The "un-named" sephirot on the Tree of Life is called Da'at. It is the Hebrew word that means knowledge. Da'at is the location, or mystical state where all ten sephirot are combined as one, each radiating divine light, and each no longer distinguishable from the other. The state of Da'at also exists at the node or centre of the cross in the labyrinth, when all aspects become one and you experience a sense of infinite oneness.

The Hero's Journey in the Labyrinth

The labyrinth represents the hero's journey that you undertake on your spiritual path. When you step into the labyrinth, you are undertaking a journey that re-enacts the hero's journey of mythology. Your journey into the labyrinth of your inner world is similar to the hero's journey described by mythologist Joseph Campbell in his book *The Hero with a Thousand Faces*. While Campbell described seventeen stages in the hero's journey, it can be condensed into three main stages: departure—the hero leaves the familiar world behind, initiation—where the hero is subjected to trials and experiences adventures, and return—where the hero returns to the world he left with greater understanding from living through his experiences.

A labyrinth walk is a microcosm of the hero's journey. You decide to leave the familiar outer world behind, if only for a short period of time. You enter the coils of the labyrinth, where the twists and turns can serve to disorientate and challenge, often resulting in new insights and recognition of inner strengths previously untapped. Your return from the centre of the labyrinth is symbolic of the hero's return home changed for the better and ready to live a renewed life. The hero's journey relates to everyone who walks the labyrinth. In being prepared to journey to your inner depths in the labyrinth, you are a hero destined to overcome the conflicts in your inner and outer worlds so that both are in union and in harmony.

Whether you know it or not, you are a hero. You are the one who is prepared to let go of the old and bring in the new. There are several levels on which you are doing this. Firstly, if you are a beginner labyrinth walker, you may not realise that this is what you are doing. You may simply consider that you are having a nice meditative walk. And so, you may be. However, the labyrinth walk is having a positive effect on you. Walking the labyrinth brings you into an altered state, however slight. It induces realizations that bring about a shift in your consciousness. You are letting go of the old and bringing in the new. You are releasing what no longer serves you and making space for new energies in your life.

On another level, you can consciously walk the labyrinth to bring about change in you. You have a deliberate intent to let go of something, to find something new, to change your life. And you are not only walking for yourself, you are also walking for all of humanity. Therefore, what you are doing is being a light of consciousness between your own internal world of conflict that might overwhelm you, and the outer world that wants to destroy you for breaking the old ways. You are a true hero—bringing about change in yourself and change in the world around you, despite the powers that might wish otherwise. You are a catalyst for change.

We have already read about the myth where Theseus entered the labyrinth to slay the Minotaur. As with most myths there are several levels at which the story of Theseus and the Minotaur can be interpreted and absorbed. Look on all elements of the myth as aspects of yourself; you are on a hero's journey into the unknown, both searching for a hidden part of yourself and embarking on a mission of saving your whole self. Through being willing to sacrifice everything, you emerge stronger and empowered.

In this story of Theseus and the Minotaur, we meet Theseus, the Minotaur, Ariadne, Daedalus, Minos, and Pasiphae. Each one of these has a significant part to contribute to the whole story. In your labyrinth journey, there are aspects of yourself that are represented by the characters in the myth. Theseus is the hero within you who partakes in a death-defying story reminiscent of many other tales and myths. The Minotaur represents your shadow side—that part of yourself that you keep hidden away for fear it will devour you! The death of the Minotaur can also be seen as a type of "death of the ego," or the uncontrollable mental forces. Ariadne is the help that is available to you, and someone who loves you unconditionally. Ariadne's thread assists and transforms the labyrinth of confusion into a clear path home. She is the goddess who guides Theseus and helps him to access the unconscious and enlightenment. Meanwhile, Daedalus represents the wisdom and assistance that is available to you from outside. As Daedalus was the inventor and creator of the labyrinth, seeking assistance from the creator as to the secret of the labyrinth can be achieved through asking, meditating. and being open to receiving the answers.

According to Fulcanelli, Ariadne is a form of *airagne* (the spider). Fulcanelli asks of Ariadne when writing about the symbolic value of the famous myth: "is not our soul the spider which weaves our own body?" (Fulcanelli 1971). Fulcanelli, in the somewhat oblique language of the alchemist, wrote in *Le Mystère des Cathédrales*, "To make the eagle fly, as the hermetic expression goes, is to extract light from the tomb and bring it to the surface … This is what the fable of Theseus and Ariadne teaches us" (Fulcanelli 1971). In your labyrinth walk, you are entering the tomb of the labyrinth, finding your true self, and bringing this back out to shine into the world, all with the help of the soul.

The following exercise draws on the symbolism and associations in the story of Theseus and the Minotaur to take a step of bravery and integration.

Exercise: How to Conduct Your Own Hero's Journey in the Labyrinth

Being your own hero entails facing your fears. The Minotaur is a symbol that represents your fears. This exercise is about meeting your Minotaur and facing your fears.

To know what your fears are you need to identify them clearly. The best way to identify your fears is to write them down. It may take a little while to compose yourself to write down your fears, because the very fact that they are fears may make this difficult for you. Yet, the first step in facing your fears is to know them. Indeed, the very act of describing your fears can have the effect of reducing their impact on you.

Take a little time to write down all your fears that you can think of. If you are finding it difficult to do this, then put at number one "the fear of writing down my fears!" Write down a heading for each fear, and describe as much as you can about them. For each, write about when you feel it, what the fear feels like, and who is involved in the fear. In what places and situations do you feel the fear? Keep writing. Describe each fear in as much details as you can, until you have nothing left to write.

If you feel that you are not ready to face all your fears, then write down those that you know you can face. You can come back to the others at another time. You will know if a fear is possibly too much for you at this time as you will find ways to avoid writing it down. You may distract yourself, or try to convince yourself that it is not a fear, or tell yourself that you don't have enough time to be doing this exercise. There are a myriad of other ways to avoid doing it. If you can come up with one fear that you are willing to face, then that is sufficient to do this exercise.

When you are finished, put what you have written into an envelope. Seal the envelope, write on the outside "Minotaur," and do a rough sketch of a Minotaur or your best effort of a horned creature that represents your Minotaur. Then underneath this image write the words "I love you."

With your envelope in your hand, walk towards your labyrinth. Remember, you are not alone on this walk; your guides are there to help you. Before you begin your walk, remind yourself that if at any time you feel that you cannot go any further in the labyrinth, you can always turn around and come out of the labyrinth.

Stand at the entrance of the labyrinth with the understanding that you are going to meet your fears in the shape of a Minotaur as you walk. You do not know where or when your Minotaur will appear; you just know that at some stage you will meet it. As you walk the labyrinth, be aware of every sensation in your body and beyond. Feel every step you make and every breath you take.

Your fear, or fears, may come to mind as you walk. As soon as a fear comes to mind, pause. Feel the fear as much as you can and then hug yourself and tell yourself that you love yourself. Imagine your fear in the shape of a Minotaur who just wants to be hugged. Squeeze your Minotaur so tightly and with such love that it brings a smile to your face. You will know when you have embraced your Minotaur enough as you will get a feeling to release. Consciously release your Minotaur and whatever fear(s) are associated with it. Let them go. Let them go with love. Let them go with the feeling and knowing that you no longer need them in your life. As you let them go, thank your Minotaur and your fears—for being companions and teachers on your journey. Continue your labyrinth walk. If you have another fear, then walk in anticipation of meeting the Minotaur of that fear. Each time you meet a fear, repeat the exercise described above.

When you reach the centre, if you still have some fears left to meet, spend some time in the centre embracing all your other fears. Consciously choose to let go of all your fears. Even if you have not let go of all your fears, give yourself a big long hug at the centre. Assume a position of power by standing erect, legs a little more than shoulder-width apart, shoulders back, chest out, and feel your power running through you. Do this for about two minutes. Then walk out of the labyrinth ready to face the world as the new you.

As soon as you exit the labyrinth, find a safe place and ceremonially burn the envelope with the list of your fears. See the fears dissolve and change into energy moving on to another dimension.

You may find that you need to do this exercise a few times to fully release yourself from some fears. Do it as often as you feel the need. When repeating this exercise, it is important to have a strong intention of meeting and releasing your fears. Also, as you release some fears, you may find that you think of some other smaller fears that you have also to release. Do this exercise as often as you feel you need to become fearless. If a memory or fear comes up that is too strong, consider if you would like to have a close companion, facilitator, or trained counsellor with you.

Reflection

Write down all the positive thoughts, feelings, and experiences that you had during the labyrinth walk. Remember what these feelings and experiences were like, and retain them for as long as you can.

6

The Labyrinth and Your Life's Purpose

The concept of having a specific purpose in life is one that many people subscribe to. It may stem from your upbringing and education, or it may arise from a sense deep within you that you are here to do something specific that will be of benefit to you and to others. Finding your life's purpose comes from knowing yourself. As you travel your labyrinth path to self-discovery, you are learning more and more about yourself, letting go of what no longer works for you, and inevitably leading to finding and living your life's purpose.

Living your life purpose brings a feeling of great satisfaction. You fall asleep in great anticipation, thinking about what you are going to do tomorrow. You want to jump out of bed in the morning to start doing what you love and what makes your heart sing. You get a buzz from feeling so alive, especially when you know that you are making progress and achieving what is important for you. There is a fullness in your life that cannot be bought, as it stems from deep inside you. You have a passion for life that you might not have felt since you were a child, a passion that stems from living your life fully, from making a difference, from making your own mark on the world.

Some people are born with a strong sense of their life purpose. We have all heard of the child who declared at a young age to their parents that they were going to be a doctor, a writer, or some other profession, and then proceeded to achieve what they had declared. For most people, such clarity is not immediately present. They need to engage in a process of self-development and exploration to reach certainty about their life's purpose.

The labyrinth is a wonderful tool to help bring clarity to your life's purpose. You can use it both to find your purpose and to explore the next steps when you have found it. If you rely on logic alone, you are unlikely to find your life purpose. Searching based solely on thinking and logic can be too mechanical, and lacks feelings that motivate you. When using the mind alone, you are limiting your possibilities and your search to what you already know. If the answers are elsewhere, you are unlikely to find them.

It is also unusual to find your purpose solely through emotion, as you can be somewhat detached from reality and may lack practicality in your approach. The labyrinth offers a means for bringing your thoughts and emotions into coherence so that you are approaching the issue of your life's purpose in a clear state of mind and in a state of balance and heightened awareness. The labyrinth also offers a quest outside the areas that you already know, opening you up to a recognition that there is a much greater you to be explored.

When you enter the labyrinth in search of your purpose, you are bringing together your conscious and unconscious mind, as well as drawing on your intuition and connection to your higher self. You are acknowledging that you are willing to step outside your comfort zone and previously self-imposed boundaries to explore parts of yourself that you have not fully met. You are also willing to meet parts of yourself that you cannot even imagine. This search can bring much joy and peace as you discover who you really are and what you are here to do. Within the safe space of the labyrinth, your ongoing self-reflection leads to greater self-knowledge, expands your awareness, and brings greater clarity in many areas of your life.

Looking back on my early interactions with the labyrinth, I now realise that I was unknowingly following my path to self-discovery. This is also true of many people who come to the labyrinth looking for insights into their life. In exploring your life purpose in the labyrinth, insights can come like a flash of inspiration or they can creep up on you gradually.

Several years ago, a woman called Mary attended a few of my labyrinth walks. She was looking for a new direction in her life and her work. She was working in a retail shop and while it paid the bills she was not particularly happy working there. The first time that she walked the labyrinth she was walking the grass labyrinth in her bare feet and she stepped on a pebble that was a little uncomfortable and caused her to stop on her walk. Reflexology popped into her mind, and she reminded herself to check it out later. She was intrigued by the practice of reflexology and ended up signing on for an evening course and trained as a reflexologist.

She didn't see how she could make a living from her reflexology. So, at a subsequent labyrinth walk, she asked the question "How am I to make a living from my reflexology?" During the labyrinth walk, she got the message, "Just advertise and see what happens." She put a free ad in a local newspaper and some notices up in local shops advertising her services. The very next day she got a phone call from someone looking for an appointment. As she was able to see clients in the evenings after work, she was able to keep her day job and gradually build up her reflexology work.

She loved working as a reflexologist, especially talking with people and listening when they shared their problems. Yet, she felt that there was more to her life purpose. At another labyrinth evening, she walked the labyrinth to seek guidance on what else she might do. She felt that she didn't receive any direct insight during the walk, but while talking with one of the other participants after the walk, they mentioned to her that she should consider becoming a counsellor as she was a good listener and was easy to talk to. This prompted her to train as a counsellor/therapist. She now runs a successful counsellor practice and is really happy in her work. She credits the labyrinth with providing the insights to take the steps she needed to find her life purpose.

The pursuit of finding and living your life's purpose is the pursuit of a fulfilled life. A fulfilled life is one that brings you satisfaction and happiness. Your life purpose is inextricably linked to your understanding of the meaning of life. Your understanding of the reason, if any, that you believe you are here on earth will influence the direction of your search for fulfilment. When you discover yourself fully, you live your life in a state of knowing yourself and being yourself. In this state, you automatically do what is right and true for you, and you feel fulfilled and full of joy.

You are only on this earth for a specific time. At some stage, your life here will end and you will pass from this earth. The desire to achieve something substantial in life is the drive that keeps you pursuing your life purpose. Your sense of achieving may come from accomplishing any goal that is personally satisfying. This can range from climbing Mount Everest to creating a new piece of art, song, book, or anything else that is meaningful to you. It may involve being of service to others, or working for the betterment of society, the environment, the animals of the earth, or some other altruistic objective greater than yourself that you consider worthwhile.

The desire to find and live your purpose ebbs and flows with the cycles of life. Just as the path of the labyrinth sometimes brings you close to the centre and other times away from it, life's circumstances also impact your attainment of a fulfilled life. When you were a child, you may have had a strong sense of what you wanted to be when you grew up. Or you may not have had any idea or thought at all about it. As a child, I loved mazes. I bought books of maze puzzles and spent hours figuring them out. I believe that this was an early connection with labyrinths that didn't fully manifest into part of my life purpose until many years later. Like many people, I lost touch with what I loved as a child for many years. The social pressures of adolescence and early working life led me in different directions for a while. The societal expectation of earning a living, getting married, buying a house, and rearing a family overshadowed the sometimes intangible life purpose aim of doing what I loved and got fulfilment from.

As a young adult, you may have specific goals and aims that you want to achieve in life. Perhaps like many people, you become involved in long-term relationships, in which the welfare of the other partner becomes equally as important as your own, and the time available for engaging in personal pursuits is often greatly reduced. If you become a parent, the welfare of your children often takes a priority for several years. As children grow up and eventually leave home, it is often only then that you revisit your own personal goals and aims. If you are reading this later in life, you are not alone in realizing that now is the best time for you to seek the fulfilment that you postponed for other worthwhile reasons. It is also important to acknowledge that part of your life's purpose may have been the devotion of some of your life's years to the support of others. On the labyrinth journey of your life, some of your life's turns seemingly have taken you away from your purpose. Yet, you were always moving forward. Now is again your time.

Happiness can be found, and if you find happiness, you most likely have also found what makes you feel alive and what is your life's purpose. Take a moment to consider what you love doing. It doesn't matter what it is as long as it inspires you and you feel excited when you think about it and talk about it. It can be anything from stamp collecting to gardening to sport to travelling to places you find interesting. Whatever motivates you is usually a part of your purpose.

Clues to your life purpose may be hiding in full view. Your hobbies and pastimes are often a good indication of what inspires and drives you. Places you visit can also be an indication of some aspect of your life purpose. If you are someone who repeatedly goes to a particular place on holidays, consider what the attraction of that location is for you. There is often something about the place that you like, even though you might not always be able to put it into words. You most likely feel comfortable there. You feel a familiarity with it, a love for the place, the people, the language, the history. If all you can think of is that you just like it, then look deeper and explore the attraction more.

Books that you buy or are given as gifts can indicate where your purpose lies. People drawn to the labyrinth in this lifetime could have worked with them in past lifetimes, or chose to recognize the labyrinth before they incarnated. So, when they come across the labyrinth, they recognize it as a symbol that previously helped them advance on their path.

The path of the labyrinth also contains clues to your life purpose. The association of the circuits of the labyrinth with your chakras can provide insights into what is your purposes. If you feel a sensation in a certain area of the labyrinth on a life purpose walk, this is indicating to you that your life purpose could be related to that energy centre. You enter the labyrinth on the third circuit related to your solar plexus. This is connected with stepping into your power, which you must do to start living your purpose fully. An insight, message, or sensation on the next circuit could be indicating that your purpose is to be found in a creative way. On the longest outer circuit related to your root chakra, feelings, and insights can indicate a job focused around safety and security.

The fourth circuit is associated with your heart and healing. Providing a loving service, helping others, and doing work for the greater good often stem from a strong heart connection. After the heart chakra, the next circuit you enter on the labyrinth is associated with your crown chakra. This is your connection to a higher consciousness and may be guiding you to a life purpose that involves knowing beyond this life and earth, and sharing wisdom about life and death. It is said that the soul enters the body at birth and leaves at death through this chakra. Roles related to this chakra include spiritual guidance and teaching, preacher, monk, meditation teacher, and other similar roles.

An active third eye chakra during the walk can indicate a life purpose related to using your intuition and psychic abilities. Mediumship, psychic readings, and other ways of helping people through these areas may appeal to you. Moving to the throat centre, issues and insights relate to using your communication skill and speaking your truth. Professions such as teachers, counsellors, psychotherapists, and even politicians can stem from a raised vibration around truth. If you are sensitive to throat energies, you may even find yourself clearing your throat as you read this!

At the centre, you are in contact with your higher self. Divine presence is being activated from above and coming down into your body. Insights received here may relate to any of your energy centres, but may also pertain to the wholeness of all your chakras being in balance. When in balance, you are really opening up to seeing the dynamics of life, the energy field of the whole planet, with nature, and beyond. When you are at one with your higher self and in balance, your purpose will become clearer.

If you haven't found your life purpose yet, then lucky you! Life becomes even more wonderful and interesting; the world is your oyster and you are looking for the pearl. You have the opportunity of living your life with curiosity. You can go out every day with expectation and excitement that perhaps today is the day. You can even make a project plan of the places you are going to go, the things you are going to do, and the people you are going to see with a view to finding out if they give you the aliveness feeling. Treat the search for your life's purpose as a great adventure, and you will be rewarded with unexpected occurrences and "aha!" moments, some of which will inevitably be guiding you in the direction of your life purpose.

When you have found your purpose, you then have to start living it. You also need to consider if you can begin straight away or if there are some things that you need to do to prepare yourself for stepping fully into your life purpose. There may be practical issues that you need to address first. While I am now full-time teaching, facilitating, speaking, writing, healing, and helping others on their path, it took me many years to step fully into this area of work. I had a mortgage and a family to support, and so for several years my passion was limited to evenings and weekends. I took several years to build up my profile in the labyrinth and holistic area, and to train in various healing therapies. Eventually when I made the decision to move full-time into the area that I am now working, I was ready on both a personal level and on a practical and financial level. I always had a passion for labyrinth work, but had to wait until it could support me before I started working with it full time.

When you come out of the labyrinth after exploring your life purpose, you then have to take steps towards what you want, including removing those things in your life that you don't want. Taking action helps you to get clear on things. Making changes is not always easy, but when you know what your purpose is, these changes often flow automatically. If you think that you have found your purpose but haven't started living it yet, then doing nothing can lead to frustration. If taking a big step is too much for you, then you need to take whatever little steps that you can. Talking to others who are already doing what you know is your purpose can be inspiring and motivating. If you need to learn more about your life purpose activities, taking lessons to move you towards being that expert person is an essential intermediate step that you can take. Just like when you are walking the labyrinth, looking too far ahead may only confuse and bewilder you. So, take the next step and you will be moving towards where you want to be. And while the labyrinth will help to bring you clarity, you will only start getting results when you take action.

Shifting into fully living your life purpose can feel like sailing in uncharted waters. You may have a fear of leaving the known behind, particularly if it means leaving secure employment to pursue your passions.

You may know deep down that it will work, yet you also know that there is an element of risk involved. It is okay to feel some fear about what you are about to do. When you are on a hero's journey with no certainty about the outcome, there are times when you have to feel the fear and do it anyway.

You are living your life purpose when you are living from your heart. Your heart is the place of love and truth. When you are fully in your heart and doing what you love, you are also accessing deeper awareness and higher consciousness to feed more into your purpose. When you are doing what you love, you are inherently happy and in tune with yourself and the world around you. Being in such a heart centred space can bring more inspiration and guidance as you are operating beyond the blocks and barriers that previously held you back. When you are doing what you love, your love comes through in everything you say, everything you do, and everything you create. Others recognize the love that you are putting into your work and want to be a part of it and to have some of what you are producing. If you were choosing someone to do work on your house, you are more likely to choose someone who really loves what they are doing rather than someone who doesn't like their work. Do what you love doing and people will love what you do.

Having more than one purpose is quite common. While most people have one very strong soul purpose, searching for that one thing that is your life purpose may be a false quest. If you feel that something is missing, then there is likely something else that you are also meant to be doing. If you get satisfaction from doing several different things, then each one of these may be part of your purpose. There are lots of things that I really love doing. The list includes inspirational speaking, spiritual healing, designing labyrinths, writing, art, energetic space clearing, visiting sacred sites, and facilitating labyrinth workshops to bring people to a higher state of awareness and consciousness. When I look at this list, I see a strong connection between them all that can be condensed into one main thing that really makes me feel alive. It is working with high spiritual energy and groups, raising the vibration so that everyone present experiences a state of high vibration and awareness. Finding that one job or purpose that is perfect for you may not be your path. You may have several life purposes that you move through over the years of your life, or you may have several roles that you fulfil at the same time, each one making you feel like you are on fire and that you want to get up and race out the door to do in the morning.

Everyone's path is different, and my way may not be your way. Yet each of us is also on the same path: the path to a fulfilled life. And you are being guided. Remember Ariadne's thread that led Theseus out of the labyrinth. That golden thread is leading you through the labyrinth of your life to finding your place and purpose in the world. That thread may come in the form of a career or profession that you were born to do. Or it may be a way of being that appeals to you above all else. And just like Theseus, you too can have an unquenchable passion and powerful connection to the work you are here to do, where your love of life and your place within it is a powerful driving force within you.

You will know when you have found your purpose, as you will be so full of life and positivity about what you are doing. When you are passionate about something you want to share it with others. My friend Michael is passionate about Ireland's ancient sacred sites. He visits them whenever he can and reads every book he can get his hands on to learn more about them. He loves talking about them, and his enthusiasm for them is infectious. When he starts talking about these "special places," as he calls them, his eyes light up, and people are naturally attracted to him and what he is saying. It is like someone has flicked a big switch and a great light starts shining inside of him.

Your passion is your purpose. Going into the labyrinth aligns you deeper in your soul. It helps you to let go of what is hindering and blocking you. The more you work with the labyrinth, the clearer your purpose will become. Every labyrinth walk is different, and every time you walk the labyrinth seeking insights into your life purpose you can receive new insights. Even when you have found your purpose, from time to time you will have questions about your next step, or the choices that you have to make in life. Continuing to work with the labyrinth will help guide you and keep you on the path of your purpose and fulfilment. The labyrinth brings you to a place where you are living life fully and loving life fully, embodying your real purpose of being completely involved in your life.

EXERCISE: HOW TO CONDUCT A LIFE PURPOSE EXPLORATION WALK (BACK TO THE WOMB WALK)

This exercise is about walking the labyrinth as symbolic of going back into the womb to remember your purpose in this lifetime. Finding your life purpose can be influenced by everything that has happened in your life to date.

Your mindset is important on this walk. You need to believe that finding your life purpose is possible. Be aware also that your purpose may not become immediately and clearly apparent, and that you need to be conscious of every signal, message, and insight that you receive.

To find your true purpose in life, you need to empty your mind of all the thoughts about it that you took on or learned. As your mind quietens while walking the labyrinth, you become more open to receiving answers to your life purpose questions.

It is important also to acknowledge that you may have some anxiety or hidden fears about finding your life purpose. Finding your life purpose may mean making some changes to your life, some of these can be radical changes. You may have an inkling what your purpose is, but are nervous of having it confirmed because it may mean substantial changes for you and your loved ones. Ultimately, you know deep down that finding your life purpose will leave you with the power to weave your own destiny.

To begin, write down in a few words or short phrases a brief description of the main life events that you have experienced in this lifetime from now back to your birth. Start with where you are now. As you remember significant events and people in your life, consciously let go of any aspects of those relationships and events that do not make you feel happy. Just let them go without any judgement. Thank the people for what they brought you, and let go of the memories that you do not wish to keep. Remember your recent years, your parents, family members, remember your young adult years, your teenage years, your college days, your school days, your childhood years, your days as a young child.

This exercise uses a finger labyrinth that you have drawn (alternatively, you can use the one on page 259), or walking a labyrinth, to travel back in time back through all the memories that you have listed. You begin at the entrance to the labyrinth representing where you are now in your life. All your life events brought you to this point. Some of them you are happy about and others not so much. During the exercise, you will be retracing your life's steps back to the time before you were born—back to the womb. As you walk, you symbolically move back through the years remembering the key memories that you have written down and some others that come to mind as you walk.

You need to customize the walk to suit your age and experiences. Whatever your circumstances, when you begin the labyrinth walk focus on your most recent experiences in life. As a memory comes to mind, allow all negative thoughts and experiences from this memory to go. Your intention is to focus on and amplify the memories that have given you joy, that made you feel alive, that make you smile even now.

Bring your thoughts back to when you were several years younger. Think about the jobs you worked at, the people you had relationships with, the places you visited. All the while, let go of what did not serve you in those relationships, and focus on what you wish to retain that made you feel good. Think about the people who were in your life, the partners you spent time with, the children you were raising. Think about the happy times, what was happening, and what you were doing.

Move back further to when you were a young single adult. Focus on those years. Remember what you enjoyed doing, especially those things that felt healthy and wholesome. Let go of any unhappy memories of people, places, and work that you did. If you went to college, go back through your college years and remember your relationships and activities there. Again, let go of the unhappy and unpleasant memories, retaining the happy times and any time you felt freedom and fully alive.

As you walk further in the labyrinth, go back to your teenage years. What were your fears and hopes when you were a teenager? Let go of any anxiety and doubt that you had at that time, and focus on the fun times you had with friends, and the things that you loved doing on your own.

Go back further to when you were a younger child, aged eleven or twelve. Remember what you loved doing. Remember what your parents had to drag you away from. What did you love doing and sharing with your friends? Remember when you were younger again and the things you did where you lost track of time. Recall how you spent your spare time when you were an eight- or nine-year-old.

Go back further to when you were only five or six years old. What memories do you have of those times? If you have unhappy memories from any part of your childhood, acknowledge them and let them go. Focus on what made you feel happy from your childhood. Find those moments and days of your childhood happiness.

You will now be getting close to the centre of the labyrinth. Think back as far as you can remember, when you were only a few years old. Hold on to the happy memories and let go of what were not nice memories at the time.

As you near the centre of the labyrinth, you will remember your earliest memories of this lifetime. You are now at a time shortly before you were born. While you may not have clear memories or images of these early years that you can recall, sometimes you have a feeling about these times that has stayed with you. You will now be at the entrance to the centre of the labyrinth. Entering the centre of the labyrinth is symbolic of re-entering your mother's womb.

When in the centre, pause, and take as much time as you need to visualize yourself in your mother's womb. This is a time when you had a greater connection with your higher self and the spirit world. Allow whatever thoughts that come to mind to grow. Do not dismiss anything. Be in a state of quiet acceptance just as if you were a warm, safe baby. It is safe to be yourself; it is safe to allow your thoughts to go where they want to go. It is safe to see, hear, and feel whatever you are feeling. See if you can go back even further to before conception took place, to before you took physical form to see what insights you get about your purpose in coming to earth. If nothing is coming to you, ask your guides to give you some insights into your reason for being here.

After a few minutes, and when you feel ready, even if you feel that you have not received any major insights, prepare to re-enact your birth and be born into this lifetime. Slowly make your way out of the womb centre of the labyrinth. As you walk out of the labyrinth, allow any thoughts that relate to what you love doing, what makes you feel alive, or what is your purpose on earth at this time to emerge. Do not judge or dismiss anything that comes to you, even if it appears not to make sense to you at the time. As you emerge from the labyrinth you are now at the point of your life at this present moment.

Reflection

Write down everything that came to you during this walk. Do not leave anything out as everything is important. When you have finished writing, consider where you are now in relation to your purpose. Do this in a nonjudgemental way. You are where you are and can now make choices.

What emotions did you feel when you were writing things down? Look for an emotion that is a little different from the others, as it may give you a clue to what you are here to do.

Consider what steps you now wish to take to progress on your journey in life. What are you going to do that's different? What are you going to do that is new for you?

You can repeat this exercise any time you feel like exploring further your life's purpose.

7
Death

The labyrinth is a symbol of death and rebirth. You release and let go of issues, emotions, and experiences in the labyrinth so that you no longer carry them with you. These issues are no longer in your life. They are dead for you. The writer and sculptor Michael Ayrton, who devoted much of his life to the study and depiction of Greek myths, takes this a step further. "Each man's life is a labyrinth at the centre of which is his death" (Ayrton 1967). In his book *The Maze Maker*, Ayton writes, "Within the great maze of a man's life are many smaller ones, each seemingly complete in itself, and in passing through each one he dies in part, for in each he leaves behind him a part of his life and it lies dead behind him" (Ayrton 1967).

Rather than consider death as negative, the labyrinth is calling us to consider the positive aspects of the many little deaths that we pass through in life, and especially the greater death of the physical body. The little deaths in life are those things, people, places, activities, and ways of behaving that we detach from, let go of, and leave behind. On your journey of self-discovery, your path of advancement is one of continually letting go of what is no longer of benefit. Ways of behaving that were the norm for you several years ago are now forgotten or seem like a distant memory. Your awareness and consciousness have changed, and you can no longer behave in ways that are not in alignment with your soul's purpose; so too with people in your life.

When you look back at your life to date, you will notice that you have spent time with different groups of people and different individuals, some of whom you no longer have any contact with. It is almost as if these people have died; your time with them is over. Letting go of what no longer serves you creates space for something new to come into your life—for the birth of something new—the new you! The advantage of some things in your life dying back is that you can move forward more easily.

Another death on your labyrinth journey is the gradual death of attachment. The more steps you take on your journey, the more you become aware of what is important in your life. Your desire to want things and to accumulate possessions for their own sake diminishes. While you can still enjoy and appreciate the good things in life, you no longer need them to feel worthwhile and whole. Your sense of identity comes more from inside than from outward appearances and possessions.

The greater death of the physical body is one that may invoke fear in you. It does for many people. It is a subject that is not talked about much today. It certainly is not talked about enough. And when it is talked about it is usually in negative terms laced with fear and even foreboding. It is okay to feel fear, as long as it does not paralyze you and prevent you from living a meaningful and fulfilled life.

For many, fear of death stems from fear of the unknown. Yet, you cannot fear the unknown because you do not know what it is. It might be *wonderful*. The fear for many people is the fear of leaving the known behind. The basis for much of the fear of death is that we are not aware of whether this is as good as life gets, or if there is something much more wonderful awaiting us after the death of the physical body. Michael Newton, in his book *Journey of Souls*, writes, "Those who have just died are not devastated by their death, because they know those left on earth will see them again in the spirit world and probably later in other lives as well. On the other hand, mourners at a funeral feel they have lost a loved one forever" (Newton 1994).

It is this sense of loss and ending, this finality to our time here on earth, that brings up our deepest fears. One of the greatest fears is the sense that there is nothing after the death of the body. Nobody has come back from the dead to tell us what happens after death. We can, however, get some indication from those who have clinically died for a short time and come back to life. For many people, accounts of near-death experiences results in a loss of their fear of death. Not all of us can experience such pivotal life-changing near-death experiences. Yet, there is a reason for those who have. It is to provide insights for them into their lives, and to provide reassurance to those of us who have not had their experiences.

You might argue that a wonderful afterlife is based solely on faith. However, you have an innate sense of the truth of the accounts of the afterlife. These accounts may trigger some subconscious, or superconscious, memory that you recognize. You may feel just a slight feeling of excitement, or a sensation deep within you that is your confirmation of the veracity of these accounts.

One reason that we consider life on earth to be the best thing to experience is that there is nothing to compare it to. Maybe life on this planet is one of the worst there is. Many people at times wish for something better. There are certainly some tough times in most people's lives. I have often described our lives on earth as being like an army assault course. We have to metaphorically climb over walls, crawl through mud, under barbed wire, jump into ice cold water, and make our way through many other physically, mentally, and emotionally challenging exercises. Newton describes the journey that many souls go through on earth as being like a battlefield from which they must recover in the spirit world (Newton 1994). You have your life experiences so that you can learn from them. Although, some of them may present as so extreme that any thought of seeing them from the viewpoint of your soul's journey through many lifetimes is often lost. The greatest of these experiences could be your death, or your fear of it.

There is also the possibility that what awaits us after death is not all bliss and wonderful. Perhaps another labyrinth is there for us to travel through. The bardo that Buddhists believe we pass through after death and before reincarnating could well be described as a type of labyrinth through which we often need help to make our way. It is thought that while in the bardo between death and rebirth, the consciousness of the deceased person can still receive assistance through words and prayers spoken on its behalf. This assistance can help it navigate through the confusion that it might be experiencing so that it can be reborn into a new life that offers a greater chance of attaining enlightenment.

The classical labyrinth can also be viewed according to John Michell as a "chart of the soul's progress from death to rebirth" (Michell 1988), embracing both the subterranean world and the rings of the heavens as described by Plato. The great majority of souls who take the path leading to the centre of the labyrinth find themselves weighed down by the earthly part of their nature, and having briefly glimpsed the heavenly centre, return out of the labyrinth and fall back into rebirth. Those few souls who attain the centre enter that region of pure intelligence farthest removed from mundane illusions.

You have a choice to enter the labyrinth of life and death or to avoid facing whatever fears are coming up for you. Fear is the opposite of love, and on your journey of self-discovery you are learning to live less in fear and more in love. Eventually all that will prevail is love. Your soul's journey in its earthly incarnations is one of learning not to be influenced or overcome by fear. Replacing this great fear of physical death with love will bring you closer to an understanding and knowing of yourself as an infinite being. When you have contemplated your death, and faced any fears that you have about it, you free yourself up to live a fearless life. When you learn how to die, you learn how to live.

Death and the Labyrinth

Some labyrinths have been associated with death and funerary rites through the ages. At Hadrumentum in North Africa there is a Roman family tomb with a fourfold labyrinth mosaic floor that has a dying Minotaur in the centre and a mosaic inscription HIC INCLUSUS VITAM PERDIT: "Enclosed here, he loses life" (Kern 2000). There is a stone labyrinth at Lassa in Uppland, Sweden, located at the end of an ancient road along which it was thought the dead would be pulled on carts to their burial sites in the cairns and mounds surrounding the labyrinth. Several other labyrinths have been found in Scandinavia close to gallows hills, serving these places of the dead.

In his article "Stone Labyrinths in Arctic Norway," Bjørnar Olsen proposes that several stone labyrinths at the northern tip of Europe "served as a material metaphor to conceptualize the transition from life into death" (Olsen 1996). A significant feature of the location of these labyrinths is that all are situated on or near Saami (Lapp) burial grounds. He goes on to write that these labyrinths played a symbolic role in this rite of passage, where the shaman entered the labyrinth as a representative of the deceased to assist them in moving through this difficult post-death phase.

There is a labyrinth carved inside an ancient underground tomb at Luzzanas in Sardinia. There are questions as to whether the labyrinth carving is of the same age as the tomb, so this labyrinth's associations with death and burial are unclear. Most of the ancient rock carvings of labyrinths in Galicia, Spain, and in Valcamonica, Italy, have their ene-trances facing west—the traditional direction associated with death, due to the sun setting in the west. Interestingly also, and remarkably, according to Kern, "the entrances of nearly all manuscript labyrinths face west. The same is true of the vast majority of church labyrinths" (Kern 2000).

The Tohono O'odham or Papago Indians of Southern Arizona have a form of the seven-circuit classical labyrinth with a human figure at the mouth, which is at the top, woven into baskets known as "The Man in the Maze." There are several interpretations of the meaning of the figure in this pattern. One is that it is a human figure representing the O'odham people, and the "maze" represents the journey to find meaning in life, with the twists and turns representing life's events. The centre represents death and the beginning of a new journey (Duryee 2007). Another is that the figure is their god I'itoi who lives on the top of their sacred mountain, Babiquovari. The labyrinth is the winding path leading to his home that is so long and torturous that no one has ever found the house's exact location.

The snakelike path of the labyrinth also carries associations of death as it changes direction several times. The turn towards the left is associated with death as it is the opposite direction to the way the sun travels. Turns towards the right are associated with life. During the whole labyrinth walk, the repeated turns in both directions symbolise the many little deaths that you undergo, and the new areas of your life that you are turning into.

The serpentine turnings also carry the symbolism of the snake shedding its old skin, emerging renewed with its new shiny coat. This is akin to us shedding our illusions and limitations in the labyrinth. On a deeper level, the snake shedding its skin symbolises death and rebirth. According to John James, the snake also "has a beneficent side—that of wisdom." And the snake that consumes itself was "the symbol of death and knowledge, of perfection and of power. It is circular, and consumes itself only to be reborn, and hence has much in common with the labyrinth" (James 1977). In the labyrinth, you are reborn into knowledge and wisdom, leaving behind the living death of unawareness.

The Minotaur in the labyrinth can also be seen as symbolizing death or our fear of death. The myth of Theseus encountering the Minotaur is a tale of death-defying magnitude. When Theseus decides to face the Minotaur without any guarantee of the outcome, he faces his probable death. Furthermore, as the labyrinth is almost inescapable, his quest most likely means that he would not return. The symbolism of Theseus no longer existing carries for us the fear of nothingness. Yet, as soon as Theseus grasps the thread that Ariadne presented to him, he gained a clue (clew of thread) to help him emerge from the labyrinth. When you decide to face the unknown, particularly in the form of your death, there is assistance and guidance available to you giving you a greater sense of determination and purpose. Facing your death gives your life meaning.

The labyrinth has many associations with moving from one state of being into another, including being seen as a supernatural doorway between this life and what comes afterwards. The symbolic representation that the labyrinth provides of death marks the end of one way of being and the beginning of another. The person entering the labyrinth leaves behind one way and is born into another.

More common associations between the labyrinth and death revolve around the labyrinth as a vessel within which the person interacting with the labyrinth explores and experiences the death of certain aspects of the personality and ego, to be reborn into a new person. Furthermore, according to Kern, "In the labyrinth, a person is surrounded by it, isolated and cut off from his or her familiar environment. For that person, familiar surroundings have died. There is no way back, only the inevitable path forward, with a change of direction at the centre. The path from a former existence into confinement, is the path of death" (Kern 2000). But it is the exploring of the death of the physical body that can bring the greatest insights into this lifetime for you.

The labyrinth offers a safe vessel within which you can access varied states of consciousness and different dimensions. As an experienced labyrinth walker, it is possible to bring yourself to whatever state and whatever place you choose. It may take practise, but in time you can access whatever wisdom you seek. Transcending your fear of the death of your physical body in the labyrinth can release you from conscious and subconscious fears that you are carrying with you. The following exercise is one way of exploring your infinite being in the labyrinth.

EXERCISE: DEATH ON THE LABYRINTH

This is an advanced labyrinth walk exercise. It is best done with someone you trust and someone who has experience working with the labyrinth such as a trained facilitator or a trained counsellor. It is a powerful and deep practice that you need to be able to carry out in a safe and undisturbed environment. You can also call on your angels, guides, and invisible helpers to be with you during the walk. You are going to experience, on a theoretical and energetic level, the death of the physical body that you now occupy.

At the entrance of the labyrinth, picture yourself as you are now in your life. Begin walking, and as you walk, see in your mind all the dreams, hopes, and thoughts that you have for the future. Work through all the things that you would like to do while you are here on earth. When you have gone through everything that you want to do, see where you are on the labyrinth. Are you near the centre? Take a mental note for later of the place where you feel that you have fulfilled all your life's work.

If you are not at the entrance to the centre of the labyrinth, slowly make your way to the entrance to the centre of the labyrinth, representative of the moment that you leave your physical body. At the point where you enter the centre of the labyrinth, imagine what it would be like for your soul to leave your physical body, or for your physical body to fade away and be no more. If you can, lie down in the centre of the labyrinth and lay still. If you feel comfortable doing so, close your eyes. Again, visualize what it would be like for you to no longer have a physical body.

Preferably with your eyes closed, allow your thoughts and consciousness to take you where it will, as far as possible. Keep your mind clear and let go of any judgement of what is happening. Stay in a state of awareness and observation, noting what you are feeling and sensing.

When your thoughts return to your physical body, focus on being fully present in your body. Keep your eyes closed for a short while longer, and when you feel ready, open your eyes. Allow yourself time to readjust to your surroundings, to being in a physical body. Feel your presence in every part of your body: your head, your torso, your legs, your feet and toes, your arms and hands. Feel aliveness in your whole body. Allow yourself plenty of time for you to come back to being fully present in your physical body. Slowly rise and get ready to make your way out of the labyrinth. The walk back out of the labyrinth is about you coming back into the world with new awareness.

Reflection

Immediately after the walk, write down any thoughts that came to you during any aspect of this walk—particularly while in the centre where you visualized yourself leaving your physical body.

Write about how you felt during the walk. Write about any fears that came up for you. Write about the people who came to mind during the walk.

Contemplate the following questions: How have your views of the death of the body changed? What will you consider doing differently after this walk? What is the most important thing for you to do in your life?

8
Rebirth and Past Lives

Rebirth follows death. To bring something new into your life you must create space for it. Through your symbolic death in the labyrinth you have let go of what no longer has life or vibrancy for you. This may be physical possessions, relationships, traumas from the past, ways of behaving, and anything else that you are holding on to that may be weighing you down at this stage of your life. Rebirth is the stage of newness after you have let go of some of these things. The labyrinth is a powerful symbol of rebirth. After letting go of what no longer serves you on your walk into the labyrinth, you then emerge from the womb of the labyrinth in a state of newness.

How you see life is reflected in the labyrinth. If you see life as primarily about death, then it may represent entrapment for you. If you see the life and the labyrinth as largely about rebirth, then the labyrinth represents release and freedom. When you focus more on the release and rebirth, that is what your life becomes. What you focus on grows.

Rebirth is soul growth. The more growth you have in this lifetime, the more advanced you will be in the next lifetime. This is karma: the bringing of learning from experiences in past lives into this lifetime. Karmic experiences can be positive as well as negative. Your soul does not forget what it learned in previous incarnations. In this lifetime, you will have chosen certain experiences to have and certain lessons to take to progress on your soul's journey. You may also have chosen to forget past life experiences for a time so that you can start afresh in this lifetime.

Rebirthing is bringing in what you already know on a soul level. Rebirthing gives you an opportunity to heal what you need to heal so you can move on. You will need to work through your current life experiences in need of healing before you can address some of your past life issues.

Issues from past lives can reappear in this lifetime. When you encounter a situation that you are struggling with on an emotional and energetic level, it is worthwhile considering if there might be a past life influence for what is happening. This is not to use past lives as an excuse to avoid addressing what is arising. Rather, once you have exhausted current life approaches and solutions, it is about being open to the possibility that you may be energetically carrying some thinking or behaviour from a past life that is dominating your approach to a situation in this life.

Remembering past lives is not just an interesting game to discover something exciting or fascinating about yourself. When you delve into past life experiences it can often shine a spotlight on some aspect of your current life that you need to address and can even provide insights into future lives. In the words of the Buddha, "If you want to know the past, look at the present. If you want to know the future, look at the present."

Past Lives

For many years, I had no idea of any of my past lives. Indeed, I had no understanding or interest in the subject. As I began to walk my own path to self-discovery, remembering my past lives crept up quietly on me without me realizing. The first memory that I had was of an immense and deep sadness that I experienced in Montsequr, France, in 2005. A group of five of us went to climb the hill and to remember those who had given their lives for their beliefs in 1244. We spent a short time in meditation at the top. My wife, Fionnuala, who is quite psychic and in-tuitive, tuned in and saw images of the five of us there back in 1244. I knew deep within me that I had been there before, although I could not logically explain it. I was overcome by a huge sadness and stayed in the energy of that emotion for several minutes. It felt like I was living in two worlds simultaneously. When I brought my attention fully back to this lifetime, something in me had shifted.

This experience seemed to open a doorway to other past life experi-ences. Several of my other past life experiences are related to the laby-rinth and some specifically to Chartres in France. One of these involved a significant healing for me on several levels in this lifetime. For many years, I had suffered with sporadic stomach pains and remember on one occasion when at a football match not being able to stand with the cramps in my stomach muscles.

A few weeks before I went to Chartres in October 2005, I went to a sweat lodge ceremony. As I crawled out of the sweat lodge, I threw my-self on the ground and pressed my bare skin against the cold, refreshing earth to cool down. I felt an energy leave my stomach and be absorbed by the earth. I had a strong sense that this had something to do with my upcoming trip to Chartres.

While waiting at the airport for my flight to Paris, I had a cup of tea with Fionnuala. At one point, Fionnuala stopped and asked me if there was a soldier in my family, as she was seeing someone in army uniform in my energy field behind me. I couldn't come up with any explanation that made sense. Later, on the flight to France, I wrote in my journal about a clear and intense dream that I experienced a few times. I wrote: "I had a vivid dream of being a soldier, running an explosive cable to destroy a building as the battle raged around me. I was and am convinced that this was a past life dream. Why it comes up now, I will find out in Chartres."

In Chartres I couldn't sleep one night, so I went for a walk at three o'clock in the morning. I walked down along the River Eure and out into the countryside. I walked for hours, always secure in the knowledge that I could see the floodlit cathedral in the distance and that it showed me my way back. Walking back into Chartres as I headed up the hill towards the cathedral, I passed a war memorial that contained thousands of names from many different wars. I sat down on the plinth with my back to the memorial, but something caused me to turn around. As I looked at the lists of names, one name particularly caught my attention, almost as if it was rising up from the stone. I knew instantly that this was significant. It was the name of a soldier who had died in 1942.

I had a pendulum with me that I used for dowsing and divining answers to questions, indicating either a yes or no answer by a particular movement of the pendulum. I began to ask questions about this name. The first question I asked was "Was this me in a past life?" and I received a strong yes. As I asked more questions and got more answers, I asked if I had been shot and got a yes. I then started asking where I was shot: In the head? ... No. In the chest? ... No. In the stomach? As soon as I asked if I was shot in the stomach, my stomach went into severe spasms and I was bent over double with the pain. I got a very definite yes. Once the pain had eased, I proceeded with my questions. I asked if I died on the battlefield, and I got a no response. "Did I die in a hospital?"—No! I asked if I died in a farm shed, and I received a strong Yes.

I told Fionnuala all about it on the phone that evening. She told me about a vivid dream that she had experienced several times years before she met me. She was a girl of about seventeen living on a farm during wartime. One day a soldier crawled into the barn on the farm. He had been shot in the stomach. She held her hands over his stomach and tried to heal him, but he died.

I was eagerly looking forward to walking the labyrinth in the cathedral a few days later, expecting to get more insights into being a soldier shot in the stomach in a past life. I was part of a group of over thirty people who were having a private walk on the labyrinth after the cathedral had closed. After preparing for the labyrinth walk through meditation and contemplation, we made our way to the labyrinth that was lit by candles placed in the lunations around the outside of the labyrinth.

As soon as my bare feet touched the cold flagstones of the floor, my perception shifted. Everything felt different, and the date 1288 shot into my thoughts. I knew that on one level, I was transported back to the year 1288 when I was a ten-year-old boy about to walk the labyrinth on the floor of Chartres Cathedral in France. Not only was I experiencing one of my own past lives, I was aware that many people in the group there with me that evening were also there in 1288. I recognized some members of the current group in different roles and different ages than they were in present-day time. Even the musical group who were performing appeared visually to me dressed in white robes of the time.

I walked the labyrinth as that ten-year-old boy. It was fun, and getting off the path to allow adults to pass didn't bother me. I had a huge smile on my face. When I looked down at what I was wearing, I had a large, baggy, woolly jumper, and my trousers were rolled up to my knees like half-length pants of the time ... and I was in my bare feet. At one stage, I glanced over to the base of one of the pillars where I always liked to sit during the day. I almost froze with fright. There was a woman sitting there dressed in black with a hooded shawl covering her head. I knew immediately that it was my mother from 1288, and that she was quite ill, which was the reason we had made the pilgrimage to the cathedral of Notre Dame in Chartres. What I wasn't sure of was if it was actually one of the present-day group or if it was an image of my past mother being shown to me just at that time. When I was finished walking the labyrinth, I made my way towards the pillar where my "mother" was sitting and sat on the steps by her feet. There was a real person sitting there: a member of the present-day group. The vivid images and palpable experiences of two simultaneous realities had me in a state of heightened awareness and still moves me when I remember it. It is still one of the most significant and relevant of my past life experiences.

Even more significant was the connection that I had with Fionnuala in that lifetime. Although it was only a fleeting few moments when she tried to heal me—the wounded soldier—I know that the reconnection is telling me that we never know when we will meet someone significant in our lives. It is a reminder to be open to the significance of every moment and the possible importance of everyone you meet.

Since the sweat lodge and my trip to Chartres I have not had any problems with my stomach. I healed a physical injury from one of my past lives that was affecting me in this lifetime. Past life memories always arise for a reason, the most common of which is to heal something in this lifetime that you have brought with you energetically from a past life. It may not always be clear what the issue is, but with time, reflection, and meditation, the answer frequently becomes clearer.

And while some of these events did not happen on the labyrinth, it was because of the labyrinth that I went to Chartres. After those events, I have a greater understanding and knowing of the interconnectedness of all of existence. I also know that healing from past lives helps us in this life in physical, mental, emotional, and spiritual ways. Past life experiences almost always show us something in this life that we are here to address. I related my experience to the group later, and it was of particular relevance for several of them. I had always considered that past life experiences were mainly for the individual experiencing them, and were for my own learning and journey. Now it appears that they can also be for others' benefit.

Over time, the labyrinth presented an image to me of togetherness. Whatever this group of people had come to experience in today's world, they had also come together for some other experience hundreds of years previously. We were taking steps on our soul's journey together over many lifetimes. And while there are some people from this group that I have never met again since this event in Chartres, there are others with whom I have developed lifelong friendships. Or, perhaps, it is more correct to say that I re-established soul friendships that have existed through many lifetimes and in the spirit world.

In life, you will find yourself in certain groups at certain times. Nothing happens by accident, particularly when it concerns people in your life. The people who are meant to be in your life at a particular time are there, whether you find their presence helpful or not. Although some people's presence in your life that you consider less than helpful is often to prompt you to choose a certain course of action that involves an advancement on your soul's journey.

In my work with the labyrinth, and particularly at workshops and events, I find that I have a soul connection with almost everyone who attends. I can feel this connection in my heart, and I can see it in their eyes. There is a knowing between us that is beyond words, and beyond the physical. It is a wonderful experience to reconnect with someone that you remember from the spirit world, and previous lifetimes. The depth of connection, joy, and recognition is full of love and a palpable excitement. There is an immediate sense of support and togetherness in this lifetime, and an image of the bigger picture of what we are here for begins to emerge.

The labyrinth is acting as a call to action and as a catalyst for people to come together, to remember their souls' journeys, and to support each other in this lifetime. If you feel a draw to the labyrinth, then follow that draw. The labyrinth is a meeting place for people that you are meant to meet on your life's journey. It is a place of assembly for soul friends and soul groups. And while the only past life recollection that I have of interacting with labyrinths was as the ten-year-old boy in Chartres, I will not be surprised if and when I discover that I had several other encounters with labyrinths somewhere in my many previous incarnations.

EXERCISE: EXPLORING YOUR PAST LIVES LABYRINTH WALK

The intention of this labyrinth walk is to seek greater awareness of some of your past lives and significant aspects of those lives that are relevant for you in this lifetime. This is so you can better understand how they might be influencing your thinking and behaviour in this lifetime and how you can begin to address them. This walk is also about going back through many lifetimes to find a common thread and purpose to get to know better your soul's purpose through lifetimes. You came to earth for a reason which you have temporarily forgotten. You may even have deliberately decided not to remember your reason for coming here so that you could overcome the learning obstacles placed in your way to strengthen and develop your soul's resolve and commitment to progression.

In preparing for this walk, take some time to reflect on the reasons that you might be here on earth or here in this room at this time. Your soul's journey has brought you to this point. The walk into the labyrinth, therefore, is a representation of tracing back through previous lifetimes—seeing significant events of previous lifetimes for the first time, or in a new light, that reveal some aspect of your progress to this point in time. When walking into the labyrinth, the centre represents the point of the beginning of your soul's journey.

Setting a clear intention before you commence your walk is crucial to gaining the most benefit from this walk. Formulate clearly what aspects of your past lives you wish to explore. Write down what you are seeking on this walk. There are several ways you can explore past lives during this walk. If you do not remember any past life, then you are seeking any information about a past life that is relevant for you and that you are ready to learn about and address. If you already have some awareness of a past life, or sense that something in this lifetime is related to a past life, then set the intention of receiving greater clarity about that past life or event. If you are looking for a common theme that is running through lifetimes that you need to address or continue with in this lifetime, then state that clearly. Visualize yourself going back in time through past lives and your time in the spirit world.

As you walk into the labyrinth towards the centre, be aware of all thoughts, insights, images, and sensations that come to you. Observe what is presenting itself to you. Allow these to develop without judgement. Judging can often halt the development of an insight, so remain as an observer until you have exited the walk and are reflecting on your experiences. Become aware of every thought, feeling, sensation, sound, and image that comes to you. Observe what you are experiencing, again without judgement. Avoid getting caught up in interpreting what you are receiving during the walk, as you may block additional information from coming through. If memories of past lives come to you during the walk, just allow the memory to flow until it reaches its natural end.

When doing this for the first time, you may have excessive expectations that are hindering access to quieting your mind, which is needed to allow past life memories to be revealed. Doing a first labyrinth walk just to quieten the mind, and following it immediately with the walk in this exercise, can help bring greater depth and clarity to this exercise. Insights received on this walk may not be obvious. Take note of anyone who comes to mind when you are walking. There is a strong possibility that someone from this lifetime who comes to mind during this walk was with you in a past lifetime. Every thought that comes to you on this walk may be a clue to a past life experience.

When you reach the centre, rest there in the centre of all of existence. You have returned to Divine Source to experience your point of origin. Allow whatever presents itself to you to penetrate your whole being. Remain in this space for as long as you feel necessary before you begin your journey back out through the labyrinth, through your soul's journey to where you are now.

As you walk out see how you have travelled as a soul. Seek guidance as to what brought you to where you are now on your journey. Allow insights to present themselves to you, particularly those that shed light on your purpose in this lifetime.

When you have finished your walk, write down everything you experienced. Describe in detail what came to you. Do not stop to interpret, just write everything down first until you have fully described your experiences. If possible leave generous spaces between paragraphs, as you will be interpreting these experiences later. Next, go back over your experiences and write down your emotions and thoughts for each significant event revealed to you. Then write down everybody who came to mind during the walk. Keep writing until you have nothing left to put down on paper.

Don't worry if you have not had any new revelations or insights. This, too, is an insight. So, consider how this might be part of your soul's journey and where you go from here.

Reflection

When you have finished writing, take a few quiet moments to contemplate what arose for you. These moments are to let whatever thoughts, feelings, and insights that came to you during the walk to settle in your conscious mind. This is a time to be quiet and just allow yourself a few special moments to be with your thoughts of your past lives.

Look back at the emotions that arose for you during the walk. Sometimes the emotion is the easiest way to get access to past life information. If you did not get any clear images or insights into a specific past life, every emotion that you experienced could be a clue or doorway to finding out more. As you consider what you have written about the emotions, keep your mind as clear as possible. Without judgement, allow whatever thoughts that come to mind to flow. If someone from this lifetime came to mind during the walk, take note of the context in which this person came to mind, and if you were thinking or feeling anything specific at the time. You may have had a different close relationship in your past lives, and may have come back together at this time to address some leftover issues, or to continue what you started in a previous lifetime.

When you have done all this, see if you can interpret what you have experienced. How does what you went through impact where you are now? What insights did you get about what you must do now in this lifetime? Consider individual events and the walk as a whole, and even tie in with other events and experiences that appear to you to be related.

If you can identify a connection to a previous existence, then consider what the relevance of this is for you. All your past life experiences and recollections are significant. The ones that are revealed to you in this lifetime are almost always to bring healing to some situation and insight into some behaviour. Be grateful for any remembrances, as they are stepping stones to greater things.

This is a deep exercise, and one during which the mind can sometimes play tricks on you. It is often beneficial to repeat this exercise.

9
Others on Your Path

Up until now, many of your interactions with the labyrinth in this book hav been focused on you as an isolated individual. You have looked at how the labyrinth represents you in many aspects of your life and spiritual development. When you have achieved a certain level of awareness and inner unity on your path to self-discovery, you move on to some of your greatest teachers—the other people in your life. Other people can shape your life as much as you shape your own, and several of your key relationships are symbolically represented in the labyrinth.

The labyrinth is a wonderful tool for exploring your relationship with the other people in a safe and insightful way. Bringing the significant people of your life into the labyrinth introduces a wider dimension to your interactions with them. It presents some of the major lessons that you chose before incarnating. However, with imposed amnesia, you have forgotten what lessons and learning you chose to experience in this lifetime. The safe and illuminating container of the labyrinth provides one way to explore and understand some of your most beautiful and most difficult human relationships.

Born into the Labyrinth of Life

From the moment you were born, and even before you were born, your life has been intertwined with others at a level you may not be fully aware of. The first group of people that you meet in the labyrinth of life are your parents. In some belief systems, it is considered that you choose your parents before birth while in the spirit world, and that the parents you choose will be best suited to present you with situations you need to encounter for your soul to progress. You owe your physical existence to your parents who conceived you, to your mother who brought you into this life, and to everyone who provided for you until you could provide for yourself.

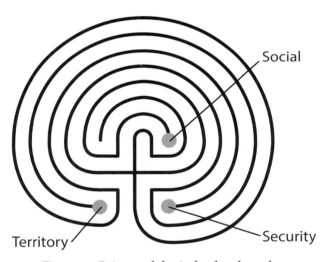

Figure 11: Points on labyrinth related to others

Several of the DNA trigger points in the classical labyrinth relate directly to people in your life and your relationship with them, as illustrated in Figure 11. The first of the nine turning points is security. You get your primary security from your mother who gave birth to you. If you have issues of insecurity, it may be possible to trace these back to the initial feelings of contact, safety, and security that you received at and immediately after your birth. While walking the labyrinth if you find yourself stopping at this turn or experiencing some other sensation at this point, then you are being guided to look at your safety and security issues, especially those connected to your mother. It is not possible to physically go back to relive your childhood, so you must revisit these issues from where you are now. Whatever your mother did or did not do for you is in the past. Yet you may still be affected by the events of your early childhood. As an adult, you can redress these issues by finding the child within you and showering it with love. On an ongoing basis, you can continue to provide the nurturing for yourself that you need in your life.

While facilitating a labyrinth walk for a group, I noticed one of the ladies in the group was stopped at this point on the labyrinth. She stood there for about five minutes. I intended to talk with her about this afterwards but didn't get a chance. She was due to meet me a few days later, so I felt that I could check in with her then about what might have been happening on this "mother" point for her. She didn't show up for her appointment with me. I phoned her to see if she was okay, and she told me that her mother had just died unexpectedly the day before. She said that her mother had been on her mind since the labyrinth walk. She had contacted her mother and they had chatted about a few things that were important to them. It seems that the labyrinth was once again working in unexpected ways to bring about a healing for the person walking it.

Giving and Receiving from Others in the Labyrinth

Your awareness of yourself in relation to others is represented by the second trigger point, territory. Wherever you are in a relationship, be it at home, work, or socially, you are interacting with people. You may notice that you are attracted to some people more than others. Certain people can trigger emotions in you that you find challenging. You are connected energetically to the people in your life, as if an invisible cord is joining you both together. Some of these energetic ties may be life en-hancing, while others may be depleting your energy. If you have ever felt drained after being in someone's company, they may be unconsciously, or consciously, tapping into your energy. Similarly, if you feel energized in another's company you may be receiving some of the higher energy vibration that they are willingly sharing.

Awareness is the key to learning from the people in your life and the emotions that you experience from their presence. It is the key that unlocks the door of understanding and progression. As soon as you become aware of an issue, behaviour, emotion, or person triggering these, you are then provided with a focus for your attention. When I recognize a certain behaviour, or reaction in myself, I begin to seek an understanding of this behaviour. I consider what is bringing up this response in me, what is taking me from my state of oneness with myself, and who am I allowing to shift me from my place of centredness.

One approach to considering your responses to the behaviour of others that is affecting you is to keep bringing it back to yourself. On the whole, other people do not do things to you, unless it involves physical or emotional violence. However, it can be easy to attribute your state of being and your state of mind to the actions of others. At times, the actions of others have such a significant effect on you that you can lose perspective on the situation and on the fact that you always have a choice as to how you behave, react, or respond in any given situation. Yet, despite the seemingly infuriating presence of some others in your life, without them the opportunity for growth would be absent and the rewards of self-advancement much less.

You may even agree with some souls before incarnating that they will play a certain role in their interactions with you that you find difficult. These can manifest in ways that are not always obvious to you, or in ways that trigger your seemingly negative aspects. It may be difficult to thank these people for bringing up these qualities in you. Yet, if you can see what is happening with others in your life, you are moving along your soul's journey: advancing beyond solely reacting—to observation and choosing a different response.

When walking the labyrinth if you feel that you want to stop at this turning point, or that there is a shift in energy around this point, this is indicating to you that you need to consider your relationship with others. Issues around boundaries with others often arise at this point on the labyrinth. During one of my labyrinth evening walks, one of the participants asked me about this point on the labyrinth and what might have caused her to stop there for several minutes. I explained that this was about her relationship with others, and particularly about establishing personal boundaries. I went on to ask her if there was someone in her life who was drawing energetically on her and if she needed to be firm about her boundaries at this time. She replied that she was currently going through a difficult divorce, and that it all made perfect sense now.

Consider where others are too demanding of your time and energy, or where you feel someone is imposing too much on you. Areas where others are trying to overly influence you can also occur at this point. In these scenarios, the labyrinth is a window of insight into your relationship with others. If you are unclear as to how to address issues that are coming up for you, entering the labyrinth with a view to gaining insights into your best approach to them is a good place to start.

The Social Labyrinth

Socialising is a necessary part of human existence. It is necessary for the continuation of the species, and it is also necessary for the majority of people to fulfil their souls' purpose. It is the fourth of the nine turning points in the classical labyrinth, and the last DNA trigger of your physical development.

You will find that as you change, the people that you wish to spend time with also change. Some of your old friends and acquaintances can fade out of your life, and new people come in. You gravitate toward people who are on your wavelength. As you progress on your life's journey you will most likely find that you are becoming involved in new groups of people.

You also begin to see and feel how different groups of people impact you. Some groups of people seem to have a negative effect on you, and you feel tired and out of sorts after being in their company. The way they talk and the way they behave is no longer in alignment with who you are. As you become more aware and sensitive, you will also become more discerning about who you spend your time with, consciously choosing groups of people that you find enlivening and who share your views and outlook.

It is also at this stage in your spiritual journey that you start becoming more aware of your soul group. Soul groups are made up of souls that you have spent many lifetimes with, and with whom you have grown and developed. You have met and travelled together with these souls in previous lifetimes and are once again connecting with them. There is an affinity with these people that goes beyond what can be easily explained. You feel a comfortableness with these people. There is a knowing in your heart that you have met before, and you can see this soul connection deep within these people's eyes.

The labyrinth can show you that you need to look at the people you are currently spending time with. If you feel a different sensation at the social trigger point on the labyrinth, or find yourself wanting to pause or stop there, consider who you are associating with and if it is in alignment with your soul's purpose.

The labyrinth is a magnet that attracts you to like-minded people. It draws in people who are on their own journey of self-development. When you are walking the labyrinth with others, everyone else is on the same path, although you are all at different places. This sharing of a common path is part of the realization of how you are interconnected to others in a variety of ways. When exploring your interconnectedness with others through the labyrinth, and while remembering that the labyrinth walk is ultimately about you, you see your relationships with others as emanating from you. Yet, there is a greater aspect to your labyrinth walk of self-discovery. Whatever you heal in yourself, you heal in others; and whatever you unite in yourself, you unite in others.

EXERCISE: WALK WITH OTHERS

This exercise is about walking the labyrinth with others. Walking with others can be quite a different experience compared to walking on your own. When on your own, you can get lost in your own world; you do not have to think about anyone else because you have the labyrinth to yourself. When walking with others, regardless of how deep you enter your own being, you are aware on some level of the others walking their path with you and of you walking your path with them. Conducting a labyrinth walk with an eye towards examining your relationships is a powerful and informative way to explore those relationships and enhance your own self-knowledge.

Walking the labyrinth with an awareness of your relationships with others helps you to apply the teachings that you are learning to the people in your life. Being aware of everything that everyone else does on the labyrinth, and more particularly with your response to it, can bring insights and clarity to relationships with significant others in your life. Everything that happens on this labyrinth walk is related to something in your life. For example, if you find that someone on the labyrinth is walking very slowly in front of you causing you to go slower than you would like, then consider who in your life may be blocking your path or preventing you doing your own thing. Or, if you sense someone walking very close behind you and feel the need to go a little quicker than you would like, then consider if someone in your life is pressuring you to make decisions or do something quicker than you want to. You will also need to pass people during your walk, as some of the other people on the labyrinth will be going in as you are coming out. Most labyrinth paths are not wide enough to allow two people to pass each other side by side, so you may have to choose if you wish to step off the path momentarily to allow them to pass. Remember, everything on this walk is about you and identifying how you are behaving in relation to others.

This exercise may take a little longer to organize than some of the other exercises. It becomes more powerful the more people you include with whom you consider you have a soul connection. While you can walk seeking insights into just one relationship, it is not uncommon for a different relationship to come to the fore when walking with representatives of significant others.

Firstly, identify each of the relationships in your life (past and present) that you consider are, or have been, significant for you. More specifically, note those with whom you feel some healing would be helpful. Write down the names of each of these people on a list. You will be choosing to explore one or more of these relationships as you travel through the labyrinth. For your first walk, it is best to choose just one relationship. For subsequent walks, you may wish to include all family or group members in the walk. You will also have to decide in what order you and the others on the walk enter the labyrinth. Once on the labyrinth each person walks at their own pace.

There are a number of ways to undertake this exercise.

The first way is to gather together as many of the actual people in your life with whom you have significant relationships as you can: parents, spouse, children, brothers, sisters, grandparents, friends, community members, others.

The second option, where you are unable or not ready to bring such people together, is to ask close friends to represent the people with whom you have significant relationships. These surrogates do not need to know who they are representing, although they can if you wish.

If you cannot bring together enough people, then gather together as many as you can, and write the names of others with whom you have a significant relationship down on pieces of paper. If you can write down the name or names of those who bring up strong emotions when you think of them, and carry it with you into the labyrinth, the walk can be quite powerful and healing.

If you do not have a labyrinth to walk, this exercise can also be done using a finger labyrinth, where you write down all the names of family, friends, and people with whom you have, or had, relationships.

This walk is solely about you, so while your walking companions may get great benefit and insights from this, it is not possible to facilitate such a walk for everyone while also focusing on your own walk. If you bring someone along to facilitate the group so that you can focus on your own walk, this person's primary focus is on you and not on the other walkers. You can set aside some time afterwards for feedback with the other participants, if that is desirable.

If you are working with just a list of relationships, take a little time to consider each of the relationships on your list. Write a few short notes on what you have received from each of these relationships, and what, if anything, you have given to each of them. It is helpful if you can identify what you consider to be the benefits, and the downsides in these relationships. When you have finished making your list, go and walk the labyrinth with an openness to receive any further insights into the relationships listed.

Walk the labyrinth in an attitude of exploration, awareness and openness. Allow any thoughts, ideas, insights, and emotions to flow without any judgement. Do not dismiss anything that comes to you. Feel free to stop at any stage if you feel you need to before moving on.

At the centre, take time to acknowledge the relationships that you had, and still have. These people are in your life for a reason. Acknowledging this helps to recognize the significance of the relationships.

The walk out represents returning to your everyday world with new insights into the relationships in your life. Walk with an understanding that this is what is happening, even if at this stage, there does not appear to be any insights. Things are changing, even if they are not obvious at this stage. When finished the walk, take time for reflection.

Reflection

The reflection after this exercise is important. People and their actions can bring up strong emotions and reactions. Emotions are your teachers, and in considering the emotions that arise, and what prompted them, you can reflect on what it is that you are carrying with you that gives rise to your responses. Write down everything that comes into your head. Do not discriminate when writing. The practice of writing everything down helps you release items on a deep, nonjudgemental level. Keep writing until you have nothing more to write.

10

Your Guides on the Labyrinth

Stop and look at the good things that have happened in your life, the kind and generous people who have helped you, the birds you heard singing in the trees, the sound of the ocean, the friends who were there for you, and those times when the right thing just seemed to happen. These things did not happen by chance. You are being watched over by your guides and angels. You are being prompted to see your way through what might appear impassable. You are being watched over particularly at the hardest times. You cannot be alone, for you are connected to everything, and this connection extends beyond the seen and heard to being in union with all life.

Your Guides Are with You

If you are drawn to the labyrinth and are reading this book, then there is a strong possibility that you have been prompted to do so by your guide. When you decided to come to earth, you went over every detail beforehand with your guide. You may have chosen learnings that seem insurmountable when faced here on earth, yet you would not have chosen them if you knew that you couldn't get through them and learn from them. And it is at the most difficult times that you can forget that you are being prompted and guided on an energetic and spiritual level. So pause now for a moment. Allow your thoughts to recede, and listen with all your senses. Feel the air moving around you; hear the voice that does not speak; tune in to knowledge that comes from a place beyond you. You are not alone. The spirit world is supporting you.

You may be fortunate enough to have already connected with your guide. Even if you have never consciously connected with your guide, you may still know that you are being watched over without being able to prove it. If you are in tune with your intuition, and find synchronicities happening to you that you cannot always explain, you are following the guidance that you are receiving. You may first become aware of this when you notice yourself choosing one thing over another just because it feels right, or having to go someplace even though it may not always make sense. I remember following an urge in 2004 to go to a health food store and restaurant in Cork. I had been there only a few days before and had stocked up on everything I needed, so I couldn't fully understand my "need" to go back there. I decided to drive by and said to myself that if I got a parking space nearby that I would go in. There was a parking space right outside the door! I went in and walked all around the shop and didn't find anything that I needed.

I moved along to the restaurant entrance where there were many notices and information leaflets about all kinds of activities, mainly of a mind, body, and spirit nature. In one of the information racks someone had left some magazines with reviews of mind/body/spirit books. I flicked through one of these and read the start of the editorial that spoke about powerful cosmic energies that were coming through in mid to late 2003 that would have significant life-changing events for many people. That was around the time that I divorced, so I was intrigued by what I was reading. Not having much time, I picked up the three or four other similar review magazines that were left there and brought them home with me to read later.

As I was going through the magazines at home, I noticed a person's name and address on the back of one of them. As I was looking to meet up with like-minded people who were interested in spiritual topics, I took a chance and wrote a letter to the person whose name was on the back of the magazine, Maureen. I received a phone call from her shortly afterwards saying that she had a meditation group at her house every Sunday evening and would I like to come along. I started going to the Sunday evening gatherings. A few months later, there was a dream workshop happening at this woman's house. It was at this dream workshop that I met Fionnuala! The woman who left the magazines in the shop was one of Fionnuala's best friends, and she didn't realise that her name and address was on the back of some of them.

You might call this following my destiny. You might say that this sequence of events was no more than a series of coincidences. Yet, I know that there was something more at work here than mere chance. I listened to the guidance that I was receiving, and I followed it, even when it didn't always make sense to me, or when I wasn't exactly sure what the outcome of my actions would be. In fact, it is often when I have no clue about where something is going that it leads me to the greatest revelations and meetings.

Your Guides and the Labyrinth

Guides love the labyrinth. In the labyrinth, your mind quietens and your awareness heightens. This is a perfect state for your guide to contact you and send you a message that you are more likely to receive. Messages from your guides can come to you in many forms. Mostly, they come as thoughts, ideas, or moments of apparent inspiration you know are significant. There are many accounts of guides helping people, and while some of them are clear, others are hidden in stories and myths that resonate with us on a deeper level that we later learn to understand. This is seen in the case of Ariadne in the story of Theseus and the Minotaur.

You have your very own Ariadne to help you through your labyrinth of life. Your guide is always watching over you and prompting you to make certain decisions and do certain things. These prompts are often in the form of something a little out of the ordinary, or something that causes you to stop, if only for a moment, and think.

The more significant of these signs will stop you in your tracks, although you may not fully understand at the time why this is happening. You know that there is something different or significant about this person, place, or situation. You know that you need to act, say, or do something, or else the moment might be missed, so you find the courage to make the move that is in your best interest.

Angels are also there to help you. Angels are beings in the spirit world who have not lived on the earth plane, while your guides have. Also, with your angels you need to ask for assistance, whereas your guides can provide assistance without you asking. You can ask your angels for help with the smallest things and with things that seem insurmountable. Asking in belief, with no thoughts on how the best outcome will unfold, allows your angels to bring about resolution to many difficult situations.

Inner Guidance

Your primary source of guidance comes from within yourself, from your own spirit. The labyrinth is a symbol of your journey to your own centre to find your true essence and to follow your own path. Ultimately what you think, feel, say, and do are the most powerful actions in dealing with your life's issues and bringing about a solution to them. The more you learn to follow your own guidance, the more you will advance on your life's journey.

Your journey of self-discovery involves stepping into your own masterhood. It first entails finding your power and accessing your inner wisdom. The more you develop and step into your power, the more you learn about yourself. You do this by starting with small steps. One step is to consider how you are feeling about any situation, and see if you can change it. Start with some everyday thing such as your feelings about the weather or something that you find you have a slightly negative thought about. See if you can change your thoughts on this issue. For example, I remember a wonderful quote from Billy Connolly, the Scottish comedian, about the weather in which he said, "There is no such thing as bad weather—just the wrong clothes." So see how you can change your thoughts, first on small everyday things, then on some of the deeper emotional issues that you are experiencing in your life.

Guides in Disguise

Guides are masters of disguise, so watch out for them and their messages in the most unexpected of ways and situations. I am an avid reader of books on spiritual and self-development topics. I have found over the years that whatever book I am reading at the time will have a significant message or messages for me. I often realise that I am reading about a situation similar to one I am currently experiencing, giving me a different perspective. What I am reading also could be about doing something new or something that I can do differently, such as a meditation technique or practice that is exactly what I need at that time. Other times I have read something new that sparks in me an epiphany of inspiration and insight.

These books have come to my attention in many different ways. Some are given to me as gifts, some are mentioned to me by people I meet, some I find on the internet, and some "call" me from the shelves of a bookshop. Each one is a guide! I began calling my favourite books "my book guides." I am grateful to the authors for what they have written, and value the authors of these books as messengers bringing me insights and advice at the time most needed.

I have lots of unfinished books. I read what I am drawn to, and if I am no longer drawn to a book that in the first instance attracted me, then I have gotten the messages that I need from that book. Sometimes, a more interesting book comes along and I start reading that. It is not unusual for me to have four or five books on the go at one time, switching back and forth between them depending on which one I am drawn to. It's great fun choosing and reading what I am guided to read at a particular time, and disregarding any thoughts that I must finish one book first before I start another one.

Books bring messages and guidance in other ways as well. I have often felt drawn to choose a certain book from the bookcase or a bookshop shelf knowing that it held a meaningful message for me. After taking out the exact book, I consciously ask for guidance as to where to open that book, and then intuitively open the book at the page that I am guided to. It is wonderfully fascinating to use books as guidance in this way.

Your guides also prompt other people to bring you messages. Your guide will often send you messages in your dreams as you sleep, because in this state you are most open to receiving the messages. Your guide will look for times when you are most receptive. Any time when you quieten your mind you are creating an opening for your guide to communicate with you. I find that in my morning meditation many new thoughts, ideas, and insights come to me. I wonder sometimes where these thoughts come from. On one level, I am connecting with the unified field of consciousness and tapping into an area on which I am ready to receive insights and guidance. On another level, I know that my guide is watching and waiting for the right time to get a message to me.

If someone is going to all that trouble for me, to help me on my path, to prompt me when needed, and to be watching over me all this time, then I want to get to know this personal guide even more. And I want to work with them more actively so that I receive all the guidance that I am being sent. Now it's time to move on to establishing a deeper communication with your main guide.

Exercise: Walking to Meet Your Guides

This exercise is about meeting your guide, or getting to know your guide better, and receiving a message from your guide. You will be walking the labyrinth with the intention of making a stronger connection with your guide. You will be asking your guide for his/her name. And you will be asking your guide for the most important message that they have for you.

Before you walk the labyrinth take a few minutes to relax your breathing. If possible, sit down for a few minutes and tune in to the walk that you are about to undertake. Write down the following three questions on a piece of paper. Are you my guide? What is your name? What message do you have for me?

You will be asking these questions during the labyrinth walk when you sense a presence or something slightly different. This difference may be in you, in the atmosphere, or in the energy around you and the labyrinth. This can be as subtle as a slight change in temperature, a slight resistance to moving along in the labyrinth, or even some apparent external distraction that catches your attention.

As you are about to enter the labyrinth, ask your guide to be with you and to give you a strong signal of their presence. As you walk, notice when you sense a shift in the energy. Pause, and ask the first question, stating that you want to hear from your guide only. Ask it three times, and each time allow time for an answer. If you receive a positive answer to your first question, then proceed to the second question. Again, ask three times, each time allowing time for an answer. Even if the first answer is fruitful, always ask the question three times. Asking a question three times is a good deterrent against receiving a false message, or of receiving a message from someone other than your guide. Ask the third question and allow time for an answer. If nothing comes immediately, ask again up to three times.

You may not receive any answers the first time that you pause or stop. Indeed, you may find that you pause or stop several times before you sense that your guide is with you. It is important to stay in an open state of mind and not get distracted if you do not sense anything on the first few occasions. The more alert and aware that you are, the more likely you are to recognize the guidance that you are being given.

Much of the guidance that you receive is through the thoughts or ideas that come to you. As your guide communicates with you mostly telepathically, you will mainly receive their guidance in a thought form. Pay attention to the thoughts that come to you. You may also receive guidance in the form of voices, visions, or feelings.

Continue your walk to the centre of the labyrinth, pausing at the centre, then making your way back out along the path of the labyrinth. If you feel that you did not pick up or receive anything, that is okay. Your guides are always with you, and are delighted with your efforts to communicate with them. Trust this connection between you and your guide and try again when you feel ready. At the end of the walk, thank your guide.

Reflection

Regardless of whether you received something or not, take time after your walk to sit still for at least five minutes. Take out your pen and paper and start writing. Write whatever comes into your head. Do not rationalize what you are writing. Write without thinking, and write down everything that comes to you. Do not read back what you are writing. You will have plenty of time for that afterwards. You may find as you are writing that you have a pause in your writing for a few moments. Allow those moments of quietness to be, and resume writing when another thought comes to you. Finish off by giving thanks for the writing that you have done and the labyrinth walk that you had the pleasure of undertaking. Later, when you have a quiet time, read back over what you have written noting anything significant or unusual. You may be surprised to see that after your labyrinth walk some guidance has come through in your writing.

Melchizedek's Labyrinth

The first labyrinth that I remember seeing in this lifetime was called Melchizedek's labyrinth. This was a seven-circuit classical labyrinth depicted on one of Angela McGerr's Angel Cards. Melchizedek is the ruler of Sacred Seven.

Angela McGerr, in her *Angel Almanac*, believes that the Holy Grail is "the chalice of the heart, as held by Melchizedek, and containing a special key." The key, according to McGerr, is the centre of Melchizedek's seven-circuit labyrinth. This is where we can "find and open our higher heart, our spiritual Divine Self." She goes on to say that "when we open the flower that is within the higher heart we can return to Oneness with all" (McGerr 2008).

The name "Melchizedek" has always held a fascination for me. I remember as a child going to Catholic mass and waiting to hear the name "Melchizedek" being mentioned. It was the highlight of the mass for me. There was something about the name that had an effect on me, resonated on a deep level, even though at the time I didn't know or understand anything about the person or energy of Melchizedek.

Figure 12: Melchizedek labyrinth healing symbol

Melchizedek

It is central to this part of your labyrinth journey to have some knowledge about Melchizedek, as it helps to understand the transformative energies that you access through Melchizedek's labyrinth. When you integrate your knowledge of Melchizedek and your experience of the labyrinth you create a fusion of mind and heart that raises you to a higher level of awareness and understanding.

We first hear of Melchizedek in the Old Testament, where he is mentioned a few times—Genesis 14 and Psalm 110—and in the New Testament in Hebrews. The name Melchizedek comes from the words melek (meaning king) and tsedek (meaning righteousness), coming together to mean king of righteousness. Melchizedek foreshadowed the ministry of Jesus Christ as both a priest and king. Jesus was a priest of God in the "order of Melchizedek" (Psalm 110:4; Hebrews 5:6,10; 6:20; 7:11,17). The word "order" refers to the manner in which he received his priesthood. In Hebrews, Melchizedek is described as "without father, without mother, without descent, having neither beginning of days, nor end of life; but made like unto the Son of God; abideth a priest continually" (Hebrews 7:3). This means that he received his priestly status directly from God. At the time of Jesus, all priests in Israel belonged to the house of Levi and were known as Levites. As Jesus was from the tribe of Judah, he is said to have also received his priestly status from God and not from human descent.

In esoteric circles, the king aspect of a person is often taken to mean their masculine qualities, while the priestly qualities are their feminine aspect. Therefore, someone who is a king and a priest, or a queen and a priestess, is considered as having their masculine and feminine sides in balance and is considered complete. It can also be interpreted to mean that as a king he had dominion over the physical realm, and as priest he had dominion over the spiritual realm. When the Melchizedek energy and the labyrinth are combined they create an immensely powerful tool for integrating your masculine and feminine as well as your physical and spiritual aspects.

We also read in the book of Genesis that "Melchizedek king of Salem brought forth bread and wine; and he was the priest of the highest God. And he blessed him, and said, Blessed be Abram of the most high God, possessor of heaven and earth: And blessed be the most high God, which hath delivered thine enemies into thy land. And he gave him tithes of all" (Genesis 14:18–20). This bringing forth of bread and wine is a forerunner to the actions of Jesus at the last supper. The act of eating bread and drinking wine in a ceremonially manner was introduced by Melchizedek after Abraham returned from battle. In ancient times victors in war might actually drink the blood of their vanquished and eat their flesh. Melchizedek made this a symbolic act and, in doing so, raised the consciousness of humanity to a higher level, in which they no longer ate the flesh of other humans. Jesus took this a stage further when at the last supper, he symbolically offered himself, in anticipation of the crucifixion, as the salvation for mankind. Man no longer needed to conquer others, or to conquer himself, as Jesus was showing the way and sharing his experience. "Do this in remembrance of me" was an invitation to all of humanity to rise above the physical body and to live consciously as soul and spirit.

When Melchizedek received tithes from Abraham it was also symbolic of the lower nature aspects being drawn up into the higher, and entering a new phase of development. Melach says that Melchizedek is a frequency that we need to "tune in to" if we are to experience the "high" frequency only accessible to those willing to jettison their weighty, illusory baggage.

If you feel an attraction or resonance with the name Melchizedek, you are being drawn to the achievement of what Frater Melach calls "the fully self-realised individual" in you. In his essay on Melchizedek, Frater Melach writes, "Interpreted microcosmically, Melchizedek is the fully awakened nature of man from which the 'gifts' of regenerative power (bread), realised oneness, wisdom and spiritual intuitiveness (wine), insight (blessing) and spirit-like ministration born of compassion for all sentient beings (tithes), flow or 'descend' into the purified mind and body of advanced man. Together these symbolise both the new powers welling up within the inner self from the essence (Melchizedek) and the fruits of initiation" (Melach, n.d.).

In Melchizedek's labyrinth, when you walk the three outer circuits you are moving through the physical body's energy centres, grounding yourself, and letting go of baggage and anything that is no longer in alignment with who you now are. You are preparing yourself, just as in the path of alchemy when you worked on spiritualizing the body for the descent of the Spirit. The Melchizedek labyrinth is both a representation of this progress of your soul becoming united with Spirit and a tool for achieving it. There is a passage in the Nag Hammadi gospels that recognized Melchizedek as a great teacher: "All the tribes of the earth will learn truth from you, Melchizedek, Great High Priest, teacher of Abraham, the prophet, about his promise for a perfect, fulfilled life" (Jacobs

2005). Melchizedek as the Hierophant is the great teacher, and one of his ways of teaching is through Melchizedek's labyrinth.

Melchizedek's labyrinth is offering you an opportunity to access greater and higher states of consciousness. Those who have achieved these higher states of consciousness are identified by their great inner light that shines from them. In the *Pistis Sophia*, an ancient Gnostic text discovered in 1773 and believed to have been written in the third and fourth centuries CE, Melchizedek is referred to by different titles, including "The Receiver of the Light," "The Great Receiver of the Light," and "The Light Purifier." In *Pistis Sophia*, Book 4, Melchizedek plays a key role in the purification of souls for entry into the "Treasury of Light," by transporting them from the domain of the Archons, or earthly rulers, into the heavenly kingdom. The more you work with Melchizedek's labyrinth, the clearer and more purified you become, and the brighter you shine.

Melchizedek's labyrinth is also a vessel for accessing Christ consciousness, the state of being in which you are in perfect alignment with all of existence. Glenn Sanderfur in his book *Edgar Cayce's Past Lives of Jesus* writes that, according to Cayce, the Master soul, or the Christ soul incarnated as Melchizedek "to teach and lead " (Sanderfur 1988). When working with the Melchizedek energy and labyrinth you awaken the transformative power of the Christ consciousness within you and begin to act in accordance with higher principles living more in awareness of your soul's purpose.

There is a beautiful carved statue of Melchizedek on the north porch of Chartres Cathedral. This doorway is known as the Porch of the Initiates, and contains many secret teachings. Alongside Melchizedek is Abraham with Isaac, then Moses, Samuel, and David. Melchizedek is shown holding a chalice, in which most observers say is bread, as the ceremony of bread and wine was first performed in the Bible by Melchizedek. The contents of the cup that Melchizedek is holding can be interpreted in another way. Rather than bread, it can be seen as a stone: the stone of consciousness, or the philosopher's stone of the alchemists. So, Melchizedek is portrayed holding in his left hand the holy grail (the chalice) within which is contained the consciousness of humanity (the stone). This cup is also symbolic of filling one's physical and energy bodies with the light of expanded consciousness. The censer held in his right hand is a symbol of the heart, with the incense smoke representing the true essence rising to heaven.

Another association between Melchizedek, the cup, and the labyrinth is found in Drunvalo Melchizedek's book *The Ancient Secret of the Flower of Life*. In it he mentions that Richard Feather Anderson associated the seven circuits of the classical labyrinth with the seven chakras, numbering the outermost circuit number one, the next outermost number two, all the way in to circuit number seven by the centre, depicted in Figure 13. In walking the labyrinth, the walker passes through these circuits in the following numerical order: 3-2-1-4-7-6-5. When these numbered circuits are indicated by short lines equal to the circuit number, and the circuits are placed one on top of the other, an image of a cup or chalice emerges (Figure 14) (Melchizedek 1999).

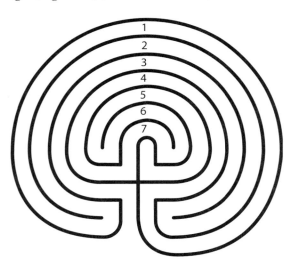

Figure 13: The chakras in Melchizedek's labyrinths

This cup is a representation of how the labyrinth aligns your energy centres to create an energetic cup of light that you become when you walk the labyrinth. When you move through the labyrinth, you connect yourself to both earth and heaven and become filled with divine light. You are the Holy Grail: the cup-shaped container within which is held the light of all knowing, all loving, and all presence. This is enlightenment, and one of the main purposes of all of us in this lifetime is to become a vessel for the light, to hold the light, and to shine the light.

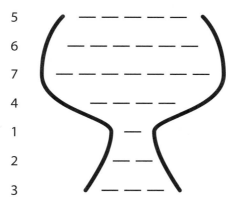

Figure 14: Melchizedek labyrinth chalice

Melchizedek Labyrinth Healing

Several years ago, I began doing a Melchizedek labyrinth meditation during my labyrinth workshops and evenings. The result of these meditations on those present was to bring everyone in each group to a higher state of consciousness. Many times groups have entered a state of peace and oneness where no thought existed, and where there was only light and love. All of us present wanted to stay in this state for as long as possible. In this state there was never a desire for anyone to speak. The energy was so high and so beautiful that nothing else was needed, and the feeling and understanding of our interconnectedness was palpable.

I began to experience the Melchizedek energy growing stronger, particularly during my morning meditations. I received insights into a form of healing based on the Melchizedek labyrinth. This healing modality, which I call "Melchizedek Labyrinth Healing," first rebalances the energy centres and energy bodies of the recipient. It is then followed by the accumulation and directing of the Melchizedek energy into the recipients' physical, etheric, emotional, mental, and spiritual bodies in this specific order. The combined effect is to ground you, and then raise the vibration of your energy bodies to assist in any healing required and in your soul's journey.

The Melchizedek Labyrinth Healing rebalances your seven major chakras as well as your seven major energy bodies: etheric, emotional, mental, causal, astral, soul, and spiritual. The rebalancing of your chakras and energy fields occurs as you move through the Melchizedek finger labyrinth, pausing when so instructed so that the rebalancing can take place. I use a divining rod to indicate where and when you need to pause as you move your finger through the finger labyrinth. I tune in to these pauses to indicate to you where the rebalancing is taking place and to give you insights into what aspects of your life and energy field are being rebalanced. These rebalancing stops can take seconds or minutes depending on what is required at the time.

During the sessions when I instruct the person to stop moving their finger on the finger labyrinth, some find that their finger is almost stuck to the labyrinth and they cannot move it. I have asked some people to try move their finger and they can't. They usually have a deep knowing themselves that they are not meant to move their finger until further rebalancing and healing has taken place. The healing energy of the labyrinth is working in an obvious way rebalancing the persons energy related to that particular point on the labyrinth. Some participants also say that they can feel their finger tingling or a pulsing sensation in their finger. Others can sometimes feel different sensations in their bodies around a particular chakra area directly related to the circuit of the labyrinth that they are on.

For the second part of the healing therapy, you lie on a therapy bed face up, while I accumulate and direct the Melchizedek healing energy into your chakras and energy fields. The healing is mainly hands-off, although I will sometimes gently place my hands on your solar plexus and on your feet during the treatment. Where required, the Melchizedek energy clears any blocks to the flow of the energy. The treatment also includes connecting you with your cosmic power source, and finishes with energetically placing the Melchizedek stone of consciousness in your energy field to provide you with a greater understanding of your life's purpose.

It is one thing to read about the Melchizedek energy; it is another thing to experience it. The following exercise is designed to bring you into contact with this high vibrational energy and help you advance on your soul's journey.

EXERCISE: MELCHIZEDEK LABYRINTH MEDITATION

This exercise is a meditation in which you move virtually through your chakras in the order in which you pass through the circuits of the seven-circuit classical labyrinth. In this meditation, you will focus on your chakras one at a time, seeing each one filled with a particular coloured light and with a brilliant white light at the centre. The order in which you move through your chakras is the order you pass through the labyrinth's circuits: 3-2-1-4-7-6-5.

Before you begin the meditation, read these instructions from start to finish. It will help to memorize this order before you begin, as opening your eyes to read instructions during the meditation can be distracting. You could also record the instructions for the meditation by reading them out loud, and then listen back to them as a guided meditation. If doing this, be sure to read slowly and consciously, and allow times of silence for when you wish to be in silence in your meditation. Also, if recording this meditation for later use, be sure to include this statement: "You should not listen to this meditation while driving." Please note that this exercise is copyrighted, so the recording that you make is for your personal use only.

To begin, find a comfortable position, preferably sitting upright in a chair with your two feet flat on the floor, or sitting on the floor with your spine in an upright position. Close your eyes. Take three deep breaths and exhale strongly to relieve your body of any stresses and tightness.

Bring your attention to your chakras in the following order, associating the chakras with their colours and qualities. Spend as long as you like in each chakra, but spend at least two minutes focusing on each.

Third chakra, located in your solar plexus area. This chakra is the colour yellow. See a ball of bright yellow light in the centre of your body in the area of your solar plexus. See a spark of brilliant white light at the centre of this ball of yellow light. See this white light expand. This chakra is associated with your power and your will. You are a powerful person with the will to manifest whatever you focus on. Now move your attention down to your second chakra.

Second chakra, located in your lower abdomen area. See a ball of bright orange light in the centre of your body in the area of your lower abdomen. See a spark of brilliant white light at the centre of this ball of orange light. See this white light expand. This chakra is associated with your creativity, your sexuality, and your emotions. You are a creative person; draw on your creativity to create whatever you want in your life. You are also a sexual person; be open and aware of your sexuality while honouring yourself and others. Your emotions are your teachers. Work with them, and learn from them. Now, move your attention down to your first chakra.

First chakra, located at the base of your spine, at the perineum. See a ball of bright red light at the base of your spine. See a spark of brilliant white light at the centre of this ball of red light. See this white light expand. The energy from this chakra spirals downwards into the earth. This chakra is also called your base chakra, or root chakra. It is your connection to the earth. It is associated with safety, security, and your right

to be here on earth. You have a right to be here. You came to earth to fulfil your purpose, and you must connect yourself solidly to the earth to
do this. Feel yourself connected to the earth through your base chakra.
See a root coming from the base of your spine and penetrating deep
into the earth until it anchors into the crystal centre of the earth. You
are fixed to the earth through this root. See similar roots coming from
the soles of your feet and anchoring your feet all the way to the centre
of the earth. You are now fixed solidly to the earth. You have brought
your energy from your solar plexus down through your second chakra
through your root chakra and have anchored yourself into the earth.
You have created a base with the lower part of your body that anchors
and fixes you to the earth. You are solid and immovable: nothing can
unsettle you.

With this feeling of being solidly anchored into the earth, bring your
focus to your fourth chakra, the area at the centre of your chest: your
heart chakra. See a ball of bright green light in the centre of your chest.
See a spark of brilliant white light at the centre of this ball of green light.
See this white light expand. This chakra is associated with love: human
love and divine love. Love is about giving and receiving. Feel the love
in your heart for the earth beneath your feet, and feel the love in your
heart for all that is beyond the earth. Allow your heart to expand with
love for everything around you, and allow yourself to receive love from
everyone who is sending it to you. Feel the love flowing from you and
to you. Find what it is that fills your heart with love, what makes your
heart sing. If you haven't yet found it, then keep looking for it, and treat
everything you do and see on your search as if it will bring ultimate joy
to you. Now bring your attention to the top of your head, to your crown
chakra.

Seventh chakra, located in the fontanel the top of your head. This
chakra is the colour purple. See a ball of bright purple light in the centre
of the top of your head. See a spark of brilliant white light at the centre of this ball of purple light. See this white light expand. This chakra

is your connection to all that is beyond the earth: the cosmos, divine energy. Allow yourself to feel this connection. See a stream of brilliant bright white light flowing into the top of your head, slowly filling the top of your head with light. Slowly bring your attention down to the centre of your head directly behind the middle of your forehead.

Sixth chakra, located in the centre of your head behind the centre of your forehead. This is your brow chakra, sometimes called the "third eye." See a ball of bright indigo light, a deep rich blue colour, in the centre of your head. See a spark of brilliant white light at the centre of this ball of indigo light. See this white light expand. This chakra is associated with your intuition. You are an intuitive person. You know when things feel right for you, and when you need to do something for yourself. Develop this intuition, and learn to trust your intuition. See the brilliant white light flowing in the top of your head, slowly moving down into the centre of your head. This light is now filling your whole head, and the flow of light in the top of your head is swelling into a torrent. It is like a waterfall of light flowing into you. There is so much light in your head that it starts to spread down your neck.

Fifth chakra, located in the throat. See a ball of bright blue light in the centre of your throat, with a spark of brilliant white light at the centre. See this white light expand. This chakra is associated with communication and, in particular, with your speech. It is through this chakra that you speak your truth, so speak your truth with love, honesty, openness, respect, and dignity for others. This is not about saying what you think others need to hear, this is about saying what you have to say because it is right for you to say it at this time. See the brilliant white light flow down into your throat area filling your whole neck and throat with white light.

You have now created a cup of yourself, with the base of your three lower chakras anchoring you firmly to the earth, a bowl created with your three upper chakras, and your heart in the middle. This cup is filled with brilliant white light. As the light flows into you from above, it fills the cup of your head and upper body and overflows so that it moves down to reach your heart. See the light fill your heart. Your heart is the bridge between heaven and earth. You are now also connected to and aware of your divine heart. It is the centre of love, the love that unites heaven and earth in us. Feel the love in your heart, and as the light flows into you from above, and touches your heart, allow the love and light out from your heart.

Send the light and love out in all directions. If you are with others, let the light touch the person nearest you. Feel the love in your heart for the person nearest to you. Now feel the light coming from your heart touch the space around you, the four walls of the room. As the light flows powerfully into you, the light now also flows powerfully out from you. See the light flowing out beyond the building or space where you are. See it spreading over the whole community where you are. Allow the light to continuously flow into you and out through your heart so that it spreads over the whole region and over the whole country.

See the light moving beyond the borders of your country, so that it spreads across the continent and the seas, moving in all directions, so that now the whole world is encircled in light that you are sending out from your heart, the light that is flowing into you. See the world like a small globe in front of you encircled in light flowing from your heart. And, as the light is still pouring into you, it flows out from you beyond the earth out into space. See it flowing out into our solar system, past the moon and the planets, so that it encompasses the sun. See the light moving further out into the galaxy, so that all the stars and constellations are bathed in brilliant white light flowing from your heart. And the light is still now flowing into you and from you. The light from you is flowing out into the farthest reaches of space, into the cosmos.

You become aware of a presence that your light is going towards. It appears first as a dim light in the distance, and as your light expands, it becomes stronger and brighter. Your light is now moving towards a greater white light that is encompassing all of existence. As the light continues to flow from you it now merges with this all-encompassing brilliant white light. You experience a sensation of immense love and joy. The light flowing into you and from you is part of a continuous flow of light that has no beginning and no end. You are in the flow of infinite light and love. This love-light is flowing in a never-ending stream to you and from you, touching all of existence, and looping back on itself and yourself. Stay in this space of the flow of love and light for a few minutes. Allow the light to flow in a never-ending circuit of which you are the centre.

When you have realised that you are both the source and destination of this light, hold this thought and knowing. Then, while retaining the experience of being in this flow of love and light, in your own time slowly begin to bring your attention back from the extremities of space. Bring your attention back through the cosmos … back through the galaxies … back through the stars and constellations … back through the planets, past the moon, so that you can now see the earth bathed in this brilliant white light. Bring your attention back from around the earth, from over the continent, from over your country, from over your region and neighbourhood, so that you are now becoming aware of your presence in the space or room where you are. Feel your feet on the floor; feel yourself sitting on the seat; feel your body; wiggle your toes; flex your fingers; move your body slowly; stretch your arms, your legs, so that you are fully aware and present in your body. Stay in this state of awareness of your body while also remembering your experience.

Reflection

Spend some time in contemplation of the experience of this meditation. Do not rush into thinking or writing: allow yourself time to dwell in the Melchizedek healing energy.

When you are ready, come out of the silence and write about how the experience was for you. How easy was it for you to expand yourself? What thoughts, positive and negative, came to you during this meditation? Write down the most significant experience for you from this exercise.

12

The Labyrinth and Your Surroundings

When you walk the labyrinth with the intention of gaining insights, the combined energetic effects of the labyrinth can help you to access previously inaccessible information. The labyrinth not only has a rebalancing and healing effect on you, but on everything that it and its energy field come in contact with. The labyrinth has a positive impact on the land and area where it is placed. Labyrinths reduce the levels of distorted electromagnetic fields of the earth and appear to have unexplained effects on underground water close to them. The labyrinth can open positive doorways and portals to otherwise unseen and unknown realms and dimensions. An appreciation and understanding of these effects and benefits will enhance your experience of the labyrinth. They will also contribute to a greater awareness of your own energy being expanded and positively impacted by the labyrinth. In discovering more about the labyrinth, you find out more about yourself.

The Energy Field of the Labyrinth

The labyrinth has its own energy field. As soon as a labyrinth is created, this energy starts to flow. I recall marking out one of my triple spiral labyrinth designs in a garden in Dublin, where I was painting the lines

171

on the gravel undersurface so the bricklayer could lay the bricks along the lines. As soon as I sprayed the last line joining up the three spirals, I received a huge positive blast of energy that caused me to exclaim out loud, somewhat disconcerting the bricklayer working with me. It was a wonderful feeling to have my work acknowledged by Spirit in such a way. It was another signal for me that I was on the right path, and reaffirmed my knowing that there is a powerful energy working through the labyrinth.

This energy field varies from labyrinth to labyrinth and time to time. When a labyrinth is first made, the energy field may be quite small. It is influenced by many things, including the energy fields of the location where it is placed. The more a labyrinth is used, the more it becomes energized. Many times, I have found myself just sitting near a labyrinth enjoying the peace that is present near the labyrinth. Next time you see a labyrinth, check to see how you feel when you are near the labyrinth.

There are a number of other considerations as to what causes the labyrinth to have an energy field. Classical labyrinths and medieval labyrinths are almost always based on sacred geometry—divine proportions built into the symbol. Labyrinths built to divine proportions also carry the frequencies of nature and its creator. These labyrinths are designed to bring harmony and balance to the person interacting with them. In moving through such labyrinths, whether one is aware of their divine proportions or not, the walker can more easily reach a state of connectedness with their own divine nature. In so doing, the walker can experience a sense of love, peace, balance, and other wonderful qualities.

Every labyrinth made also carries the energetic imprint of all other similar labyrinths constructed. This is an element of the consciousness field of the labyrinth where the simple act of creating the symbol connects it with its related labyrinths and energizes it.

The Labyrinth Effect on the Earth

Labyrinths positively affect the energy field of the area in which they are located or placed. Labyrinths have a neutralizing effect on negative earth energies and geopathic stress. Geopathic stress is the harmful energy that emanates from the earth where the natural energy of the earth is disturbed by weak electromagnetic fields created by some underground streams, sewers, fault lines, tunnels, caves, and mineral formations. Living in a house with high levels of geopathic stress, or spending long times in such areas, can have ill effects on the health and well-being of the people living there.

When I was training as a space clearing practitioner, the class was doing a divining exercise to measure the levels of geopathic stress in a given area. We did this by checking the level of geopathic stress on a scale of one to ten, with ten being the highest. In the particular area where we were checking, most people got a measurement of seven or eight. (Note: it is not unusual for different diviners to get slightly different measures; what is important is the before and after comparison measurements from the same diviner.) After we had all checked the levels in this area, I then spread out my labyrinth on the area, which took about two minutes. We all then took our measurement of geopathic stress again. This time, most diviners recorded a measurement of two or three out of ten.

The trainer on that course told us that one time when she went to do a space clearing for a client, she had difficulty getting a reading for the level of geopathic stress on the property. She was standing outside the front of the house and was getting a zero level for geopathic stress. She checked several times and each time the result was that there was no geopathic stress. This is most unusual, and she thought that she may have unintentionally been influencing the results. She was considering leaving and coming back another day to see if she might get a different reading. Before leaving she decided to have a look around the property and walked into the back garden. In the middle of the back garden there was a large labyrinth. She smiled at the further evidence she had received of the positive effect of the labyrinth in eliminating geopathic stress and healing the land.

The labyrinth had an instantaneous effect dramatically reducing geopathic stress levels in the land. The healing qualities of the labyrinth have a positive effect of neutralizing harmful earth energies in an area, and healing the earth. If you think that your property and land needs an energetic lift, building a labyrinth is a great way of raising the energy of where you live.

The Labyrinth Effect on Water

Labyrinths have an ability to affect underground water. Sig Lonegren, geomancer and dowser, tells an interesting story of a modern Chartres labyrinth at Benton Castle in southern Wales. Within weeks of the labyrinth being constructed, it was noticed that a water dome was present underneath the centre of the labyrinth, where there had not been one before the construction (Lonegren, n.d.).

A water dome is a column of pure water that rises from the centre of the earth towards the surface. Often these water domes do not reach the surface, and are sometimes known as blind springs. They follow the path of least resistance as they rise through the earth's crust. It seems the labyrinth not only cleared the land energetically, but it also created a vortex with a magnetic effect a certain distance all around the labyrinth, drawing in the water to underneath the labyrinth. You can often experience some of these positive effects of feeling clearer and more centred when you are near the labyrinth, and especially when you walk the labyrinth. Perhaps the draw that some people feel towards the labyrinth can be partially explained by the high water content in our bodies being positively affected by interaction with the labyrinth!

The Labyrinth as a Portal

A portal is a gateway, or entrance, to another dimension. Portals can be one-way or two-way, allowing information and energy to pass through the portals in one or both directions. Portals can be positive or negative depending on what energies pass through them. The labyrinth acts as a positive portal, and by accessing and entering the portal, information previously unavailable can be accessed.

Walking the labyrinth, or tracing the labyrinth symbol with your finger, helps generate the labyrinth portal. Many people have had insights and revelations on the labyrinth that they have not had elsewhere. The activity of circling towards the centre creates an energy vortex that forms an opening into otherwise concealed information. The more a labyrinth is used, the more effective it becomes as a portal. The energetic force is usually most concentrated at the centre of the labyrinth. However, the node or centre of the cross in the classical labyrinth is sometimes more powerful. This is the spirit point in the classical labyrinth from which everything else emanates.

While I am not aware of anyone physically travelling through the labyrinth, I have experienced another dimension while on a labyrinth and at the centre of the labyrinth. My experience of a vivid past life experience while walking the labyrinth at Chartres when I was transported back almost eight hundred years can be attributed to it functioning as a portal. On one occasion when I was giving a labyrinth workshop, one of the participants came out of the labyrinth with tears running down her cheeks. I checked in with her to see what was happening for her. She said that they were tears of joy. As she walked the labyrinth, she said that she became enveloped in a brilliant white light. It was as if she was walking in the middle of immense love and light. When she reached the centre, it was as if there was no one else on the labyrinth but her. She felt that time was standing still and that she was at the centre of something so wonderful that words were not sufficient to describe it.

She wondered if she should ask a question, but she felt that she had no need for answers at that moment. She was experiencing a great depth of feeling and heightened awareness, and just wanted to stay in that beautiful space. Then she realised that this beauty was inside her and that it was always with her. So, she walked out of the labyrinth with tears of joy streaming down her face.

On another occasion when walking my back-garden labyrinth, I had an experience that I can only describe as interdimensional. I had walked into the labyrinth and was standing in the centre. After a few moments, I noticed a subtle movement of the energy field around me. Remaining as detached as possible, I observed the movement progress so that it felt like the ground underneath me was slowly moving downwards, then gently upwards. These waves of energy that gently raised and lowered me became more frequent. As I looked across the circuits of the labyrinth the whole labyrinth was moving in undulating ripples. I lost all awareness of my physical surroundings and experienced myself being held and floating in a sense of timelessness and spacelessness. It was as if I was being held on a giant wave of creation. I was aware of a sense of nothingness, and was also aware of everything. I was transported for those few moments into another dimension—through the portal of the labyrinth.

Exercise: How to Tune in to Your Surroundings through the Labyrinth

At this stage of exploring the labyrinth it is time to move on to increasing your awareness of what is happening around you. In this regard, it is helpful to see what aspects of the labyrinth's energy field you are aware of. This walk is about sensing what is happening outside of you. Through developing a heightened awareness of what is happening around you, you become more aware of what is happening within you. The more you discover about the world around you, the more you learn about yourself.

Your intention at the beginning of this walk is to seek awareness of any labyrinth effect that the labyrinth is having on the land where it is located. Your focus is not on you, but on the land around you.

This is slightly more difficult if using a finger labyrinth. However, it is not insurmountable. Use the finger labyrinth as a model for a larger labyrinth placed on the land, then proceed as if you were physically walking a labyrinth on the land while your finger moves around the labyrinth.

You will need to tune in to the land where you are. Bring your attention to the land where you are situated. How does it feel to you? What are you sensing about the land? When physically approaching the labyrinth, see if you can sense where you enter the energy field of the labyrinth. This can be quite close to the labyrinth, or it can be quite a distance away. It can often feel like a change in temperature, or the air feels a little heavier, or lighter. You are focusing on any subtle shifts in the atmosphere around the labyrinth. Every labyrinth is different, so you can try this exercise every time you encounter a new labyrinth. You can then compare your findings and begin to learn what places are more positive and beneficial for you to be in, even without a labyrinth.

Before you start your walk, stand for a few moments at the entrance to the labyrinth. Quieten yourself by taking several deep breaths. When you inhale, feel the air going deep into your lungs. When you are ready to breathe out, exhale with a deep sigh, letting go of all tension from your body. As you stand at the entrance to the labyrinth, feel your feet on the ground, and allow yourself to become aware of everything around you. Asking in your mind to be shown the labyrinth effect on the land will help in your sensing of the labyrinth effect.

Begin walking the labyrinth in a peak state of awareness. Your every attention is on detecting subtle shifts in the energy field. You may feel very little the first time you do this, so don't be disappointed if that is the case. You may also feel many different sensations. You may find that the air seems heavier in one place than another. You may feel colder, or warmer, in one part of the labyrinth. You may feel that you have to stop at a particular point, or walk slower in some parts, and even walk faster in others. Give yourself the freedom to stop where you feel a shift in the energy. Where does it appear easier to walk? Where does your labyrinth feel more sluggish? If you notice something as you are walking the labyrinth, it is okay to go back a few paces to re-experience what you just passed through. This is about you becoming more aware of what is happening around you.

It is not always possible to differentiate between what you are feeling from the labyrinth and what you are feeling within yourself. Walking the labyrinth is an integrative experience, and sometimes trying to separate yourself from your surroundings is not desirable and can even be counterproductive. If your walk becomes one of integrating what is within with what is without, then allow that to be also.

If distracting thoughts come into your mind, acknowledge them. Then allow them to pass on. I have often been distracted on the labyrinth, and have sometimes walked a labyrinth twice: the first time to quieten my mind, and the second time to get a better feeling of that particular labyrinth. If you still feel that you have too much going on at this time, then give yourself permission to come back at another time to do this exercise.

The second level in undertaking a walk such as this is to ask the spirit of the land to communicate with you and tell you what changes the labyrinth has brought to the land. Allow your mind to quieten and tune in to the spirit of the place. See if you can sense back to when there was no labyrinth on the land. What did the land feel like then? How does this differ to how the land feels now?

Reflection

Take a few minutes to write down what you sensed and felt during this walk. If this is your first time doing an exercise such as this, then it may be helpful to just write without thinking or trying to make sense of what you picked up. If you think that you felt nothing, then write down that you felt nothing. There is no right or wrong in this exercise. You can always do this again at a different time and see if you get any different results.

13

The Interconnectedness of All of Existence

You are related to and connected with much more than you might first realise. You have already seen and experienced how the labyrinth is a symbol of you and that it contains your different aspects and elements. The labyrinth also embodies much of the world around you. The cross in the seed pattern represents the four directions: north, east, south, and west. It also illustrates time in the placing of the solstices on the vertical axis and the equinoxes on the horizontal axis; the Celtic cross quarter days are found at the dots in the seed pattern. When combined with its associations with the four elements, your chakras, and the planets, the labyrinth is a multi-dimensional instrument that has a matrix of layers and levels for you to access and interact with. We will now move on to explore the labyrinth's appearance in crop circles, plans of cities, and epic tales that serve to further illustrate the connections between your outer and inner worlds; as without, so within.

Gaining a deep understanding of the labyrinth as a symbol of the interconnectedness of all of existence is a path through many stages from initial awakening to enlightenment. The stages of this journey are represented by the path through the circuits of the labyrinth as the initiate makes the journey to become a master. We are all masters; some of us just don't realise it yet! Part of stepping into your masterhood is recognising and acknowledging that you are part of the wisdom, part of the knowing of the interconnectedness of all of existence.

Through the labyrinth you can see how things are connected by numbers, by form, by vibration, and by similarities in spiritual paths. As your knowledge and awareness expands you begin to realise that there are more similarities than differences in the physical and energetic world around you. The labyrinth is a central part of the network of connections. It not only reflects and illustrates many of the associations and links that you have explored up to now, it also plays an active part in unifying the different aspects into a coherent whole. As Richard Feather Anderson says about the labyrinth: "All of the patterns and all of the processes of all of the forces, archetypes and symbols of our universe are packed into that thing" (Montana, n.d.).

Oneness with Your Environment

In walking the labyrinth you are connecting on many levels. On a basic level, your feet are connected to the earth. Your mind is connected to the thoughts that you are receiving. Your energy field is connected to the energy field of the labyrinth. As you progress through the labyrinth of your life's journey you develop a growing state of oneness with yourself, and your awareness of the world around you increases. Your understanding of your environment expands out to encompass a sense of caring for the places you work, rest, and play. You most likely begin to notice that you are altering your behaviour slightly so that you are more in communion with the earth. You become more conscious of littering, pollution, organic farming, and activities that honour or take from the earth.

You may also find your attitude and approach to the creatures on the earth is changing. There was a time when it didn't bother me if I accidentally or deliberately killed small creatures such as flies, wasps, and others. Now, I find myself stepping over crawling ants so as not to harm them. Sometimes, I go to great efforts to set free insects trapped inside the windows of my house. You too may find yourself moving into a space where you respect all forms of life and can no longer consciously harm the creatures of the earth. You are becoming at one with nature and your environment.

The world around you is also sending you messages that you begin to receive and understand. The behaviour of animals, the shapes created by the earth, and images that appear in plants and in the clouds take on new meaning. There is a wealth of information being presented to you if you are aware enough to recognize it. One mysterious method that the consciousness of the earth uses to communicate with humanity is through crop circles.

Crop Circles

There are as many explanations for crop circles as there are unanswered questions. The mystery surrounding crop circles, and the manner in which they appear in complex formations in a relatively short periods of time, lead many to consider that there is a super-intelligent nonhuman energy involved in their creation. The increasingly intricate and detailed patterns, that are sometimes identified as having multifaceted associations, link crop circles with many other geometric, cosmic, and spiritual phenomena.

Crop circles are found worldwide, although Wiltshire in England is recognized as the centre of crop circle activity. While undoubtedly some crop circles are man-made, there are others whose creation can be attributed to nonhuman forces. These are characterized by the stalks of the grain not being broken when they are flattened to form the pattern, and continuing to grow after being flattened. Also, the nodes of the stalks in "energetic" crop circles become enlarged.

Several labyrinthine patterns have appeared in crop circles. Intricate walkable paths such as the double spiral type designs found at Portsdown Hill, Hampshire, on June 10, 2004, and Windmill Hill on July 13, 2011, indicate that a crop circle of one of the ancient labyrinth types may emerge at some stage. The crop circle that appeared at Redlynch, Somerset, on June 22, 2015, is a circular labyrinth of Ottfrid design. At first it appears that it is a complete labyrinth, although on closer examination, the second circuit from the outside is not accessible. It is possible however to pass through the other six circuits on your way from the outside to the centre.

If you apply the seven-chakra association to this crop circle labyrinth, then the second chakra is blocked. This could be a message about the current state of humanity's creativity and sexuality. We, as a human race, need to be more creative in how we address some of the issues facing us and the earth. We need to unblock our creativity. It could also be an indication that the suppression of our sexuality is still happening, and we need to embrace fully all aspects of our humanity and spirituality.

One other crop circle with labyrinth connections worth examining is a crop circle that was formed near Lewisham Castle near Aldbourne, in Wiltshire, on August 6, 2004. This circle is sometimes referred to as a "squares" pattern, although Andy Thomas of *Swirled News* writes that Geoff Stray is "pretty sure that the Lewisham Castle formation is a rendition of the magic square of the moon" (Thomas 2004).

Magical squares consist of numbers arranged in a square where the lines of numbers all add up to the same total: up, down, and diagonally. Known in many ancient cultures, magical squares were a way of expressing the order of the heavens in numerical values. Each magic square represents a planet or heavenly body, and the magic square's size relates to the planet's speed as it appears to move in the sky, from the slowest (Saturn) to the fastest (the moon). So, the magical square of Saturn is a 3x3 grid, and the magical square of the moon is a 9x9 grid of numbers.

The magic square of the moon has a total of 81 squares each containing a different number from 1 to 81. The numbers are arranged in the grid so that each horizontal, vertical, and diagonal line adds up to 369 (Figure 15).

Eighty-one is a significant number where the moon and the earth are concerned. The moon is moving through space at 81 times the speed of the earth; the moon at 2,268 miles per hour, the earth at 28 miles per hour. Also, the mass of the earth is 81 times that of the moon.

When you shade in all the uneven numbers in the 9x9 grid in Figure 15, you see a pattern identical to the seed pattern for drawing the classical labyrinth. The magical square of the moon holds the key to drawing the classical labyrinth, and is one of the reasons why the classical labyrinth is sometimes called Luna's labyrinth; Luna is the Roman goddess of the moon.

37	78	29	70	21	62	13	54	5
6	38	79	30	71	22	63	14	46
47	7	39	80	31	72	23	55	15
16	48	8	40	81	32	64	24	56
57	17	49	9	41	73	33	65	25
26	58	18	50	1	42	74	34	66
67	27	29	10	51	2	43	75	35
36	68	19	60	11	52	3	44	76
77	28	69	20	61	12	53	4	45

Figure 15: Magical square of the moon

The crop circle at Lewisham Castle clearly shows a seed pattern for the classical labyrinth with an equal-armed cross, L-shaped brackets in each quadrant, and four dots. However, the cross of the seed pattern in this crop circle is drawn diagonally, as opposed to the usual way of vertical and horizontal lines. If a labyrinth were to be drawn from this seed pattern it would appear at an angle of 45 degrees. Also of interest is that there are thirteen different square patterns in the formation. Thirteen is a lunar number as the moon travels around the earth thirteen times in a solar year. There appears to be three squares missing from each corner of this crop circle, although these could also be three "flattened" squares. It is not clear what significance might be attributed to them. Yet, as there is almost always an importance and meaning to every aspect of a crop circle, I eagerly await a full interpretation of this formation.

Labyrinth Cities

In exploring the interconnectedness of all of existence through the labyrinth, the associations that the labyrinth has with certain cities often reveals hidden connections and messages for us. Over the years, the labyrinth has been associated with, and even used to depict, cities such as Troy, Jerusalem, Jericho, Constantinople, Scimangada in Nepal, and others. There are several explanations as to why these cities have been represented by a labyrinth symbol, and there are a number of levels on which you can view these labyrinth cities and the insights that they can provide into your life.

Most commonly, the labyrinth was used to represent the defences of the cities such as Troy, Jerusalem, Jericho, and the fortress of Lanka in the ancient Indian epic poem, the Ramayana. The city is representing something valuable, something worth protecting, something worth an effort to seek out. Jeff Saward writes that "The labyrinth has often been employed as a symbol for the omphalos, the sacred centre or city" (Saward 2009). John James, in writing about the alchemical text *Ars Chemica* says, "God lies within the bosom of the city" (James 1977). Seeing the labyrinth as representing the city, the centre serves as a sacred place wherein God dwells. When you see the labyrinth as both a symbol of the city and of you, then Spirit resides within you, and you have to travel the circuitous path of the labyrinth of life to access it.

Troy

Labyrinths are sometimes known by names connected with Troy. The association between Troy and the labyrinth dates back as far as 600 BC when the Etruscan inscription "Truia" (Troy) was written within the paths of the labyrinth on a ceramic wine jar found at Tragliatella, Italy. The names "Troytown," "Trojeborg" in Swedish, and "Caerdroia" in Welsh are often used to describe labyrinths. Other Troy-related names that labyrinths have been called are "City of Troy" and "Walls of Troy."

Legend has it that the walls of Troy were impregnable, and so the labyrinth symbol may have been used to illustrate the complex and confusing construction of the walls and the difficulty in impregnating these walls. When you consider the most famous tales about Troy concerning Helen of Troy, both Helen and the labyrinth take on significant symbolism in the context of your own personal journey. Helen, who was stunningly beautiful, is symbolic of the beauty that is within you. The task of seeing this beauty in yourself is akin to breaching the labyrinth of Troy's impregnable walls. And that is what you do on your journey to wholeness when you seek, unveil, and accept the beauty that lies within.

Scimangada

The ancient city of Scimangada, in the Himalayan foothills in Nepal, had defensive walls that have been represented by a classical labyrinth. The walls enclosing the city were entered at one place. The way to the city passed four fortresses, placed at the ends of the two lines making up the classical labyrinth.

Despite the strength of these defensive walls, they were breached by treachery. The story relates how an aggrieved minister plotted to overthrow the king of Scimangada. He pointed out the weakest spot in the defensive walls to the army of the rival Muslim emperor. This spot was where the two lines making up the labyrinth cross each other. This is the spirit point in the seed pattern. If you cross the lines at this point you will be almost at the centre, illustrating to you that this story carries a message: directly seeking Spirit in your life can significantly shorten your quest for enlightenment.

Jerusalem

The associations of the labyrinth with Jerusalem appear to have originated in medieval times. Some cathedral labyrinths in northern France are called "Chemin de Jérusalem," or "Road to Jerusalem." The name most likely came from the practice of substituting a pilgrimage to the Holy Land with a pilgrimage to a cathedral city such as Chartres or Amiens, due to the dangerous nature of such a pilgrimage to the Holy Land at the time. Jerusalem is also renowned for its defensive walls, and the labyrinth formation may here also have been another representation of the city and its defences.

There is a belief that Jerusalem is the place on earth where God will reveal himself. When you see Jerusalem represented by the labyrinth, and the labyrinth as a symbol of you, then God will reveal himself in you. Jerusalem is used symbolically in Revelations 21:2 to describe man's redeemed state: "And I John saw the holy city, new Jerusalem, coming down from God out of heaven, prepared as a bride adorned for her husband." By having breached or destroyed the walls of the physical illusion represented by the walls of Jerusalem, you reach the true centre, the centre of knowing, the centre of understanding of all of existence, the centre of you.

Jericho

Jericho's association with the labyrinth stems from the story of Joshua and the Israelites' arrival at Jericho and the subsequent conquering of the city. As in many biblical stories, there can be several interpretations and layers of meaning. The story of Joshua and Jericho relates that after Moses died, Joshua was entrusted to lead the children of Israel into the Land of Canaan: the Promised Land. The city of Jericho was the first city they met, and a major obstacle in their way. The walls of Jericho were so high and broad that they were considered impregnable. The Israelites gave siege to Jericho.

In Joshua, chapter 6, we read that the Lord instructed Joshua as follows: "See, I have given you control of Jericho, including its king and soldiers. Have all the men of the camp walk around the city. Circle the city one time. Do this for six days. Seven priests will carry seven ram's horn trumpets before the ark. On the seventh day, you will circle the city seven times, and the priests will blow the trumpets. When the ram's horn sounds, when you hear the sound of the trumpet, let the people shout loudly. Then the wall of the city will fall down, and each person can go straight in" (Joshua 6:1–5).

It is significant that the number seven is found so prominently in this account. The Bible often uses the symbolism of the number seven to describe the human body and brain/mind. Interpreting this story on a spiritual level, the city of Jericho represents the mind, and the wall circling the city represents the division between your physical and spiritual self, a division that you are working to eliminate so as to integrate your physical and spiritual bodies.

The number seven also symbolises the seven main energy centres, or chakras, located along your spine. To progress on your spiritual path, your energy centres must be aligned and imbued with consciousness so that you recognize yourself beyond your physical presence or illusion. Seven was also important as it symbolised completion, in this case the completion of spiritual enlightenment. In raising consciousness through the seven gates (chakras) you experience true Christ consciousness, removing the veil of separation between the physical and spiritual aspects of your being. The walk around the city walls on the first six days represents moving through your lower six chakras. Walking helps integrate the physical and spiritual bodies, and walking the labyrinth expands your consciousness. By repeatedly walking in silence as in the labyrinth, your attention turns within. The power of meditative walking is in turning the focus inwards where you are preparing yourself for an experience of the Divine.

The Holy Land of Israel, or Canaan, can represent for you a spiritual life to be attained. As Jericho was the first city that the Israelites met after crossing the Jordan, Jericho can be seen as a symbolic barrier to your spiritual development and growth, an obstacle on the road to enlightenment. The warning to the Israelites not to rebuild Jericho is relevant advice for you also, as this would only lead to a return to the old ways and re-erect obstacles to your attainment of greater self-knowledge and understandings. A further spiritual lesson to be taken from the Jericho story is that by trusting in a power greater than yourself, impregnable walls can crumble and the "promised land" can be reached.

The culmination of the fall of Jericho involves a sound (trumpets and shouting) that ultimately brings down the walls, which only worked once the seven priests had walked around the city seven times. This is the climax of the story. You have moved your consciousness through your seven energy centres, and as the veils of separation are removed your physical and spiritual bodies are integrated. With one great sonic effort from every cell in your body, your mind is conquered/awakened, and you achieve enlightenment. When you walk the path of the classical labyrinth, the last circuit that you walk before entering the centre is the fifth, associated with your throat chakra. It is only when you have purified all your other centres that you can speak your truth and your words carry real power.

On a practical level, this story gives added meaning to doing something seven times, or seven times on the seventh day! Sometimes, things can take more than one attempt to succeed. It certainly illustrates that the number seven carries a certain power and energy. A further connection between the seven-circuit, or Luna's, labyrinth is that the name "Jericho" means "Moon City."

There are similarities between the stories of the fall of Troy, Jericho, Scimangada, and Jerusalem. While we can view these stories as purely factual, many myths and stories carry hidden meaning not immediately visible. As detailed above, these cities are representations of the true self.

The defeat of the city and the breaching of the walls is not necessarily to be seen as a negative occurrence. But, it is as a breaking down of the protective barriers that you have erected around yourself in the past. The accounts of trickery or treachery to breach the walls is a metaphor for the way to access the true you at the centre of your being. To overcome the dominant mind, you sometimes need to "trick" it by some unexpected action or approach.

Other cities associated with the labyrinth, such as Constantinople, Nineveh, and Babylon, have given their names to labyrinths in different locations. Such associations are generally related to the walled nature of these cities, especially those that at one time or another were held to be holy cities at the centre of the world. The analogy with your own divine centre is recognisable to those who can see.

Ancient Indian Epics: Mahabharata and Ramayana

The labyrinth features in the ancient Indian epic the Mahabharata that originated over five thousand years ago. The Mahabharata is an account of the Kurukshetra war and the fates of the Kaurava and Pandava princes. The Kaurava princes had Drona the magician devise a troop formation to help ensure victory. This formation was known as chakra vyuha, a labyrinth with a spiral at the centre drawn from a "Y" seed pattern. Chakra means "wheel" in Sanskrit, and Vyuha is a battle formation. Abhimanyu, son of the Pandava prince Arjuna, knew the plan of the chakra vyuha and fought his way to the centre. However, he had not learned the way out of the formation and was killed by arrows fired from all sides.

It is said that Abhimanyu learned about the chakra vyuha when he was in his mother's womb, but he did not learn how to escape from the formation. In the womb, the soul remains in contact with the spirit world and has ongoing direct access to knowledge and guides as support. While most incarnations result in loss of memory when passing through the veil of forgetfulness, this was not the case with Abhimanyu.

Having made his way to the centre of the chakra vyuha labyrinth, he had become at one with himself, and did not need to return. The account of being killed by arrows from all sides is a symbolic representation of letting go of everything related to the physical existence, and moving fully into an understanding of yourself as a spiritual being.

In the Indian epic the Ramayana, Sita, the wife of Rama was abducted by Ramana, the demon, and imprisoned in the castle at Lanka. Rama attacked the castle with his army of apes (and in some versions, is accompanied by the god Hanuman), then killed Ramana and saved his wife. After successfully storming the castle, Rama circles the ramparts seven times in Ramana's stolen chariot.

This account of a female character at the centre of a city represented by a labyrinth is similar to accounts found in other cultures. The woman at the centre of these city stories is representative of the feminine aspects of yourself. The walls and defensive systems show how difficult it can be to access the feminine and unite it with the masculine. The practice of circling seven times are symbolic of aligning and balancing your seven main energy centres. To fully integrate your masculine and feminine aspects you must also be master of your seven chakras. The seven-circuit classical labyrinth is a symbolic representation of both the stories and the practice of becoming at one with yourself.

EXERCISE: DEMOLISH YOUR WALLS WALK

This labyrinth exercise is based on the labyrinth as a series of walls that represent barriers to realization of the true you. Similar to going seven times around the walls of Jericho, each circuit of the classical labyrinth, or part of a circuit on the Chartres labyrinth, represents one of your defensive walls that you are symbolically demolishing as you walk the labyrinth. And it is not only a walk that breaks down the barriers for you to access your centre, it also demolishes the walls that separate you from the world, the universe, and all of existence.

Prepare for this walk by focusing on the unknown and unseen barriers that you are carrying with you. Hold the intention of them about to be demolished as you walk the labyrinth. Start your labyrinth walk, and with each step feel the wall that you are currently walking around begin to weaken. As you reach the turn on the labyrinth, visualize the energetic wall that you have allowed to build up around you crumbling to dust at your feet. Pause to allow this to happen and sink into your consciousness.

Move on to the next circuit and repeat the same process. Be aware of every thought and sensation that you are experiencing. Tune in and see if you can sense your walls beginning to crumble. As your walls begin to disintegrate on your walk you may begin to feel expanded and liberated.

On the other hand, you may begin to feel somewhat exposed. This feeling of being uncovered is because you no longer have the walls that separated you from the world. See these feelings and thoughts as revealing the real you to yourself and the world. Feel your connection to everything growing and expanding, merging into a feeling of oneness with all of existence. This is the feeling that you are aiming for, even if at first it may feel alien and unnatural to you. Focus on the positive and enlightening aspects of this unveiling, and allow yourself to feel the freedom of shedding your layers. If you feel uncomfortable at any stage, and not fully ready to lower all your walls, you can decide to stop knocking down your walls and continue on the walk, keeping some of your walls standing. You can always come back at another time and do this exercise again if you wish.

When you reach the centre, all your walls have been demolished. There is nothing, only you. You have revealed your true self to yourself. Focus on this connection with yourself and experience what it is like to connect with yourself. You can carry this feeling with you wherever you go, and you can access this feeling whenever you choose. When you are ready, begin your walk out of the labyrinth. You are now walking on a journey where the walls are still demolished. You are walking in heightened awareness. You are walking into a world where your awareness of yourself and your connections with all of existence are enhanced. As you leave the labyrinth give thanks for what you have received.

Reflection

Immediately after this walk take some time to remain in the feeling of having all your walls demolished. Write down what you now feel, and how it felt to bring down your walls during the labyrinth walk. When you are finished writing, pause, and consider how you are now feeling. Do you feel liberated or exposed? If you feel uneasy and not yet ready to let go of all your walls, you can consider if you wish to temporarily re-erect some walls around you before you fully re-enter your everyday life. Over time, and especially the more you practise this exercise, you will find less and less need to have any walls around you.

14

Awareness of the Intangible

We have considered many of the physical connections between man, earth, and the labyrinth. In this chapter, we move almost fully into the realm of the intangible. Your five senses (sight, hearing, taste, smell, and touch) will be less important to you than your sixth sense and all the senses that you possess beyond the five physical senses.

You possess several nonphysical senses. Some of these such as intuition, telepathic reception, and ESP are well known, while others are so subtle that they are often grouped together under the heading of psychic ability or intuition. Fully appreciating and accessing all that the labyrinth has to offer involves using all of your senses. These senses are your guides to interacting with and benefitting from the labyrinth and its consciousness field.

Oneness

Central to this book is the theme and concept of oneness: that all-encompassing, all-knowing, omnipresent existence of which we are all a part. Some of the earliest written theories of consciousness are those found in the Vedas, written by the Vedic rishis of ancient India. Their teachings are of an all-encompassing field of pure consciousness as a universal self, called Brahman or Atman. This field of consciousness was considered the whole cause of all existence and included within itself all individual human consciousness. This field of consciousness is accessed by using meditative techniques that allow the practitioner to experience union with the universal field of consciousness, often described as ultimate bliss. Walking the labyrinth is a meditative technique that helps bring about an altered state that brings insights and ultimately enlightenment.

Unified Field of Consciousness

The unified field of consciousness is another term for oneness. In the unified field of consciousness everything is interconnected—there is no separation. While you may have an understanding and a knowing that this is the truth for you, others require more tangible or scientific proof of its existence.

For years scientists, particularly physicists, have been seeking a workable unified field theory: a theory of everything that ties together all known phenomena to explain the nature and behaviour of all matter and energy. According to Michio Katu, a theoretical physicist at the City College of New York, those in pursuit of a unified field theory seek "an equation an inch long that would allow us to read the mind of God" (Rouse, n.d.).

Knowing the mind of God and becoming one with the ultimate Source is a spiritual quest that more and more people are recognizing as their primary journey. So, while scientists and physicists are seeking a theory and formula to identify and explain a unified theory, many on the spiritual path know in their hearts that everything is connected; there is ultimately only one. Indeed, there are some traditional societies that have held a belief and understanding of this one consciousness for thousands of years.

Scientists and physicists are getting closer to finding this ultimate proof. M-theory could potentially be the unified field sought by Einstein, reconciling the incompatible aspects of his theory of relativity and quantum theory. The "M" can stand for a number of things depending on who is describing it. The most common are "Mother of all theories," Magic, Mystery, and Matrix. I wonder what will happen when scientists prove the existence of the unified field. Perhaps it will be similar to many other scientific discoveries. People will accept what is within their sphere of reference and understanding, so those who believe and understand the scientific proof will accept it and those who do not, won't.

The concept of a unified field of consciousness has been described by Allen Roland as having three basic tenets. The first of these tenets is "the basic underlying healing force of the universe is a psychic energy field of universal love." Second, "the consciousness of the observer is the determining factor in being able to perceive the unified field." Third, that "the pain of not feeling loved for oneself and being seemingly separated from our original state of soul consciousness and the unified field" result in a left brain imbalance as well as the denial and forgetting of our connection to the unified field and the love and joy and a state of soul consciousness deepest within us (Roland 2014).

Within this field of universal love are found the four main forces: gravitational and magnetic fields, and strong and weak forces in the atom. As well as these, this field also possesses all other forces of nature and paranormal events such as clairvoyance, telepathy, precognition, and near-death experiences. The primary characteristic of this field of universal love is its propensity to unite, complete, and fulfil all living things with a constantly evolving loving plan. This field of love is the absolute in the universe, within which time and space do not exist, and we are instantly joined with the past, present, and future.

The depth of your sensory experience is what determines your level of consciousness, which in turn determines you being able to perceive the unified field. The more you surrender to what is deepest within you, the more profound a sensory experience you will have, and the more you experience the love and joyful state of soul consciousness. Your awareness of the field of universal love and taking responsibility for your part in it are fundamental to experiencing the unified field as soul consciousness. The state that can limit or deny your perception of the unified field is ego consciousness, where it appears that you are separated from your soul consciousness and the unified field. You could think of the ego consciousness as a protective shell that is gradually being shed, revealing the unified field as a type of all-encompassing matrix of luminosity joining together all of existence within its energy field of love.

The consciousness field of the labyrinth is an element of this unified field of consciousness, and is contained within it. Working with the labyrinth can bring you closer to and within the unified field of consciousness. The effect of the labyrinth in reducing the dominance of the left brain and bringing about a whole-brained state is helping you on your path of achieving understanding of, and union with, this unified consciousness. Within this consciousness field of the labyrinth you access a wisdom called labyrinth wisdom, which in effect is accessing your own wisdom as well as the wisdom of the ages through the labyrinth.

The essence of the unified field is it is everywhere. Therefore, the unified field is not outside of you somewhere, it is part of you. Your journey is to know that this field is all around you and within you and seek to become more and more a conscious part of it. Accessing this field at will is not always easy, as you may be carrying barriers to such access. Yet, as you are advancing on your spiritual journey, you are beginning to tune in to the nonphysical world. Your growing awareness of the nonphysical world is bringing you to the next step in the attainment of states of heightened awareness, or altered states. Your ultimate aim is to access such states when you choose, and eventually to reside in this state all the time.

For now, accessing the consciousness field of the labyrinth may not yet be something that you can consciously choose at will. By this I mean that accessing the consciousness field of the labyrinth up to now has "happened" rather than been intended by you. Some of this is because it exists on several dimensions at once, just as in M or string theory where strings can exist in multiple dimensions at once. Therefore, to access it, you must either tap into the field on this dimension, or elevate yourself to another dimension and access it there.

You start to access the consciousness field of the labyrinth by immersing yourself in the labyrinth and its effects. The level and depth to which you immerse yourself depends on how much you can allow yourself to access the knowledge and wisdom of the field. Your energy field is the key by which you unlock the levels of the consciousness field of the labyrinth. If there are blocks in your energy field, then these will hinder your access to some areas of the consciousness field.

The beauty of the labyrinth is that the more you use it the more refined you and your energy field become. When I began using the labyrinth, I often walked with a single intention or focus. If I was feeling unsettled, I walked to seek peace. If I was feeling sad, I walked seeking happiness. If I was feeling low, I walked seeking greater aliveness. At times, I walked the labyrinth with a question, or seeking insights to some of my life's issues. Other times, I just walked to be open to whatever experiences presented themselves to me. Looking back, I can see the pattern of my use of the labyrinth progressing to higher and higher levels: helping release emotional blocks and becoming clearer and accessing deeper parts of myself and of the consciousness field.

Your interactions with the consciousness field of the labyrinth is not one-directional. By working with the labyrinth and adding to the labyrinth experiences of humanity, you are enhancing and expanding the consciousness field of the labyrinth. Every new labyrinth activity: walking, tracing, drawing, painting, writing, et cetera expands further the consciousness field of the labyrinth. Every expansion in the consciousness field of the labyrinth brings it to the attention of more people. As the field expands, more people become aware of the labyrinth. Many people today are telling of how they are being drawn to the labyrinth. This attraction is a direct result of all the labyrinth activity up to this time. The benefits, insights, joy, peace, pleasure, and all other benefits that people receive through the labyrinth are enhancing the consciousness field of the labyrinth, and are then available to everyone else who accesses the consciousness field.

The consciousness field, while not tangible, is most certainly palpable. There is a certain presence that can be felt when in contact with the consciousness field of the labyrinth. The typical attributes of this consciousness field are a sense of heightened awareness—a focused attention in which you become more aware of your surroundings, your physical senses are heightened, and your perception is sharper and more acute. It is often recognized by a shift in the energy of the space in which you are present. When in conscious awareness of this field, you are knowingly operating at a higher level where the mind is quietened and you are receiving all signals clearly. Sounds, smells, sights, and even tastes are heightened. You feel more alive. And in feeling more alive, the quality of your life is enhanced. This is the space in which you can begin living a vibrant, fulfilled life.

Your greatest indicators and receptors for accessing the consciousness field of the labyrinth are found in your auric or energy bodies. These bodies are beyond your five physical senses, and constitute a subtle, yet at times profound presence that interacts with the space around you. The more refined your auric body, the further it penetrates the consciousness field. Your emotions, thoughts, and more are contained in your energy bodies.

While science has not yet developed sensitive enough instruments to identify and measure the energetic component of your emotions and other feelings, many people recognize how emotions can have a noticeable effect on their physical bodies. Terms and expressions such as a knot in your stomach, a lump in the throat, and weak at the knees are all physical experiences brought about by emotions. Teachers of energy and the auric field generally agree that weaknesses and issues in our energy bodies can directly affect your physical body. So too can weaknesses and blocks in your energy body affect your ability to access the consciousness field of the labyrinth, and the greater unified field of consciousness. To explore this area further, you first need to understand your auric or energy bodies.

The Aura and Energy Bodies

Your aura is one of the most important parts of your nonphysical existence. It is comprised of interpenetrating layers known as energy bodies, some of which can be seen by visibly sensitive people. However, even among those who can see some aspects of the aura, not everyone can see all your energy bodies, especially the higher-vibrating spiritual bodies. There are many classifications of the energy bodies. Different traditions and different schools have different names for the various energy bodies. Most schools have divided the aura into seven main parts, although it is not unusual to read of more layers, and even that each layer has seven sublayers.

Barbara Ann Brennan classifies the human energy field into seven levels, each with a different frequency of vibration. The three innermost layers (etheric, emotional, mental) are associated with our life as human beings, and the three outer layers (etheric template body, celestial body, ketheric template) are associated with our spiritual being, while the fourth layer, associated with our fourth chakra, the heart, is the mediator between our human and spiritual aspects. Brennan is clear that the layers of the energy field are not like the layers of an onion. She writes, "Each level penetrates through the body and extends outwards from the skin. Each successive layer is a 'higher frequency...' Each extends out from the skin several inches farther than the one within it of lower frequency" (Brennan 1988).

As you move out from your physical body through your energy field, each layer vibrates at an increasingly higher frequency. Indeed, as one comes to dwell more in the higher layers, approaching union with the Divine, then one's energy field becomes merged, and the levels become one. Your energy field is more like a continuum of energy with the lowest vibration and densest matter in your physical body moving gradually (and without any clear divisions) to the highest vibrating edge of your energy body—your spiritual body.

You do not always reside in only one layer at a time. You can occupy and move through layers depending on your state of being at any given time. Therefore, some days you begin the day primarily in the mental body with issues, thoughts, and other considerations on your mind, while you end the day in communion with your angels in one of the higher spiritual bodies. Moving up and down through the bodies is common, and the more you work on your personal and spiritual growth, the more time you will begin to spend in the higher spiritual realms.

Your Seven Light Bodies

You are a being of light. Your physical body is energy that has slowed and become dense so that it can be seen and touched. For the purposes of clarity in this book, I am using a sevenfold division of your energy body and using the following descriptions of your seven energy bodies beyond the physical: etheric, emotional, mental, causal, astral, soul, spiritual. The different layers of your energy body perform different functions. Understanding the different layers of your energy body can help you in identifying and healing weaknesses and blocks in your energy field.

The physical body is the usual starting point from which you explore and understand your other energy bodies. Your physical body is the body of matter that you see and touch. It is your physical eyes that are reading this book. It is linked to and surrounded by your other energy bodies. Your physical body enables your soul to act and perceive in the material existence. It serves as a base and connection for other parts of your energy field.

The etheric body is found next to the physical body and usually extends one inch from the physical body. It can sometimes be seen as a white shadow or glow around the physical body. It holds the blueprint of the physical body. It is a web of energy lines that create a structure around the physical body helping to maintain the health of the physical body. The etheric body can be weakened by factors including electromagnetic radiation, poor lifestyle and diet, and karmic patterning from the causal body.

The emotional body is found outside your etheric body. Your emotional body contains the feelings that you have about yourself and that you hold about others. Your emotions present as different colours in your emotional body. Common expressions such as green with envy, red with anger, and feeling blue often emanate from how certain emotions show up in your emotional field. Emotions can accumulate in your emotional body. Light emotions will present as bright and alive and moving, while emotions that are suppressed show as heavy, stagnant clouds in your emotional body. Negative emotions held in your emotional body can eventually impact the health of your etheric and physical bodies.

The mental body is where your thoughts, ideas, beliefs, and mental activity, both healthy and unhealthy, find expression. Your mental body responds to your activities by giving you thoughts about what is happening. A healthy mental energy body pulses with a bright yellow light. A heavy mental body can impact negatively on the emotional body below it. The thinking that you do generates a web of mental activity that can impact your emotional and physical well-being.

The causal body is your energy body where experiences, primarily those from past lives, are stored. It is sometimes called the karmic body. While the energetic imprint of past life experiences can be found and have an impact in many of your energy bodies, their root is in the causal body.

The astral body is the soul's vehicle in the astral realms, where we go after the death of the physical body. It is a field of energy that is being impacted by thoughts, feelings, and patterns from the astral levels of humans, nonincarnated beings, and the cosmos. It likewise can impact on these beings and fields of energy. It not only encompasses the lower vibrational energy bodies, but is also integrated through them.

The soul body is the house of your soul on a spiritual level. It is where you receive and process soul guidance from your other bodies, and from other sources such as your guides. It is your energy body that holds your intuition, guidance, and knowingness, and where you act on this information. It is where you come to a final decision about your soul's journey in relation to the information received. The more you progress on your spiritual path, the more you operate in this energy body. It is not always easy to reach or stay in this body as you can be preoccupied with the denser energies of your lower energy bodies that make it difficult for you to access this energy body. At this level, you feel immense love that goes beyond duality. When you awaken to the consciousness of this energy body, you begin operating from your soul consciousness, seeing all other people as souls, and seeing their actions as their learnings on their soul journeys.

Your spiritual body, which I also call the oneness body, is the level of your being that understands and experiences your existence as being at one with the divine mind. It is at this level that you operate in pure consciousness and create infinite realities. When in this energy body, you see the divine plan in everything that happens, and know your true nature, feeling your connectedness with all of existence. Your spiritual body contains within it all your other bodies. It is also everyone else's oneness body, for when you are in oneness there is no separation. Your spiritual body is a body of potential, holding the image of oneness for you. As a soul incarnating in a physical body, you may only briefly touch on your spiritual body from time to time. Yet you have a knowing that it exists and that your purpose is to be fully engulfed in your spiritual body and be merged with all that is.

Your Energy Bodies and the Labyrinth

Your energy bodies correlate with the circuits of the classical labyrinth starting with the physical body at the centre with the next closest the etheric body, then your emotional, mental, causal, astral, soul, and spiritual bodies. The labyrinth is a container that holds all of you, while outside the outer circuit of the labyrinth is a symbolic representation of the nonexistent boundaries of all of existence.

Layering your energy bodies onto the labyrinth sets a course for your soul's journey to incarnate in human form. When you are in the spirit world and ready to go to earth for another lifetime the path of the labyrinth shows the stages that you go through. Placing your future physical body at the centre of the labyrinth, you move through your energy bodies in the following sequence: astral, soul, spiritual, causal, etheric, emotional, mental, and physical. When you enter the labyrinth on the third circuit, you are in your astral body, which is your soul's vehicle in the astral realms. Next you move out to access your soul body, where you take on the information from guides and learnings from past experiences. You then move into the outer circuit of the labyrinth representing your spiritual/oneness body and encompassing not only all the labyrinth and you within it, but also representing the ultimate goal of your soul's journey to which your incarnation will bring you closer.

Next you jump into the fourth circuit and your causal body. It is here that you deposit past life experiences for working through in this lifetime. As the body that you are to occupy develops in the womb you go to the circuit representing your etheric body where the energetic matrix for the body you are to occupy is being created. Moving out through your emotional and mental body circuits is a recognition of their existence and the part that they will play in your forthcoming life through your emotions and your mind. Finally, you enter the centre of the labyrinth representing your physical body for this lifetime.

When you use the labyrinth to map your soul's journey to incarnate, the journey out symbolically represents your journey through this lifetime. From the physical, you become a thinking being accumulating thoughts, ideas, and beliefs. You gather emotions through your life's activities and incidents. Then you begin to develop an awareness of your energy bodies as represented by the circuit for your etheric body. You move through your causal body accessing past life experiences that assist you to clear and heal in this lifetime. You move into the outer spiritual body touching on a growing knowing within you that there is only one and you are part of it. You move into your soul body and receive an understanding of you as a soul and everyone else in your life as a soul. Finally, you move into your astral body ready to leave this physical body at its death, so you can move on to the spiritual world and process all your learnings from this lifetime.

The labyrinth is a tool to consider your different energy bodies and understand their place in purifying your soul as your transformational process unfolds. As you consider the different energy bodies and their relatedness to your soul's journey, you begin to understand that your personal and spiritual growth is inherently connected to clearing and purifying your energy bodies. The more you work on yourself, the more your soul's purpose and plan will be revealed to you and, in particular, your soul's plan for this incarnation.

The seven energy bodies also correspond with the seven levels of Mithraism and the seven stages of alchemy. Moving from one stage to the next is indicative of increasing living in and functioning from the next highest vibrating energy body. Other belief systems also carry associations with the seven energy bodies, particularly the seven spheres of the Gnostics.

Gnosis—Seven Bodies

The original Gnostics lived in communities in the eastern Mediterranean in the late first century AD. They believed in the duality of existence: darkness and light, with God residing in the realm of light. They considered the soul containing the "pneuma" or spark of divine substance to be imprisoned in the physical body on earth; the realm of darkness. Gnosticism taught that salvation of the soul is achieved through gnosis (special or secret knowledge), usually dealing with the soul's relationship to the transcendent being.

Gnosticism taught that the soul travelled through seven "spheres" on its journey to incarnate on earth and the soul in man was encased in seven related but reversed soul vestments. Irving and Jonas wrote, "As in the macrocosm man is enclosed by the seven spheres, so in the human microcosm again the pneuma is enclosed by the seven soul vestments originating from them." They went on to write that the order in man is reversed: "What is outermost and uppermost in the cosmos is inner-most in man, and the innermost or nethermost stratum of the cosmic order, the earth, is the outer bodily garment of man" (Jonas 2001).

These seven layers can be seen as separating us from Spirit, or as a means for coming into union with Spirit. Related to our own energy bodies on a macrocosmic scale are the seven cosmic shells that Gnostics consider to enclose the earth, separating man from God. John Michael Wenzel writes that Gnostics consider that these are "the seats of the Archons (rulers), which are the seven planetary gods borrowed from Babylonian astrology. The Archons collectively rule over the world, and each individually in his sphere is warder of the cosmic prison" (Wenzel 1996). These Archons bar the way of the soul that seeks to ascend after death in order to prevent their escape from earth and their return to God.

The true person is the innermost soul, whose origin is not of this world. The soul, or true identity, is so encased in these layers that it is not aware of its existence. Henry describes these layers as "vestments" or "soul-garments," and states that "the only escape is to acquire self-knowledge and to ignite the divine spark" (Henry 2006). Gnostics aimed to work through the layers in which man is encased and return to the natural state in union with the light. Knowledge of the spheres in which the earth is enclosed helps the Gnostic to understand what he has to achieve, so that he can open the spheres and pass through them and move towards union with God, just as when the body dies, the soul travels up through these spheres discarding each layer.

When layered onto the labyrinth, your journey has several similarities with the work of the Gnostics. You can see your seven energy bodies as being similar to those described in Gnostic texts. Awareness is gained through gaining knowledge and awakening the soul, just as you are doing with the labyrinth. Becoming more aware of these bodies is part of the process of working through the barriers associated with the seven cosmic spheres of the cosmic architecture. Labyrinth work assists you in becoming more aware of your energy bodies so that you can work with them and progress on your spiritual path, gaining enhanced self-knowledge and illumination.

EXERCISE: EXPANDING OUT THROUGH YOUR SEVEN AURIC BODIES

The exercise is designed to assist you in becoming aware of the seven energy bodies that surround your physical presence and encompass your soul, or divine light. This exercise is best done with a finger labyrinth, preferable one that you created yourself imbued with your energy, although you can also walk a labyrinth as part of this exercise. Because this exercise delves into your soul's purpose, ask for the assistance of your guides during this exercise.

Before you begin, read these exercise instructions from start to finish. It will help to memorize this order before you begin, as opening your eyes to read instructions during the meditation can be distracting. You could also record the instructions for the meditation by reading them out loud, and then listen back to them as a guided meditation. If doing this, be sure to read slowly and consciously, and allow times of silence for when you wish to be in silence in your meditation. Also, if recording this meditation for later use, be sure to include this statement: "You should not listen to this meditation while driving." Please note that this exercise is copyrighted and the recording that you make is for your personal use only.

With a finger labyrinth, trace the path to the centre of the labyrinth. This is symbolic of moving through the outer fields of your energy body to arrive at the core of your energetic and physical being. A key element of this exercise is going inwards and outwards simultaneously; as within, so without.

When you have reached the centre of the labyrinth, take several slow deep breaths. Now become aware of your physical body and sense the outer extremities of your physical body. See yourself in the centre of the labyrinth. Feel your presence in your physical body. Feel your hands, arms, feet, legs, torso, and head.

Slowly bring your awareness to your etheric body, your energy body that is immediately outside your physical body, most of which extends out about one inch. Allow your awareness to occupy the whole space of your etheric body. You may become aware of the connection between your physical and etheric bodies through tingling or goosebumps on your skin. See your etheric body as a clear bright light all around your physical body, and feel the aliveness in your etheric body. Scan your whole body to see that your etheric body is clear, and pour light into any areas that appear to you to be a little dull.

Next move your attention out to your emotional body, extending about nine inches out from your physical body. It is here all your emotions are found. Allow your mind to become still and see if any particular emotion comes up for you. If something comes to mind, release it with your intention. Allow it to dissolve into brilliant white light. If nothing comes to mind focus on seeing your emotional body as completely clear and bright.

Now move your attention out further to your mental body. What thoughts come to you? Are they positive, or negative? If any negative thoughts emerge, visualize them as existing about twelve inches from your physical body, and see them becoming filled with brilliant white light, and then dissolving in the light.

Extend your focus out further into your causal body. See if any specific thoughts, images, or feelings come up for you. If something arises, pause, and see if you get an indication that this has come from a past life. Allow yourself to receive whatever information is necessary for you to understand what you are receiving. Even if you do not receive any specific information, your focus is on having your causal body as clear as possible. See your causal body as a brilliantly clear field of light surrounding you.

Move out now into your astral body. The energy of this body is quite subtle and you may not be able to directly detect it. However, holding the intention of accessing this energy body will bring you into contact with it. As you contemplate this body and visualize your awareness in your astral body gently ask for any aspects of your soul's purpose in this lifetime to be revealed to you. Allow a few minutes for any information to be imparted.

Now move your attention out to your soul body. While you may not be able to visualize exactly where your soul body begins and ends, focusing on the thought of your soul body is sufficient to bring your attention to it. Your soul body holds the blueprint of your soul's purpose in this lifetime, and also how it relates to past and possibly future lives. Your soul body in this lifetime is connected to your guide who is currently working with you. Allow your energy and attention to rest in the energy field of your soul body and allow guidance from your soul's essence to be revealed to you. This can be very subtle so do not dismiss any thoughts that come to you.

Also, your guides can communicate with you through the energy of your soul body, so allow some time also for your guides' messages to filter through your energy fields into your consciousness. If you feel your thoughts drifting, refocus on your soul body to bring your attention back to this layer of your energy body. As already said, it is not always easy to reach or remain in this high vibrational state for long periods of time at the beginning.

When you feel that you have received all that you are able to receive at this time, and holding the highest vibration that you can, move your attention out to your spiritual body. Slowly allow yourself to merge with oneness. You have no thoughts in this infinite field and you are receiving information through your feelings and knowings. Allow yourself to become aware of whatever aspects of the divine plan that are being revealed to you. You are in a place of nonjudgement, and you are allowing everything to be.

Your spiritual body contains within it all your other bodies, and is your connection to everyone and everything. Even if you cannot easily feel your connection with oneness, your spiritual body is a body of potential, holding the image of oneness for you. It is always there for you. It is just a matter of time when you connect with and become part of this oneness. Practicing this exercise will help you initially to briefly touch on your spiritual body. In time, this connection will strengthen and the periods that you can spend there will grow. Ultimately, you will be fully engulfed in your spiritual body and be merged with all that is.

When you feel that you have spent enough time in your spiritual body, slowly begin to bring your attention back through your energy bodies. Allow your attention to settle in whichever body or bodies feel comfortable for you. Do not rush back into everyday activities, but slowly re-orientate yourself to your everyday life.

Reflection

Spend time after this exercise in a quiet space. This is a powerful exercise and you need to allow yourself time to process what you have experienced. This exercise involves working with very subtle energy bodies, so while you may not appear to receive any direct communication, interchanging of information is happening on a high level that you may not always be aware of.

Taking time to write down your experiences can help reveal what has been imparted to you. Furthermore, taking time to pause and write automatically when you feel the prompt is a useful way of recording what initially seemed inaccessible. Write down any thoughts, ideas, visions, and other aspects of your experience during this exercise. When you are finished, give thanks for becoming more connected with your energy bodies.

15
Cosmic Consciousness

Cosmic consciousness is an expansion of your consciousness in which you are fully aware of your interrelatedness with all of the cosmos. While it encompasses the physical cosmos, it is primarily an energetic consciousness that transcends the physical. It is as much an experience as it is an understandable concept. The labyrinth is an excellent tool for illustrating the many cosmic layers and dimensions and accessing this state. In exploring the layers of the cosmos inherent in the labyrinth, you gain a greater knowledge of the concept and bring yourself closer to the experience and state of cosmic consciousness.

There are several steps that you take to progress on your path to cosmic consciousness. The beginning point is often an awareness of your connection with the cosmos—a fascination with a specific star or constellation, perhaps. The initial attraction is often with one of the well-known constellations such as Orion or the Pleiades or individual stars such as Sirius or Polaris. This can indicate a transit point on your soul's journey to earth and can show that you are remembering some aspect of your soul's journey prior to incarnating on earth this time.

Your cosmic consciousness develops to encompass a connection with all of the cosmos. You begin to see the patterns and movements in the heavens that are reflected in your life—there is no separation between you and the cosmos. Cosmic consciousness brings into alignment all aspects of yourself and all aspects of the cosmos. In the words of Vera Nazarian, "When you reach for the stars, you are reaching for the furthest thing out there. When you reach deep into yourself, it is the same thing, but in the opposite direction. If you reach in both directions, you will have spanned the universe" (Nazerian 2010). Not only are you contained within the cosmos, but the cosmos is contained within you.

The sense of the planets and galaxies of the cosmos being within you is a powerful and humbling experience. When you have accessed this state of cosmic consciousness, even for a few moments, your understanding of your place and role in life shifts to a higher level and your realization of the interconnectedness of all of existence becomes ingrained in you.

As Above, So Below

Central to many religions and esoteric traditions is that heaven and earth are interconnected. This is summed up in the alchemical maxim "As above, so below," which originated in the Emerald Tablet of Hermes Trismegistus in ancient Egypt. The connections between the labyrinth and the cosmos span a range of scales, levels, and dimensions. The labyrinth is not just one representation of an aspect of the cosmos. It contains many associations with different aspects and parts of the heavens. The labyrinth is a map of the cosmos, a route map for astral travelling, a plan of Mercury's path in the sky, an astronomical calendar, and a model of cosmic consciousness. In exploring the individual relationships that the labyrinth holds with the cosmos, it is important to bear in mind that all the other connections exist at the same time. When you are interacting with one aspect, you are connected to all. And when you layer the already explored labyrinth aspects of you on top of these cosmic connections, the labyrinth becomes a vibrant symbol of your earthly and cosmic presence.

A Map of the Cosmos

The classical labyrinth has been used to depict the seven visible heavenly bodies with earth at the centre. They can be represented in the order as they appeared from earth with man at the centre and the planets in order of their closeness to man on earth: Moon, Venus, Mercury, Sun, Mars, Jupiter, and Saturn. The heliocentric view denotes the planets as revolving around the sun, with the sun at the centre, and each heavenly body placed in a circuit in accordance with their closeness to the sun, as follows: Sun, Mercury, Venus, Moon, Earth, Mars, Jupiter, Saturn.

In using the labyrinth to represent these planets, one is connecting with the energy of the planets while also journeying through them. This journey, as we have already seen, is also related to the alchemical path, and to the Mithraic initiation path. In each of these, the labyrinth is the connection between the heavens and the earth, and you are the catalyst for the interactions between them.

In *The Yoga Sutra of Patanjali*, a collection of aphorisms or sayings, one sutra says that "By practicing samyama on the sun one gains knowledge of the universe" (Prajnanananda 2011). Samyama may be described as the combination and interconnection of concentration, meditation and realization. In this sutra, practicing samyama on the sun helps you gain knowledge not only of the physical universe, but also of the seven planes of existence. When placing the sun at the centre of the labyrinth, and with the focus of your walk being on the sun, your labyrinth walk then is an exercise in concentration and meditation with the intention of realizing cosmic consciousness.

Zecharia Sitchin in his book *When Time Began* attributes the seven-day week and the significance of the number seven as related to earth to the fact that the earth was the seventh planet the Anunnaki encountered on their journey to the centre of our solar system. "Seven was the number that represented our planet, the Earth. Earth was called in Sumerian texts 'the seventh,' and was depicted in representation of celestial bodies by the symbol of the seven dots because journeying into the centre of our solar system from their outermost planet, the Anunaki would first encounter Pluto, pass by Neptune and Uranus (second and third), and continue past Saturn and Jupiter (fourth and fifth). They would count Mars as the sixth (and therefore it was depicted as a six pointed star) and earth would be the seventh" (Sitchin 1993). The seven-circuit labyrinth may actually be a more accurate representation of the journey through the outer planets of the solar system to reach earth, as the planets are almost never in a straight line; if one was travelling from outer space to earth and was to pass by each planet, the journey could be quite circuitous, just as it is in the labyrinth.

Your connectedness to the cosmos is multi-layered through your chakras and energy bodies. You are not separate from the cosmos. You are an integral part of the cosmos, and everything that happens in the cosmos is reflected in you. So, when learning about the cosmos, you are learning about yourself.

There is a stage that you reach in your understanding and experience of yourself and the cosmos that Alice Bailey calls the stage of love wisdom. "When this stage is reached and men realise the unity of the solar system not only theoretically but also as a practical reality with which they have identified themselves, then there is borne in upon their consciousness a something which transcends consciousness altogether and which can only be expressed by the limiting word identification. This identification is a cosmic and not a systemic process, and is itself sevenfold in nature. This sevenfold process for lack of a better term we call the sevenfold cosmic Path" (Bailey 1973).

Mercury's Orbit

The classical labyrinth is a route map for the planet Mercury's annual movements in the heavens as seen from planet earth. Sig Lonegren observed that Mercury goes direct (i.e., appears to travel clockwise in an east to west direction along with the rotation of the "fixed" stars in the sky) about three times each year, and goes indirect, or retrograde, about four times each year. He goes on to write that "this follows exactly the path of a left-handed classical seven circuit labyrinth" (Lonegren 2015).

He also draws the connection between Mercury, or Hermes, as the messenger of the Gods and the labyrinth. "Modern uses of the labyrinth permit us to receive messages from the Gods—answers to dilemmas that don't seem to yield themselves to rational, logical approaches." When you walk the labyrinth with the intention of replicating the movement of Mercury in the sky, you are tapping into your communication energy on a deep level. If you are looking for answers to questions that entail communication, this walk can be particularly insightful.

The Labyrinth and the Octaeteris

In many ancient traditional societies, time was often calculated by observing and recording "heavenly bodies." However, the two main heavenly bodies, the moon and the sun, had quite different cycles that didn't evenly match each other. The Greeks around 600 BC figured out a way of reconciling these differing cycles and introduced the octaeteris, an eight-year solar cycle that contains ninety-nine lunar cycles, so that at the end of the eight-year cycle the moon phase occurred on the same day of the year plus one or two days. Attributed to Cleostratus, who was born in 520 BC, the octaeteris contained five years of twelve months each, and three years with thirteen months.

However, even before the Greeks calculated the octaeteris, there is evidence that it was known to many ancient cultures. As it was relatively straightforward to calculate from observation of celestial events such as solstices and equinoxes, and some basic counting skills, it is not inconceivable that nomadic and "primitive" societies used such a calendrical system.

The relationship between the octaeteris and the labyrinth is explored by Lance W. Latham in an article entitled "The Classical Maze and the Octaeteris." Latham argues that the classical maze was "a common and dominant calendric pattern for many early societies. As such its choice was not arbitrary, and its exclusive use as a symbol of calendric structure and religious ceremony was assured for centuries" (Latham 2006). One can trace the path of the labyrinth related to the turning points of the sun beginning with the winter solstice as one enters the third circuit of the labyrinth at the start of the walk. There are eight turns to reach the centre, whereupon the walker, having no exit available, turns around and retraces the path making a further eight turns to bring the number of turns to sixteen, or eight for each of the winter and summer solstices.

The walker also generally slows down to take turns, just as the north and southward progress of the rising sun appears to slow down near the solstices. When associated with the octaeteris, the walker walking the labyrinth is re-enacting the path of the sun across the skies over an eight-year period. There is also a connection between the labyrinth dance and the sun's movements in the sky. Matthews writes that "Ariadne's dance was symbolic of the sun's course in the sky, its intention being by sympathetic magic to aid the great luminary to run his race on high" (Matthews 1970).

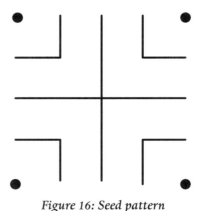

Figure 16: Seed pattern

As a symbolic representation of the octaeteris, the seed pattern of the classical labyrinth can be seen as a representation of an eight-fold division of time. The number of arcs required to complete the labyrinth is eight, while the number of endpoints and dots is sixteen, as can be seen in Figure 16. Indeed, it may have been that the commencement of recording the movement of the sun began with the first arc drawn near the centre of the labyrinth at winter solstice.

The eight-year period of the octaeteris is also quite synchronous with thirteen cycles of Venus around the sun, and with five Venusian visibility cycles or synodic periods. In other words, if Venus is visible beside the moon at the start of the octaeteris, they will both be close again at the end of the eight-year cycle. The ancient Greek name for Venus was Hesperus when it appeared in the west as the evening star. The Hesperides were nymphs of the evening star and golden light of sunset. They were also known as nymphs of the west, the direction that many ancient labyrinth openings faced. They guarded the golden apples beyond the ocean. Depending on the source, there were either three, four, or seven Hesperides, each an integral labyrinth number.

Ursa Major (The Great Bear)

Those familiar with the night sky and versed in navigation via the stars will know that the North Star, or Polaris, is found by first seeking out the Great Bear, also known as the Big Dipper or the Plough, in the night sky. In the northern hemisphere, it is via the North Star that you find your bearings and your way. Drawing a line between the last two stars of the "pan" of the Big Dipper creates a line that points directly to Polaris. In Patanjali's *Yoga Sutra*, it is written, "By practicing samyama on the polestar, knowledge of their movements is gained" (Prajnanananda 2011). Prajnanananda writes that the polestar represents the inner point of concentration in the ajna centre, or soul centre, or an experience of inner light.

Similarly, the labyrinth is a method of finding your way and navigating through the complicated earthly world. As you may see by now, everything is interconnected, and this connectedness between Ursa Major, Polaris, and the labyrinth occurs on several levels. While your initial understanding of the location of the stars in the night sky is to provide physical direction, they are also energetically guiding you on your life's journey. Each star represents a certain quality, and by using the labyrinth to journey through the stars and their energetic equivalent you will arrive at the fixed state represented by Polaris.

Here, at the centre of the labyrinth, you have found your place, and now you see that the world and the cosmos revolves around you. Polaris provides a point of re-orientation for you. From here you can make any readjustments necessary, and continue on your path in a more secure way. The stars of Ursa Major corresponding to each of the seven circuits in the labyrinth are Dubhe, Merak, Phecda, Megrez, Alioth, Mizar, and Alkaid, as shown in Figure 17.

Figure 17: Ursa Major in the labyrinth

The constellation of Ursa Major is intimately related to the number seven and its vibrational frequencies, and resonates with the cosmic labyrinth on many levels. Hindu tradition sees the seven stars of the Big Dipper as the abode of the Seven Rishis. Rishi means "the one who knows." Theosophy teaches that cosmic spiritual energy from the galactic logos is focused through the seven stars of the Pleiades to the seven stars of Ursa Major, and on from there through Sirius to the sun, where it is transmitted to the human race. In resonating with the number seven, Ursa Major connects you to the labyrinth and to all sevenfold connections found on earth and beyond. While the path does divide into seven, just as in the seven circuits of the labyrinth, there is in fact only one path leading you on.

Seventh Heaven

The labyrinth is your path to seventh heaven. In today's world, seventh heaven means great joy or contentment. In many ancient traditions seventh heaven was seen as the place where your soul is closest to Spirit. It has its origins in ancient teachings, and is derived from the highest of seven levels in the heavens. Judaism, Islam, Buddhism, and the West African Bambara people mention seven heavens or count seven levelsof perfection. As seven is significant from an earthly point of view and also from a cosmic perspective, the seven circuits of the labyrinth embody the seven heavens, and your journey through the cosmos: from physical presence to enlightenment.

Sufism has seven cosmic planes: Zat, the not-expressed; Ahadiat, the conscience; Vahdat, the self-interior; Vahdamiat, the internal light; Arwah, the spiritual plane; Ajsam, the astral plane; Insaam, the physical plane (Alavijeh 2013). Sufi whirling, or turning, is a form of physically active meditation through which dervishes aim to reach the source of all perfection. This is achieved through abandoning all desires, focusing on God, and spinning one's body in repetitive circles that is a symbolic imitation of the planets orbiting the sun. The effect of dancing is closely related to the experience of the walker in the labyrinth. As the dervish yields to the movements, their consciousness changes to assume a freedom from thought, just as the mind quietens during a labyrinth walk. Through the dance, the dervish understands the possibility of the eternity of the soul, while on the other hand the body is not denied.

Beyond the realm of the seven planets, there are further layers of cosmic connectedness to be found in the labyrinth. One of these aspects is found in the works of Alice Bailey and Djwhal Khul writing about the seven cosmic paths. Bailey writes that there are seven cosmic paths all of which lead eventually to the central spiritual sun: path 1, the path of earth service; path 2, the path of magnetic work; path 3, the path of planetary logos; path 4, the path to Sirius; path 5, the ray path; path 6, the path of the solar logos; path 7, the path of absolute sonship. These paths are for advanced souls that are masters of wisdom and compassion. As we progress and reach a higher point of development, the significant of the path unfolds and we choose a particular path to travel. Bailey goes on to write that "these seven paths, when trodden, prepare a man to pass certain cosmic initiations, including those upon the Sun Sirius" (Bailey 1973). Each path describes a method of work, endeavour, and aspiration where you pass onto "specific cosmic paths or streams of energy, making in their totality one great cosmic way."

The first path of earthly service involves respect for all life and reverence for the earth. It is an energetic path that involves harmonizing the dissonant energies of duality and requires strength of soul to alleviate the suffering of many beings. On a cosmic level it contributes to the advancement of humanity and planet earth. The second path of magnetic work involves the law of attraction and the use of the cosmic stream of energy to manifest the cosmic will.

The third path of the planetary logos comprises work to reinstate the original blueprint and "law" governing the earth's planetary body. The fourth path to Sirius is the path which links higher and lower mind bringing the energy of Sirius to earth through the sun. The fifth "Ray path" is taken by those with a clear understanding of the laws of vibration, responding to vibrations that contribute to holding our solar system in equilibrium.

The sixth path of the solar logos is the path the logos himself is on and is taken by certain sons of men who reach a high level. It means specialising in the inner sight, and the development of a certain measure of cosmic vision to work with the plan for the solar system. The seventh path of absolute sonship includes all who are close to the logos in a personal and intimate sense who have moved on to this seventh path. They know his wishes, his will, and his aim, and to them he entrusts the carrying out of his behests.

These paths are to be seen more as streams of energy, that blend and merge to form one path. So, while the labyrinth is a model of the seven paths, there is no real separation, as their combination makes the whole.

The Cosmic Consciousness Point in the Labyrinth

In addition to the seven circuits of the classical labyrinth representing many aspects of a sevenfold cosmos, there is a specific point in the classical labyrinth that represents cosmic consciousness. This is the eighth of nine turning points identified by Vincent Bridges. It is the turning point where you move from the fourth circuit into the seventh circuit, where you bring love from the fourth circuit into the divine connectedness of the seventh circuit. The cosmic consciousness point on the labyrinth is connected to trigger point number four, social. Just as the social trigger prompts you to enter into relationships on a human level, the cosmic consciousness point propels you into a relationship with "sentience on a galactic scale" (Bridges 2012).

You Are a Star

I wonder sometimes how information comes to us. I know that when my mind is quietened, thoughts and ideas seem to come to me out of nowhere. One such flash of insight came to me one morning while meditating. It was a realization so clear and so strong, that I immediately knew I had to write it all down and share it. The writing flowed easily, and when I stopped I had eight pages written. The main theme of what I received and wrote is that you have your very own star in the heavens.

There are over three hundred billion stars in the Milky Way galaxy. There are over two hundred billion known galaxies. Together that is an incomprehensible number of stars. If you consider that there are almost eight billion people on earth, there are many times more stars than there are people. There are plenty of stars to go around; and, there is a star in the sky that is just for you. As Frances Clarke says, "There wouldn't be a sky full of stars if we were all meant to wish on the same one."

Your Spirit Star

Your own personal star is called your spirit star. Everything comes from Spirit, the one absolute Source that has many names: God, Goddess, Universal Energy, the Source, Great Spirit, Brahma, Oneness, or whatever name works best for you. When you connect with your spirit star through the spirit point of the labyrinth, you are connecting to yourself on a higher dimension.

This connection to your spirit star serves several purposes on your soul's journey, and in your life on earth. It is a source of information and wisdom that you can tap into. It is a stopping off point on some of your lifetimes as you go between the spirit world and earth. It is a place of comfort and peace for you. That spirit star is your home base, your place of rest and refuge. Your spirit star is an energy that holds you and nurtures you when you are in physical form and when you are not.

Connecting with Your Spirit Star

You can find, connect with, and draw on the energy of your star whenever you wish. You can make and maintain your connection with your star through the labyrinth. You can also be connected to your cosmic power source during a Melchizedek Labyrinth Healing session. Your star connection is found at the node (the centre of the cross) of the classical labyrinth as shown in Figure 18. In the Chartres labyrinth, it is at the offset cross between the fifth and sixth circuits from the outside. When you enter the Chartres labyrinth, it is just beyond you on your right before you take your first 90-degree turn to the left, as shown in Figure 19.

Figure 18: Spirit point in the classical labyrinth

Figure 19: Spirit point in the Chartres labyrinth

The point in the labyrinth where you connect with your star energy is called the spirit point. This is the ninth and final point in the nine DNA triggers/turning points in the labyrinth that we saw earlier. You make your connection to your star in the labyrinth through your solar plexus, your power source, while standing on these points in the labyrinths.

While standing on the spirit point is the easiest and most direct way to connect to your spirit star, there are other ways to connect with it through the labyrinth. I found that drawing the labyrinth can automatically connect you to your star, although this is usually subconscious. Walking the labyrinth can also do this. If you want to consciously connect with your spirit star, then do the exercise at the end of this chapter.

If the thought of being connected directly to your own star seems a little strange to you, see if you can first find a connection with the cosmos as a whole. Go outside on a clear starry night and gaze at the stars. Allow your mind to quieten, and take in the vastness of what is appearing above you. There are billions of stars in our galaxy. They all have a purpose. One of these stars is calling you and connecting with you. It may also help to switch your thinking around being connected to a star. Ask yourself, "Why shouldn't I be connected to a star? If there are so many of them there, is it possible that there is one specially connected to me?"

Understanding your star connection is an aspect of seeing yourself as unique. When you see yourself as unique, everything in your life is happening because of you. The more you see yourself as a unique person, the more gateways to other possibilities open. When you leave this body, you can choose to return to your spirit star for a period of recuperation and rest. Returning to your spirit star does not mean that you are stranded there all alone, it just means that you can recharge your batteries much more quickly there. You are always connected to Spirit. Your spirit star is God's gift to you—your divine battery charger. Just as you have a guardian angel, you also have a spirit star. And as your guardian angel watches over you, your spirit star energizes you.

Once you have made the connection with your own star, it cannot be lost. You may not always be aware of this connection, yet when needed you can call on it. If at first you do not get this connection, don't worry. Hold the intention of this connection being made and allow the bond to form and strengthen. Initially, there may be some bandwidth issues that do not permit the full connection or download of energy. If you make a connection but the energy does not appear to be flowing, then focus on quietening your mind and allowing the energy to flow to your solar plexus. Walking the labyrinth helps strengthen this connection.

Labyrinth Star Connections

There are several other star connections with the labyrinth. The English healer Jack Temple had a labyrinth in the grounds of his healing centre. He identified seven significant turning points in the labyrinth. He dowsed for rocks to place at each of his seven turning points. He then dowsed to connect each of these to a specific star or constellation. The seven star constellations that he connected to were: Orion, Capricornus, Corona Borealis, Pegasus, Scorpios, Taurus, and Sirius.

Jack Temple does not indicate in his book if these stars are the associations in every classical labyrinth, or just in his own. "At each of these turning points there is a small stone lodged in the earth and pretty much grassed over. Every stone connects to a specifically dowsed for star or constellation and—coming from the same immensely ancient organic root—it attracts cosmic energy and a vibrant colour from a 'sister' star." He goes on to say that his discovery showed him "how the ancients knew that the labyrinth could be a kind of telescope, a means by which to read the stars" (Temple 2002). He further wrote that each chakra connects to a specific star, planet, or constellation, and labelled the labyrinth a "star trap." He compared the labyrinth to a gigantic magnet that pulls and holds the healing wisdom and power of many eons. He added, "we need this cosmic energy every bit as much as we need nourishment from food."

I have found that these star connections are not the same in every labyrinth. There can be different stars for each of the turning points depending on where the labyrinth is made, and on who makes the labyrinth. There is also a star connection at the centre of the labyrinth. The centre usually represents the star connection of the person creating the labyrinth and/or the star connection of the person for whom the labyrinth is being made. So for your own labyrinth you may have two places where the labyrinth is extra powerful.

In a book called *Between Death and Life*, Dolores Cannon, a regressionist with over forty-five years of experience in hypnotic research and past life therapy, recounts a near-death experience that was told to her by a woman called Meg. In this story, Meg had died in a hospital and had passed through to the spirit world where she was brought from the typical "tunnel" into another place. At one stage in her story, Meg went on to say, "I looked up and the sky was suddenly darkened, and it was filled with stars. Some were huge and some were medium and some were tiny, and they were of varying brilliances but not one outshone the other. Even if there was a tiny one next to a huge, brilliant one you could still see each with equal clarity. And I knew the stars were souls. I said, 'Well, where's mine?' And someone said, 'There it is.' I looked behind me and there was my star. It had just risen off the horizon. And suddenly I was there, in the place where my star was. And I felt like I was interwoven into fabric. In that instant, I knew that we were all totally connected and that no matter what happened we could not be destroyed. Even if something came and ripped the fabric, the fabric would hold. I knew that I could not be not be destroyed, nor could anyone else. That I was as I was as I am" (Cannon 1993).

Star Lines

Star lines connect you with the stars. Your strongest star line connects you with your own spirit star. You are shining through that star, and it is shining through you. It doesn't really matter where exactly your spirit star is, for when you look into the sky you will know. You will feel a special bond or connection in a particular area of the sky. The connection that you feel is the energetic bond, or star line, that exists between you and your star.

The labyrinth is a container that anchors these star lines to the earth. Certain turning points and other specific points on the labyrinth connect certain star systems to earth through star lines. The classical labyrinth is a vessel for holding and transmitting these star energies. Jack Temple was tapping into these star lines when he dowsed for constellations to connect with the turning points of the labyrinth.

You have at least one star line: your main, or primary, star line. As you become more aware and conscious of the energies of the stars, and as you work more with the stars, you will form connections to many different stars and star systems. When you are resonating with your spirit star, you are in a state of star resonance. This is an aspect of cosmic consciousness. Star resonance implies that you are resonating with the energy and vibration of a particular star. When you are connected to several star systems you can then choose at will which one, or ones, you wish to be in communion with at any given time.

When your vibration is synchronized with the energy of those stars, you are in a state of coherence and are also transmitting their positive healing energies. You absorb the healing energies from the stars for yourself then transmit that particular healing and loving energy to others. For example, I have a very strong connection with Sirius, which is connected to heart-based people. On a clear night, I am drawn automatically to it. I can look at it for ages, feeling a real connection. I know that I was there many times, and I know that I will be there again. When I was in Egypt in 2008 I was in the Temple of Man in Luxor one evening after dark. I was sitting in the "heart" area of the temple and was drawn to look up into the sky. It was a cloudy night and I couldn't see any stars. Then, a gap appeared in the clouds and I was transfixed by a brilliant star shining between the clouds. I felt a strong energy in my heart, as if my heart was expanding, and I knew that something special was happening. I couldn't identify this star as there were no other stars visible at that time. Then, the clouds began to disperse, and I was able to identify Orion. From there I confirmed that the star that was "calling" me was Sirius. I know deep within me that I came through Sirius on my way to earth. You also came through a star or star system on your way to earth.

Finding and exploring your own spirit star connections is an empowering and enlightening aspect of your soul's journey.

Stardust

You are stardust. As well as having an energetic connection to your own star, you are also physically connected with the cosmos. Every atom in your body is billions of years old. Your body is made of the burned out remains of stars that were released into the cosmos in massive explosions billions of years ago that found their way to earth. This stardust carries an energy that inextricably links you to the cosmos. You are resonating with all the stars from which your body was created and the vibration of your own personal star. Just as the stars emit light, so do you. You are emitting the light and love of many star systems.

Connecting with your star may sometimes seem detached from what is happening here. While your greater emphasis will always be focused on earthly happenings, there is so much going on beyond the earth that it can be difficult to understand or comprehend. The people of the light who are ready to connect and transmit healing star energy will know themselves when they are ready. You may already have heard the call. You have travelled your path in this lifetime, and in many past lifetimes, to bring you to this state of readiness. It is time now for you to look up, to connect, to draw down. It is time to be the connector, and the transmitter, that you came here to be. You are a Star.

Searching for your star is a wonderful journey to take and to be on. It is an exciting search that brings you into a state of heightened awareness of your place in the cosmos and the place of each and every star in the universe. The following exercise is designed to help you connect to your spirit star.

EXERCISE: CONNECTING WITH YOUR COSMIC POWER SOURCE

This exercise consists of walking the labyrinth to connect with your spirit star. Before you begin your labyrinth walk, hold the intention that you will connect with your spirit star. This exercise is best done on a starry night when you can see the stars in the sky. However, it can be done during the day, although this will often only give a general sense of the area of the sky where your star is located, and you will not be able to see it.

Walk the labyrinth attempting to let go of any obstacles in the way of making your spirit star connection. Walk with a sense of anticipation and expectation. Walk through the labyrinth as if you are travelling through the cosmos. When you have reached the centre, pause there for a few moments. Then, bring your attention to the sky above you. Slowly move around in a circle becoming more aware of the cosmos all around you. When you feel that you have established a connection to the cosmos, make your way to the spirit point (node) of the labyrinth. This is the centre of the cross in the classical labyrinth.

Stand on the spirit point of the labyrinth. This is where you connect with your cosmic power source. With your awareness fully on the sky above, slowly turn around in a circle, sensing where in the sky you are being drawn. You may feel something immediately, or you may find that you have turned full circle and are not sure if you have felt anything.

If you are certain that you have felt a connection to a certain area of the sky, stop when you are facing in that direction. If you wish to double check that you are feeling something, slowly move away from the direction where you found your connection and see if you can notice when you lose that connection. Then slowly turn back to re-establish the connection to the particular area of the sky that you were originally facing.

If you are not sure if you felt anything, pause for a few moments and try again. This exercise is also about heightening your awareness, so a little practise will help. It is also important to get out of your head, and to be focused in your heart or your solar plexus power centre. If you get any sense of a connection, trust that the bond has been made.

Whether or not you have found a definite connection with a particular part of the sky, you can move on to the second part of this exercise. This will either help you find your connection or will reinforce the connection.

The second stage involves bringing your attention to your solar plexus/ third chakra/navel area. When you have brought your attention fully to your solar plexus area, feel an energetic cord going from your solar plexus up into the night sky. Follow that cord in the direction it is going. This cord may go straight up in front of you, or you may sense that the cord is connecting with your spirit star in a different part of the sky. If you feel this cord turning, then staying on the spirit point, slowly turn around in a circle following the direction in which you are being drawn by the cord. Keep turning with this cord until you feel that it is stopped. This cord will lead you to your spirit star.

Again, if you do not feel anything, do not worry. Sometimes this can take a few attempts, especially if your mind is not fully clear or you are distracted in some way. You can repeat this exercise immediately or whenever you feel that you are ready.

When you feel that you have made your connection, stay in this connection and appreciate what you have joined with. This is your power source. If you wish you may draw down energy from your spirit star. You do this with your intention. You can also use your hands to reach out and catch the energy flowing to you and then bring this energy into you by placing your hands over your solar plexus.

When you have made the connection, stay tuned in to the energy and see if you can feel or sense anything. Be open to receiving insights or messages through your spirit star in any number of ways: telepathically, psychically, through clairvoyance, clairaudience, or clairsentience. Once you have made this connection you can draw on this power at any time. You do not always have to be in a labyrinth to make the connection, although being in the labyrinth makes it easier to establish and maintain the connection until you have perfected the art of connecting with your star at any time, any place.

When you are finished connecting with your spirit star, thank your spirit star for having made the connection. Then, slowly make your way back to the centre, maintaining the connection with your spirit star as best you can. When you are ready, slowly make your way out of the labyrinth. This walk out is symbolic of you returning to your everyday life with new insights, and, in this case, new connections. When finished with your walk, give thanks for what you have received—and smile!

Reflection

You have just completed a powerful exercise. It is helpful to acknowledge this, and to remember everything you can about the connection that you made. Once the connection is made, it is always there, although the more you practise having the connection, the stronger it will get.

Take some time after this walk while still focused on the connection to write down all your experience. You may find as you write that information, insights, and ideas come to you. Write down as much as you can about these and, if it feels right, write automatically. This walk can also enhance your understanding of your life's purpose, and empower you to start living it.

If you did not connect, write down everything you can about your experience during the exercise. This exercise is one that will eventually bring you to a connection, so writing how far you got will make it easier to go farther the next time.

If you are doing a second or third walk, then refer back to your writings to see how far you came on your previous walk. Always walk with an open mind and the expectation of receiving; then allow to happen what happens.

16
Consciously Creating

The labyrinth is a gift to humanity to be used for the benefit of all humankind. So far in this book you have been using the labyrinth to address your individual issues: to look at your own life events seeking answers and insights. You have looked at your relationship with others, with your environment, with the cosmos, and with all of existence. It is now time to look at using the labyrinth for the benefit of humanity. While this always begins with yourself, you are now ready to go further than you have gone before to using the labyrinth as a tool for creating the future of humanity.

The labyrinth has many associations with fertility, creativity, and the birth of new life. The labyrinth is a place of safety and rejuvenation from which creativity in its many forms emerges. For example, you might enter the labyrinth with the seed of an idea, then during the labyrinth walk that seed can germinate and gestate to bring you greater insights, and you emerge from the labyrinth ready to bring your idea to life.

You are living on the edge of creation. You are always creating. What you are about to do is create consciously and actively. Active creation is a conscious act, where you choose how you want to be and how you create your reality. You have a unique contribution to make to the advancement of our human family. William Blake summed this up when he wrote in his book *Jerusalem*, "I must create a system, or be enslaved by another man's. I will not reason and compare: my business is to create" (Blake 1802–1820). Your business is also to create.

Act of Creating

In reflecting on how I have been creating and contributing over the years, every thought, every word, and every deed of mine has created something. Many of my creations were unconscious and were not necessarily positive ones. I was not operating from my current level of understanding and awareness. Indeed, most of the time I was not aware that I was creating at all. As I began walking the spiritual path, I learned how I create in every moment. As my awareness grew I began to seek positive creating within myself, and from there to create for the benefit of humanity.

After working with the labyrinth for a short while, I realised the depth of insight and wisdom that was coming to me through the labyrinth. Through walking the labyrinth, insights into a different way of being emerged. Then as I realised the benefits of these insights to others, I began bringing the labyrinth to people. I held workshops to teach people about the labyrinth. I designed, created, and built labyrinths. I also started painting labyrinth images. I have no art training and wasn't even sure if I could draw or paint until I began. Some of my early paintings were not very good, yet others seemed to carry an energy of something greater than what I was putting into them. I could see and feel that the images I painted were coming from some place deep inside me, or even from within the greater consciousness field of the labyrinth. The labyrinth enhanced and empowered my creativity in this area.

You too have the potential within you to do what you think at first you cannot do. There is something that you are here to create. It may not be art, but it could be writing a book, playing music, creating a beautiful garden, singing, or some other activity that enlivens you and inspires others. Other less recognised acts of creating might involve developing a new method of working at the office, using whatever materials you have to fix something broken, or putting together whatever ingredients are available to make dinner. You just need to start, and once started, it is just like walking a labyrinth, taking one step at a time.

The labyrinth assists you in creating space for the new. It meets you where you are at, and helps open a door to the next most appropriate level of knowledge, wisdom, and understanding. When you have reached, or can touch, the stage where you are aware of your thoughts, your actions, and your part in creating your reality, then you can actively begin creating the present and the future.

Evolutionary Creativity

Humankind has been evolving for several hundreds of thousands of years. The earth has been evolving for billions of years. The universe and cosmos have been evolving for approximately fourteen billion years. This evolution is continuing. All around you, evolution is happening: the earth is changing, society is changing, you are changing. These changes are not happening in isolation. All changes are interconnected. Change in one area is reflected, mirrored, or counterbalanced in another. You are part of this change. You may think that you are just an observer, watching all that is happening with wonder, or concern, or maybe even fear. But, as proven by the observer effect, being an observer affects the results.

The Observer Effect

In 1998 the Weizmann Institute of Science in Israel conducted an experiment on electrons passing through a slit. This experiment demonstrated that when under observation electrons are being "forced to behave like particles and not like waves. Thus the mere act of observation affects the experiment's findings" (ScienceDaily 1998). In the context of evolution, and in particular creative evolution, you cannot be an observer without also influencing the outcome. The very fact that you are observing means that you are contributing your energy to the experiment, the process of evolution.

Furthermore, what this experiment also means is that when you are looking at something at a quantum level it behaves like a particle, and when you are not observing it behaves like a wave, vibration, or energy. Therefore, everything in the universe is ultimately energy, and energy is influenced by the mind of the observer.

In the world of quantum physics, electrons and events are considered to have potential rather than physical existence, that is until someone looks. The act of observing, then, results in a determination as to which potential is realised. Therefore, all of existence is basically an unlimited quantum field of energy, of infinite possibilities. Everything is energy, and energy can be influenced by the mind. Your thoughts create your reality.

I was talking about this to a group I did a mindfulness class with and told them a story of when I was checking into my hotel earlier that day. I was in a hurry to get to my room and had a long walk from reception to my room. On the way to my room, I thought this key probably won't work. When I got to the room, the key wouldn't open the door and I had to go back down to the reception to get another key. The following day one of the people at the class told me that she was late going home on the bus after the class and needed to get home as quickly as possible. She was hoping the bus wouldn't break down. What happened? The bus broke down! This is how the Law of Attraction works. What you focus on most of the time, you get.

You now know that it is up to you to choose how you want to influence evolution. Your role on earth is to be a conscious creator of a new way of being. By consciously deciding and creating, you are playing your part in giving birth to a new reality. You are the next step in fourteen billion years of creation and evolution.

On the Threshold

Humanity is on the threshold of a quantum leap forward that will propel humankind away from the ego-based, never-ending striving for material wealth and growth. It is not fully clear what it will take for this shift to happen. Daniel Pinchbeck considers that it will "require a mutation in consciousness that can only be self-willed and self-directed." He further states that "according to this paradigm, it is as if physical evolution has done billions of years of work on our behalf to get us to this point. Right now, it is our choice whether we would like to go forward or fall by the wayside" (Pinchbeck 2012).

Kingsley Dennis thinks that the influences of a certain number of individuals who are in conscious contact and communication can create an exponential level of conscious force. These individuals are "now shifting up a gear and raising levels of awareness on this Earth at unparalled speed … The needed shift in collective and planetary consciousness is unfolding, it appears, according to the law of evolutionary design" (Dennis 2011).

If you are reading this book, then you are most likely one of these conscious individuals who is impacting on and contributing to the evolution of humanity at this time. You probably know other people or friends who are like-minded and living a life of personal and spiritual awareness and growth. As Dennis says, "It is required that we traverse two paths simultaneously; one path requires inward travel, while the other requires that we balance our outer lives so that our intellectual, emotional, and physical faculties are in a harmonious relationship" (Dennis 2011).

Furthermore, you are not alone. Your journey to greater awareness and connection is bringing you into relationships with certain people with whom you will be making a greater contribution than if you were working solely on your own. The work of contributing to a shift in consciousness happens more strongly in groups. You may find that you are drawn to like-minded people and that the conversations and energy around your interactions are contributing to raising the vibration around you and, consequently, of all of humanity.

Apart from talking, there are several tools that already exist that you can use to assist in your creative endeavours. When you incorporate these into your labyrinth practice, you create a multiplier effect greater than the sum of their parts. Two of these tools that we will consider here come from the ancient Vedic traditions and teachings. They are an understanding of the seven lokas, or planes of existence, and the use of the Gayatri mantra. Incorporating them into your labyrinth practices enhances their effect even more.

Seven Lokas (Spheres or Planes of Existence)

To create consciously, it helps to consider on what level you are creating and what has brought you to this point in your own journey of creation. Every day, new events happen without your conscious participation, but it is much more exciting to participate! Being aware of the levels of existence can further enhance your own creative forces and abilities, and put your existence in the here and now in context. In the words of Sri Krishnamurti, "What you are, the world is. And without your transformation there can be no transformation of the world." In other words, there is no separation between you and all of existence.

Certain ancient Indian texts, such as the Puranas, talk of the seven lokas or spheres that describe the universe. Sri Yukteswar, a master of Kriya Yoga, in his book *The Holy Science*, writes that the universe has been distinguished into seven different spheres, "commencing from the Eternal Substance, God, down to the gross material creation" (Yukteswar 1949). Moving from our sphere of physical existence, each loka is more spiritually advanced than the previous one. You can progressively move through these realms and ultimately merge with the Supreme Being. The lokas are sometimes known as the seven heavens, and each loka corresponds to a circuit of the labyrinth. The seven lokas as described by Sri Yukteswar are:

- Bhur Loka—Sphere of gross material creation: the physical world.
- Bhuvar Loka—Sphere just beyond the earth: the astral plane. The gross matters are absent from this sphere.
- Swar Loka—Heavenly Sphere: the sphere of magnetic auras. It is "characterized by the absence of the fine material things."
- Mahar Loka—Sphere of the Atom. This loka is the connection between the spiritual and material worlds. It is called Dasamadwara, the door.
- Jana Loka—Sphere of spiritual reflection, "wherein the idea of separate existence of self originates." It is called Alakshya, the Incomprehensible.
- Tapo Loka—Sphere of the Holy Spirit, the Universal Spirit, which is eternal patience, as it remains forever undisturbed. Known as Agama, the Inaccessible.
- Satya Loka, or Bhrama Loka—Sphere of God. God, the only real substance (Sat) in the universe.

The first three lokas (Bhur Loka, Bhuvar Loka, and Swar Loka) make up the material creation, sometimes called "the Kingdom of Darkness." The last three (Jana Loka, Tapo Loka, and Satya Loka) comprise the spiritual creation, "the Kingdom of Light." In between these is Mahar Loka, or the sphere of the Atom. It is the communication between the material and spiritual creation. It is called Dasamadawara (the tenth door), or Brahmarandhra, the way to divinity. The middle of the seven spheres, just as the heart chakra is the centre of the chakras, is the bridge between the physical and spiritual worlds. This is reflected in the fourth circuit of the labyrinth, that serves to symbolically unite our lower chakras with our higher spiritual chakras. It is also representative of the bridge between the alchemical lesser work (the spiritualisation of the body) and the greater work (the embodiment of the spirit).

The lokas are sometimes describe a little differently, with variations on their names. Yet their essence and existence remains predominantly the same. Sri Swami Sivananda describes the seven lokas as like "different kinds of light in a room such as kerosene oil light, mustard oil light, petromax, candle light, electric light; the various lights interpenetrate in the room," with each interpenetrating the matter of the plane next below it. The astral plane, or Bhuvar Loka, interpenetrates the earth plane and extends for some distance beyond it. And so on for each of the other planes. In the words of Sivananda, "In each plane the soul develops a new and higher sense of power" (Sivananda 1946).

He continues, "When you pass from one plane to another you do not move in space. You simply change your consciousness." He also writes that you have different vehicles, or parts of your energy field, that correspond to and function on the different planes. So, "In the dreaming state, your astral body functions. In the deep sleep state, your causal body functions." And as each plane is formed by matter in different degrees of density, using a subtler and different energy body you can function in any plane. And in the mental plane, you can get everything by "mere willing" (Sivananda 1946). Think of a person and he is in front of you; think of a place and you are there. There is no separation.

So, working to create depends on what level you are operating on. You can influence positive change on any level. And, your impact will be greater the more knowledge and awareness you have of the levels that you can create on. The higher a level you work from, the greater will be the effect that you have.

Working from Higher Dimensions

In the *Magus of Strovolos* we see Daskalos stress, "We must not confine energy into invisible matter or substance of the three-dimensional world. Because even invisible matter belongs to the three-dimensional world. We have also the fourth-dimensional, fifth-dimensional, the sixth and seventh-dimensional universes. The mystic is working with his superconsciousness" (Markides 1988).

He goes on to say that to affect gross matter you must "start working from the highest dimensions and descend through the lower levels until you reach the gross material plane. You must begin from the higher noetic world. The world of ideas, laws, causes, the world of noumena. From there you proceed to lower the vibrations. You pass through the lower noetic world, the world of images and forms. Then you reach the psychic plane and further down you arrive at solid matter." The labyrinth is a wonderful tool for raising your vibration, and for bringing you to a higher state of existence. In using the labyrinth to raise your vibration, you can then create from a higher level. It does not mean that you always have to exist and operate in these higher dimensions. Initially, it can take time and effort to reach higher levels of vibration. With practise you will find that you can exist and operate in a higher level for longer and longer periods until that state becomes your normal state of existence. Then you look to move temporarily to an even higher level. Initially for short periods of time, then longer, and so on to higher and higher levels.

The Gayatri

Om Bhur Buvaha Svaha, Tat Savithur Varenyam. Bhargo Devasya Dheemahi. Dhiyo Yonaha Prachodayath.

The Gayatri is an ancient chant from the Rig Vedas, which was written in Sanskrit about 2500 to 3500 years ago. It is found in Chapter 36, Mantra (verse) 3 of the Yajur Veda, and is also known as the Savitri mantra. The mantra is probably much older and may have been chanted for many centuries before that. According to ancient Hindu scriptures, the sage Vishwamitra was given the Gayatri Mantra by the Supreme Being as a reward for his many years of deep penance and meditation. This was to be a gift for all humanity.

The Gayatri Mantra is known as Vedamata, or Mother of all Vedas. The language, sound, and rhythm of the Gayatri Mantra make it the most powerful mantra for spiritual practice and enlightenment. The words of the Gayatri Mantra were arranged in such a way that they not only convey meaning, but also create specific powers of "righteous wisdom" through being uttered. The syllables of the mantra are said to positively affect all the chakras or energy centres in the human body. Chanting the Gayatri Mantra removes all obstacles in your path to increased wisdom and spiritual growth and development.

It is said that chanting the Gayatri Mantra purifies the chanter, and listening to the Gayatri Mantra purifies the listener. By chanting this mantra, divine spiritual light and power is infused in each of your seven chakras and connects them to these seven great spiritual realms of existence (Chandra-Shekar). It is also said that this sacred prayer spirals through the entire universe from the heart of the chanter, appealing for peace and divine wisdom for all.

Translations of the Gayatri

There are many translations of the Gayatri. The following two convey a sense of the source of power that is being connected with.

1. "May the divine light of the Supreme Being illuminate our intellect, to lead us along a path of righteousness" (Quora 2016).

2. Radiant divine soul from which we all came
   Awaken the same brilliant divine Light in me
   So that inner radiance consumes all thought and emotion
   Teaching and guiding me to realizing reality (Mehta 2016).

Understanding the Gayatri

Because of the detail and attention that went into the creation of the Gayatri, proper pronunciation and enunciation are important. When learning or downloading the Gayatri, seek to get as pure a version as you can. Each word and syllable carries a meaning and invocation. When chanting the Gayatri it is important to chant with understanding, intention, and integrity.

The Gayatri begins with the cosmic sound "Om"—the sound of creation. This is the divine sound, and salutes the nameless, formless, absolute One. Next come the words Bhur Buvaha Svaha that describe the physical, astral, and celestial planes. "Bhur" means the earth, "Bhuvah" the planets, and "Swah" the galaxy.

"Tat" again represents the supreme being. "Savithur" means the radiating source of life with the brightness of the sun. And "Varenyam" means the most adorable, most desirable.

"Bhargo" means splendor and lustre. "Devasya" means supreme or divine, and "Dheemahi" means "we meditate upon." "Dhiyo" is our understanding of reality, our intellect, our intention. "Yo" means "he who" and "Naha" means "our." "Prachodayath" means may he inspire, guide.

The Gayatri Mantra begins with the cosmic sound "Om." This gave rise to the seven Vyahritis of Gayatri, which enable man, living on the material plane, to rise to the spiritual plane of consciousness. Light is associated with consciousness, and in the outer world, the sun does the same work as the soul does inside us. Both include the process of awakening, so that when the soul is awakened into the consciousness of Brahman, we can see the light of Brahman. Thus, light and consciousness are inseparable. Also, the reference to light does not refer to sunlight only, but to the inner light from where the seven vibrations have descended from the "Brahma-plane" down to earth and living beings.

The Labyrinth, Lokas, and Gayatri

The Gayatri informs us that what is contained in the macrocosm is also contained in the microcosm—as above, so below. The light vibrations descended as seven planes of consciousness into man. These seven planes are represented by the seven circuits of the labyrinth. The labyrinth is a model, or representation of man—of you. You are a seven-layered being corresponding to a structure like the universe. These seven layers, or lokas, are your seven chakras along your spinal column. The seven vibrations of the Sapta Vyahritis are contained within the universal sound "Om"—the Divine One. Chanting the Om is an act of uniting you with divinity. It is a recognition and invocation of all.

When walking the labyrinth as the planes of existence, you return to the point of oneness at the centre of the labyrinth. Chanting the Gayatri while walking the labyrinth enhances this experience and supports the walker in their intention. The names of the seven lokas are sometimes chanted before the Gayatri. In the following exercise, you will use a combination of the labyrinth, lokas, and Gayatri to consciously create for the benefit of humanity.

EXERCISE: EVOLUTIONARY CREATIVITY LABYRINTH WALK

The key purpose of this exercise is to bring you as far back in time as you can experience and through all the planes of existence to rest at zero-point—the point before any material world existed, the point of infinite potential—and in the awareness of oneness in the centre of the labyrinth. Then, expanding from that point, to emerge from the labyrinth at the present moment of evolutionary creativity, ready to create what you want to create in your life and for humanity.

This walk is the accumulation of everything that is covered in this book. While it may not be always possible to be consciously aware of all the associations and connections, you will be carrying them subconsciously with you on the walk—a witness to the interconnectedness of all of existence.

This is a walk of conscious creation that takes you back as far as you can go in your awareness of your creation. From there, you expand to the being that you are today ready to play your part in the continuing expansion of conscious evolution. In your walk you will be going back to the point of creation and simultaneously moving up through the planes of existence to the highest spiritual plane.

The centre of the labyrinth is zero-point. Dwell in the centre of the labyrinth to be this point of infinite potential: live it; feel it; experience it until you are ready to manifest and create. If you are walking a Chartres labyrinth, you can further enhance your experience of this exercise by standing in each of the six petals and contemplating the realms they are associated with. By connecting with the realms of mineral, plant, animal, human, angelic, and divine you move through the ever-increasing vibrations of these realms and are ready to create from the highest possible level. When you stand in the centre of the labyrinth you are then at the point of nothing and of everything.

As you begin your return journey out of the labyrinth, you will draw on the latent capacities that are within you, accepting your individual and collective role and responsibility towards your future and the future of our human family. This is your purpose on this labyrinth walk: to consciously create your future and to participate in the creation of a new world view. In walking with others you are recalling the past exercises of being at one with yourself, with others, and with all of existence. Your walk out of the labyrinth coincides with the journey of the expansion of the universe. Indeed, this expansion of the universe marks your journey to this point, as you and the universe are one. Not only has the universe shaped the development of your physical being, it has also been involved in shaping your emotional, mental, and spiritual evolution, bringing you to where you are at this point in your existence. As you are an infinite being, your awareness of creation may extend beyond a mental understanding, and you may become vividly aware of the infiniteness of your existence.

The questions to consider on your journey from the point of creation are: What are you bringing out of yourself? What are you creating? What are you contributing to humanity / our human family?

To add power to this exercise, before entering the labyrinth you will consciously connect with the seven lokas by chanting their names. You are not only recognizing and honouring the planes of existence, you are also connecting to the energy of those planes to assist in your transformation and your creating. This is a multi-dimensional labyrinth walk, where you will be consciously or subconsciously connecting with all aspects of your creativity.

When engaged with a pure intention, you are also engaging these planes to assist in the transformation of humanity, raising the existence of all to a higher plane. Connecting with, engaging, and invoking the higher planes is done by chanting the names of the seven lokas. As Sanskrit is one of the most ancient languages, its sounds carry an energy and power. You will use their Sanskrit names when chanting, beginning with the gross physical world and moving through the spheres of existence with each world or sphere becoming more refined. *Om bhur, om bhuvar, om svar, om mahar, om jana, om tapa, om satya.*

By chanting the introduction, you're telling the energy created by Gayatri to progressively work through from the grossest physical level of your being to the highest, most refined aspect of you, purifying all. You become purer, more refined, and more translucent—divine in all aspects. Chanting the seven lokas harmonizes you with all the spheres of existence and prepares you for chanting the Gayatri, which raises your vibration and the vibration of your forthcoming labyrinth walk.

When you are creating, your thoughts and feelings are all that are needed. You do not have to use words. You just need to feel it in your being. Determine what it is that you want to create, and as far as you can get into the feeling of that creation. Think it, feel it, see it in your mind's eye. In the words of Abraham: "When you are consciously aware of your own thoughts and are deliberately offering them, then you are the deliberate creator of your own reality—and that is what you intended when you made the decision to come forth into this body" (Hicks 2007a).

To begin the walk, first consider what you intend to create for yourself and for humanity. Then, chant the names of the seven lokas. Chant the Gayatri seven times. When you are ready to walk the labyrinth, enter and walk through the circuits as representing you walking back to the point of creation. One way to assist you in this exercise is to see the first circuit as you going back through your current physical life. You can visualize, or work through, the next circuits as representing your previous lives where you incarnated, your existence between these lives, your existence in other energetic forms, your existence at the point of creation, your existence as a part of God.

When at the centre, chant the Om (the sound of creation) at least seven times. Start by making an "O" sound in your stomach, allowing it to rise through your chest finishing at the top of your head with the "M." Feel your whole body resonate with the sound. Your body is the bridge between heaven and earth; it is the alchemist's vessel, the cauldron of creation.

You are now merged with the divine creative force, and have begun your journey of creation. To be in the centre (the centre of the labyrinth and the centre of existence) is to simultaneously be at the beginning of time, and at your point of departure to something new.

When ready to bring your creation into being, begin your walk out of the labyrinth. Take as long as you need. You will be aware of how creation has evolved. Walking from the point of nothingness, see the cosmos being created; see the solar system being created; see the earth being created; see the rivers, lakes, oceans, mountains being created; see them still being created, as creation is a living thing. The earth is still creating. See the creatures of the earth, the fish of the sea, the animals being created; see the human family being created; see yourself being created in your current human body, and as you are brought up to the present day, see the new world being created. Visualize, think, and create the world in which you wish to live, the world you wish your children, grandchildren, and seven generations into the future living in. See how people will relate to each other, how they will relate to their environment, to all of existence. Allow your creative powers to create the best of all there is; the possibilities are limitless.

Pause just before exiting the labyrinth. As you exit, you are now at the edge of creation, about to re-enter your everyday world having created what you wish to be manifest. Then step out of the labyrinth into the new you in the new world.

Reflection

Seek a quiet space, and be in the awareness of what you have created and what you have experienced. Reflect on how you, as a divine immortal being, have created and are continuing to create in every moment, through big and little ways. Write down your thoughts, draw your images, and enjoy.

Take some time to bring your awareness back to your everyday life. Fully ground yourself. One great way to ground yourself is to use the first three stages of the Melchizedek labyrinth meditation. First, focus on your solar plexus. Bring your attention from there down to your second chakra and then into your root chakra, concentrating on the energy glowing from your lower three chakras deep into the earth.

17
Your Destination Is Your Origin

You are coming close to the beginning! Your path to self-discovery is one of beginnings and endings that in time merge into a complete state of self-knowing and being. You may think that this book is nearing an end, yet it is the beginning of something new and wonderful for you. In the words of T. S. Eliot in his poem "Little Gidding," "What we call the beginning is often the end / And to make an end is to make a beginning. / The end is where we start from" (Eliot 1943). Further on in the poem, Eliot writes, "We shall not cease from exploration / And the end of all our exploring / Will be to arrive where we started / And know the place for the first time." Your journey of exploration is just beginning.

In regards to this book and your labyrinth journey, you have come full circle. You have entered the labyrinth to access its wisdom, and you have returned. You have experienced beginnings and endings. Your experiences of these beginnings and endings are a microcosm of the endlessness (and beginninglessness) of oneness. You have experienced the alpha and the omega. You are back where you started, and yet you are not. For just as the exit of the labyrinth is the same as the entrance, you have changed, you have moved on, and you are now seeing the same place through different eyes.

You are not exactly the same person or soul that commenced this journey. You have evolved. You are never the same. All of the time there is movement. All of the time there is change. You have moved. You have changed.

You are unique. Only you have the qualities that you possess in the quantities that you possess them. You bring something special to the world. You bring your presence to the world. You are the only one who can do what you are here to do. You are the only one who can bring what you are here to bring. You are the only one who can share what you are here to share. You are the one.

In your journey of self-discovery, there is only you. While this may be a great source of reassurance, it also carries with it great responsibility. No longer can you wait for someone else to do something for you. The only one who can take your steps for you is you. While there is help along the way for you, it is up to you to take the first step. The more steps you take, the easier the next one gets. You now know that you have to take the steps that will bring you into contact with the people you have to meet. You have to take the steps that will bring you to the places you have to go. You know that you have to live and operate from that space of knowing deep within you that leads you to every place and everyone you are meant to meet on your soul's journey.

Your labyrinth path to self-discovery has brought you to a special way of knowing and being. When you think about who you are and what you are doing, you may feel like shouting a great big YES. You then start living your life in the knowledge that every moment is significant. Live in the vibrancy of every moment, in the wonder of every moment, in the aliveness of every moment, and every moment becomes vibrant, wonderful, and alive.

The Magic of the Labyrinth

There is one last aspect of the labyrinth that I want to bring to your attention. When considering the many settings and situations in which people have used the labyrinth over the centuries and millennia, there is undoubtedly a magical aspect to the labyrinth that cannot be fully explained. The magical qualities of the labyrinth have been called on in many different situations and uses.

Labyrinths have been used as protective symbol at doorways and entrances to homes, churches, and cathedrals. In parts of India there is a tradition of painting geometric and complicated art forms, including labyrinths, with rice flour on domestic thresholds. It is known by different names in different parts, such as "muggu" in Andhra Pradesh, "kolam" in Tamil Nadu, and "alpana" in Bengal. The threshold is a significant concept in the Hindu worldview. It not only represents a passage between one space and the next, but is seen as a bridge between the physical and the spiritual realms. The use of symbols on the threshold sanctifies the space and can affect the well being of persons crossing the threshold. Such symbols are believed to trap bad luck, illwill, and negative energy while also helping to cleanse and imbue the person passing over the patterns with good luck, positive energy and renewed spirit. The use of the labyrinth symbol in such spaces is another example of its cleansing and healing properties.

Hundreds of years ago, Scandinavian fishermen also used the labyrinth as an entrapment device. They built labyrinths on shorelines with the intention that any malevolent spirits that were attached to or following them would be ensnared in the coils of the labyrinth, so the fishermen could safely go on their fishing trip. Similar accounts exist in Sweden where the labyrinth was used as binding magic by shepherd boys as protection against wolves, and in Lappland for magically protecting reindeer herds against wolverines.

Scandinavian fisherman also believed that walking or running the labyrinth was beneficial to collecting strong winds. According to Pennick, the Scandinavian labyrinths were used for "raising the wind magically, giving protection against the perils of the sea and also increasing the catch" (Pennick 1990). Helen Curry writes that "wives of fishermen would run the labyrinth when bad weather approached and the fishermen were out on the water, to propitiate the storm energies drawing them away from the boats and into the labyrinth where they would do no harm" (Curry 2000).

The magician priests of the Batak tribes in the northern Sumatra part of Indonesia had small bark books of spells, some of which included images of the classical labyrinth. Next to the labyrinth in one of these books is an inscription that is translated to read, "This is the drawing that should be made on protective leaves, to send evil spirits home, to avert the magic of strangers" (Pennick 1990).

In another Indian connection, women in India have used the labyrinth to relieve pain, particularly in childbirth. The Chakra-Vyuha form of the labyrinth was used to focus the mother's attention. It involves rubbing ochre (saffron) with water and using this to draw the labyrinth pattern on a metal plate. It was then rinsed off and given to the mother to drink.

In England, there are accounts of wise women using what were called "Troy Stones" to achieve altered states of consciousness. The Witchcraft Museum in Bocastle, Cornwall, houses one such stone, which is a piece of slate about 15 x 45 cm on which is carved a classical labyrinth. Nigel Pennick related, "The wise woman would trace her finger over the labyrinth, back and forth, whilst humming a 'galdr' (ceremonial call), until the transcendent state was reached" (Pennick 1990). This Troy Stone was handed down from wise woman to wise woman, and the galdr used was kept secret. A related use of galdrs comes from Scandinavia where they were used by women for the practical purpose of making childbirth easier.

When all these protective and magical uses of the labyrinth are taken together, the labyrinth emerges as a powerful symbol for healing, transformation, transmutation, and protection. Similar modern uses of the labyrinth are beginning to emerge. The common practice of walking the labyrinth to ask a question and seek insights into specific situations could be viewed as a form of invoking the magic of the labyrinth to gain beneficial outcomes. My own Melchizedek Labyrinth Healing therapy is taking the use of the labyrinth to a different level of magic. The exercise at the end of this chapter is based on the traditional invocative uses of the labyrinth and designed to bring about positive transformative change in you, which brings you closer to self-realization.

It's a Dead End!

While walking a public labyrinth on the streets of Cork during a labyrinth festival, I was stopped by an elderly passerby who had been observing my walking and studying the labyrinth pattern. He loudly announced to me, "It's a dead end!" and indicated by his expression that I was engaged in a fruitless and futile exercise.

Having considered his observations many times over the years, I am grateful to this gentleman for helping me to see my labyrinth walking and my life in different ways to how some others see them. Perhaps on an immediate physical level, labyrinths and life look like dead ends. Yet, when you step beyond the threshold into the world of the unseen, the world of energy, the world of spirit, you are beginning a journey of exploration with infinite possibilities.

One man's ending is your beginning. The labyrinth is a multi-dimensional device where you can experience endings and beginnings on many different levels and dimensions. So just as the physical path of the labyrinth appears to end, a new path on another level or dimension is available to you when you are ready to enter it.

Every moment that you experience, every thought that you have, every word that you speak, and every action that you take is a new beginning. It is your choice whether you choose to see your life as a series of endings or beginnings.

Having travelled the path of the labyrinth in this book you may be asking yourself the question "Am I there yet?" This frequently posed question is one for the linear mind and presupposed a goal somewhere in the distance. Yet, the labyrinth is not linear. You are not linear, and your soul's journey is not linear. In seeking something outside of yourself, even via the labyrinth path, you are distracting yourself from the knowing that the ultimate "there" is "here" within you and all around you. Therefore, the question to ask yourself is...

"Am I here now?"

EXERCISE: YOU ARE ONENESS

This exercise is one that takes you to new levels and dimentions, and at times will bring you into a transcendent state where you experience oneness. Just as every labyrinth walk is different, each time you do this exercise you are different and so will have a different experience.

You will need a classical finger labyrinth, perferably one that you created earlier imbued with your energy. You can also use the labyrinth on page 259, one that you have printed on paper, or a finger labyrinth with a groove that you can trace with your finger. Before you begin, take a few moments to allow yourself and your breathing to settle. Then start tracing the path of the labyrinth at a speed comfortable to you. As you trace the path of the labyrinth say out loud: "I am Oneness."

Keep repeating these words in the form of a mantra while you trace the path of the labyrinth with your finger into the centre and back out to the outside. When you come back out to the entrance begin tracing the path inwards again so that your tracing is a continuous flow of following the path inwards and outwards. Trace the path while repeating the invocation until you feel that you do not need to do so anymore. When you finish your exercise take some quiet time for reflection.

Reflection

Sit quietly, allowing whatever thoughts, ideas, and anything else that arose during the exercise to come to the forefront of your awareness. You may find that you just wish to sit with the energy of the exercise and remain in that state for a while. If you consider that you had no experience—even better. Sit with this experience of nothingness.

When you are ready to begin writing, do so, and keep writing until you have nothing left to write.

Finally, give thanks for the labyrinth in your life.

Finger Labyrinth

Associations of the Circuits of the Classical Labyrinth

See chart on the next page.

Circuit	Colour	Chakra	Heavenly Body	Metals	Endocrine Glands	Alchemy Stages
1	Red	Root	Saturn	Lead	Gonads	Calcination
2	Orange	Sacral	Jupiter	Tin	Adrenals	Dissolution
3	Yellow	Solar Plexus	Mars	Iron	Pancreas	Separation
4	Green	Heart	Venus	Copper	Thymus	Conjunction
5	Blue	Throat	Mercury	Quicksilver/Mercury	Thyroid	Fermentation
6	Indigo	Third Eye	Moon	Silver	Pituitary	Distillation
7	Violet	Crown	Sun	Gold	Pineal	Coagulation

Appendix 2
Major Arcana and the Labyrinth Parts

Number	Name	Labyrinth Part	Short meaning and comments on the labyrinth journey stages
0	The Fool	Outside	Trust, faith, open to possibilities, choice, no fear, feeling protected. The Fool is outside the labyrinth as he is the one making the journey—not necessarily part of the journey.
1	The Magician	Short entrance path	Spiritual Father: representing new beginnings, sense of self, consciousness, starting something, using skills and talents.
2	The High Priestess	First turn	Spiritual Mother: female sense of self, inner wisdom, waiting, esoteric knowledge, self-reliance.

Number	Name	Labyrinth Part	Short meaning and comments on the labyrinth journey stages
3	The Empress	First path / third circuit	Physical Mother: feelings, self-expression, giving birth to something new; grounding your energies on the first circuit.
4	The Emperor	Second turn	Physical Father: leadership of self, sense of control, getting the best out of something; experiencing wholeness and unity with the self, integration of the elements.
5	The Hierophant	Second path / second circuit	Teacher: receiving your education from the Hierophant; intuitive guidance, truth and understanding, giving / receiving advice.
6	The Lovers	Third turn	Combining elements of heart and head, feeling and intellect; choice; relationships mirroring inner sense of worth; integrating masculine and feminine in self; passion—choosing what motivates to prove oneself.
7	The Chariot	Third path / first circuit	Setting off on a quest; self-control, harnessing all your forces towards your purpose.

Number	Name	Labyrinth Part	Short meaning and comments on the labyrinth journey stages
8	Strength	Short path to fourth circuit	Strength to continue; love for what you do; reaching goals; can represent first success—mastery of self and the world.
9	The Hermit	Fourth turn	Solitude: seeking and finding, completion of a cycle; holding the light for the way ahead.
10	Wheel of Fortune	Fourth circuit	Consequences of actions; things are already set in motion, unexpected developments, change in circumstances.
11	Justice	Fifth turn	Decisions to be made at this turn. Balancing all areas of your life; receiving consequences of past actions; insights from past experiences; possible new beginnings.
12	The Hanged Man	Short path to seventh circuit	Suspended action; Looking at things from another point of view; trials and challenges, leading to a defeat; sacrificing something; transition from one state to another.
13	Death	Fifth path / seventh circuit	Endings, new beginnings; painful endings that could crush, yet a time of transformation; giving up sense of self, merging with cosmos.

Number	Name	Labyrinth Part	Short meaning and comments on the labyrinth journey stages
14	Temperance	Sixth turn	Testing yourself, maintaining balance, blending aspects of your life in a new way.
15	The Devil	Sixth path / sixth circuit	Meeting the Devil on the path: adverse conditions, fears, doubts, self-imposed limitations, feeling trapped without options.
16	The Tower	Seventh turn	Upheaval, unexpected events, sudden change; not nice when happening, but miracle that saves!
17	The Star	Seventh circuit	First glimmer of hope; spiritual regeneration; living by own truths and values. Faith in self and the future restored.
18	The Moon	Eighth turn	The illusion of the Moon appears on the final turn. Bewilderment and confusion can arise from deep-seated fears and anxieties. Yet the way ahead is being lit.
19	The Sun	Short path to centre	Clarity, understanding, and wisdom prevail. Success and recognition of own achievements. Enlightened by the Sun.

Number	Name	Labyrinth Part	Short meaning and comments on the labyrinth journey stages
20	Judgement	Centre	Awakening to a new life. Discovery of reason for incarnating and ready to follow that purpose. Now time to decide if willing to fulfil his purpose.
21	The World	Node point	Point of oneness: everything emanates from the point of oneness represented by the central point of the cross in the labyrinth. The beginning and end of cycles. Order is restored.

References

Alavijeh, Ali Zamani. 2013. "A Comparative Study on the Significance of Number Seven in Different Social and Religious Contexts." *Asian Journal of Social Sciences & Humanities* 2 (4): 301–309.

Artress, Lauren. 1995. *Walking a Sacred Path: Rediscovering the Labyrinth as a Spiritual Practice.* New York: Penguin.

Attali, Jacques. 1999. *The Labyrinth in Culture and Society.* Translated by Joseph Rowe. Berkeley, CA: North Atlantic Books.

Ayrton, Michael. 1967. *The Maze Maker.* Bantam Books.

Bailey, Alice. 1973. "The Nature of the Cosmic Paths." In *A Treatise on Cosmic Fire*, by Alice Bailey. Lucis Press Ltd.

Blake, William. 1802–1820. *Jerusalem: The Emanation of the Giant Albion.* London.

Brennan, Barbara Ann. 1988. *Hands of Light, A Guide to Healing Through the Human Energy Field.* New York: Bantam Books.

———. 1993. *Light Emerging: The Journey of Personal Healing.* New York: Bantam Books.

Bridges, Vincent. 2012. *Notes on the Labyrinth, DNA and Planetary Alignment.*

Burckhardt, Titus. 1997. *Alchemy: Science of the Cosmos, Science of the Soul.* Louisville, KY: Fons Vitae.

Cannon, Dolores. 1993. *Between Death and Life.* Huntsville, OR: Ozark Mountain Publishing.

Chandra-Shekar. n.d. *The Magic of Gayatri.* http://www.magicofgayatri.com/pages/magic-of-gayatri.html.

Cumont, Franz. 1903. *The Mysteries of Mithra.* Translated by Thomas J. McCormack. Chicago: Open Court.

Curry, Helan. 2000. *The Way of the Labyrinth: A Powerful Meditation for Everyday Life.* Compass.

Dennis, Kingsley L. 2011. *New Consciousness for a New World: How to Thrive in Transitional Times and Participate in the Coming Spiritual Renaissance.* Rochester, VT: Inner Traditions.

Duryee, Kent. 2007. *The Man in The Maze.* http://www.coyotetale.net/mim/index.php.

Eliot, T. S. 1943. *Four Quartets.* Harcourt.

Fulcanelli. 1971. *Le Mystère des Cathédrales.* Translated by Mary Sworder. Las Vegas: Brotherhood of Life.

Gardiner, Philip. 2007a. *Gateways to the Otherworld.* Franklin Lakes, NJ: The Career Press.

———. 2007b. *Secret Societies: Gardiner's Forbidden Knowledge.* Franklin Lakes, NJ: New Page Books.

———. 2007c. *Secrets of the Serpent.* Foresthill, CA: Reality Press.

Henry, William. 2006. *Mary Magdalene: The Illuminator: The Woman Who Enlightened The Christ.* Kempton, IL: Adventures Unlimited Press.

Hicks, Ester and Jerry. 2007a. *The Teachings of Abraham Book Collection: Hardcover Boxed Set.* Hay House.

Hicks, Esther and Jerry. 2007b. "Ask and It Is Given—Perpetual Calendar." Carlsbad, CA: Hay House.

Incognito, Magus. 1918. *The Secret Doctrine of the Roscirucians*. Chicago: Advanced Thought Publishing Co.

Jacobs, Alan. 2005. *The Gnostic Gospels*. London: Watkins Publishing.

James, John. 1977. "The Mystery of the Great Labyrinth Chartres Cathedral." *Studies in Comparative Religion* (Perennial Books Ltd) 11 (2): 128.

Jonas, Hans. 2001. *The Gnostic Religion*. Boston: Beacon Press.

Jung, C. G. 1955. *Mandalas*. Zurich.

Jung, Carl. 1967. *Collected Works*. New York.

Kern, Hermann. 2000. *Through the Labyrinth: Designs and Meanings over 5,000 Years*. Translated by Abigail H Clay. NY: Prestel.

KJV, Bible. 1611. *King James Bible*. London.

Latham, Lance W. 2006. "The Classical Maze and the Octaeteris." *Caerdroia, 36th Edition*, 68.

Lings, Martin. 2005. *Symbol & Archetype: A Study of the Meaning of Existence*. Louisville, KY: Fons Vitae.

Lonegren, Sig. 2015. *Labyrinths, Ancient Myths and Modern Uses*. 4 Rev Upd edition. Glastonbury: Gothic Image Publications.

———. n.d. "The Benton Castle Labyrinth." *Mid Atlantic Geomancy*. http://www.geomancy.org/index.php/mag-e-zine/mag-e-zine-1996/no-2-summer-solstice/the-benton-castle-labyrinth.

Mariboe, Knud. 1994. *Encyclopedia of the Celts*.

Markides, Kriacos. 1988. *The Magus of Strovolos: The Extraordinary World of a Spiritual Healer*. Penguin.

Matthews, W. H. 1970. *Labyrinths and Mazes: Their History and Development*. New York: Dover Publications.

McGerr, Angela. 2008. *The Angel Almanac: An Inspirational Guide for Healing and Harmony*. London: Quadrille.

McGowan, Kathleen. 2010. *The Source of Miracles: 7 Steps to Transforming Your Life Through the Lord's Prayer*. New York: Touchstone.

Mehta, Anmol. 2016. *Gayatri Mantra Meaning, Benefits, Power.*

Melach, Frater. n.d. *Melchizedek King of Salem.* http://members.tripod. com/~Keter_Magick/melchizedek/index.htm.

Melchizedek, Drunvalo. 1999. *The Ancient Secret of the Flower of Life: v. 1 (Ancient Secret of the Flower of Life).* Light Technology.

Michell, John. 1988. *The Dimensions of Paradise.* Rochester, NY: Inner Tradutions.

Montana, Cate. n.d. *Labyrinths: Transformational Paths to Peace.* Accessed 2017. http://whatthebleep.com/.

Nazerian, Vera. 2010. *The Perpetual Calendar of Inspiration.* Los Angeles: Spirit.

Newton, Michael. 1994. *Journey of Souls: Case Studies of Life Between Lives.* Woodbury, MN, Llewellyn Worldwide, Ltd.

Olsen, Bjørnar. 1996. "Stone Labyrinths in Artic Norway." *Caerdroia 27* 24–27.

Ozaniec, Naomi. 2002. *Initiation Into the Tarot: A Powerful System for Personal Spiritual Awakening.* London: Watkins Publishing.

Pennick, Nigel. 1990. *Mazes and Labyrinths.* London: Robert Hale Limited.

Pinchbeck, Daniel. 2012. "The Intention Economy." In *Mysteries of the Ancient Past: A Graham Hancock Reader,* by Glenn Kreisberg, edited by Glenn Kreisberg, 310. Rochester, Vermont: Bear & Company.

Plutarch. n.d. *The Parallel Lives.* Loeb Classical Library edition.

Prajnanananda, Paramahamsa. 2011. *The Yoga Sutra of Patanjali.* Vienna: Prajna Publications.

Quora. 2016. *What is the meaning of the Gayatri Mantra.* https://www. quora.com/What-is-the-meaning-of-gayatri-mantra-How-can-it-help-someone-Is-there-any-scientific-reason.

Renander, Zara. 2011. *Labyrinths: Journeys of Healing, Stories of Grace.* Sarasota, FL: Bardolf & Company.

Renard, Gary R. 2006. *Your Immortal Reality: How to Break the Cycle of Birth and Death*. Carlsbad, CA: Hay House.

Rhodes, J. W. 2008. "Perceived Effects of Labyrinth Walking on a Variety of Physical and Emotional Traits, Additional Results." *Labyrinth Pathways* (Labyrinthos) 31–37.

Rigby, Greg. 1996. *On Earth as it is in Heaven*. Surrey: Rhaedus Publications.

Roland, Allen. 2014. "Allen L Roland's Web Blog." *The 12 Truths of Roland's Unified Field*. Accessed 2016. http://allenlrolandsweblog.blogspot.ie/2014/04/the-12-truths-of-rolands-unified-field.html.

Rouse, Margaret. n.d. *Unified Field Theory or Theory of Everything (TOE)*. Accessed February 2016. http://whatis.techtarget.com/definition/unified-field-theory-or-Theory-of-Everything-TOE.

Sanderfur, Glenn. 1988. *Edgar Cayce's Past Lives of Jesus*. Virginia Beach: A.R.E. Press.

Saward, Jeff. 2009. *The Centre of the Labyrinth*. http://www.labyrinthos.net/centre.html.

ScienceDaily. 1998. *Quantum Theory Demonstrated: Observation Affects Reality*. February 27. Accessed July 29, 2017. www.sciencedaily.com/releases/1998/02/980227055013.htm.

Sitchin, Zecharia. 1993. *When Time Began: The First New Age*. New York: Avon.

Sivananda, Sri Swami. 1946. *What Becomes of the Soul After Death*. The Divine Life Society.

Steiner, Rudolf. 1910. *Genesis: Secrets of Creation 1957 Edition*. Translated by Dorothy Lenn. London: Anthorposophical Publishing Company.

Stevens, Anthony. 1998. *Ariadne's Clue: A Guide to the Symbols of Humankind*. Princeton, NJ: Princeton.

Temple, Jack. 2002. *Medicine Man*. Findhorn: Findhorn Press.

n.d. *The Tree of Life.* http://www.corax.com/tarot/index.html?tree-of-life.

Thomas, Andy. 2004. *Numerical Magic in Two of 2004 Masterpieces.* http://www.swirlednews.com/article.asp?artID=748.

Tzu, Lao. 1963. *Tao Te Ching.* Translated by D. C. Lau. London: Penguin.

Ward, Geoff. 2006. *Spirals: The Pattern of Existence.* Sutton Mallet: Green Magic.

Wenzel, John Michael. 1996. "Early gnostic Christianity." *jewishchristianitylit.com.* April 24. http://jewishchristianlit.com/Courses/New-Test/Papers/Old/gnosticism.html.

Yogananda, Paramahansa. 1946. *Autobiography of a Yogi.* Self-Realization Fellowship.

Yukteswar, Sri. 1949. *The Holy Science.* Los Angeles, CA: Self-Realization Fellowship.

To Write to the Author

If you wish to contact the author or would like more information about this book, please write to the author in care of Llewellyn Worldwide Ltd. and we will forward your request. Both the author and publisher appreciate hearing from you and learning of your enjoyment of this book and how it has helped you. Llewellyn Worldwide Ltd. cannot guarantee that every letter written to the author can be answered, but all will be forwarded. Please write to:

Tony Christie
⅗ Llewellyn Worldwide Ltd.
2143 Wooddale Drive
Woodbury, MN 55125-2989

Please enclose a self-addressed stamped envelope for reply,
or $1.00 to cover costs. If outside the U.S.A., enclose
an international postal reply coupon.

Many of Llewellyn's authors have websites with additional information and resources. For more information, please visit our website at http://www.llewellyn.com.

GET MORE AT LLEWELLYN.COM

Visit us online to browse hundreds of our books and decks, plus sign up to receive our e-newsletters and exclusive online offers.

- Free tarot readings • Spell-a-Day • Moon phases
- Recipes, spells, and tips • Blogs • Encyclopedia
- Author interviews, articles, and upcoming events

GET SOCIAL WITH LLEWELLYN

Find us on   @LlewellynBooks
www.Facebook.com/LlewellynBooks

GET BOOKS AT LLEWELLYN

LLEWELLYN ORDERING INFORMATION

Order online: Visit our website at www.llewellyn.com to select your books and place an order on our secure server.

Order by phone:
- Call toll free within the US at 1-877-NEW-WRLD (1-877-639-9753)
- We accept VISA, MasterCard, American Express, and Discover.
- Canadian customers must use credit cards.

Order by mail:
Send the full price of your order (MN residents add 6.875% sales tax) in US funds plus postage and handling to: Llewellyn Worldwide, 2143 Wooddale Drive, Woodbury, MN 55125-2989

POSTAGE AND HANDLING
STANDARD (US):
(Please allow 12 business days)
$30.00 and under, add $6.00.
$30.01 and over, FREE SHIPPING.

INTERNATIONAL ORDERS,
INCLUDING CANADA:
$16.00 for one book, plus $3.00 for each additional book.

Visit us online for more shipping options. Prices subject to change.

FREE CATALOG!
To order, call
1-877-
NEW-WRLD
ext. 8236
or visit our
website

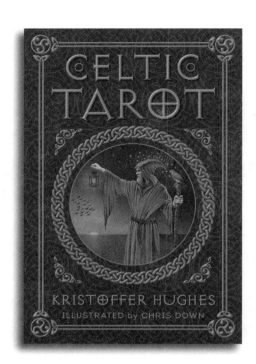

CELTIC
TAROT

KRISTOFFER HUGHES

ILLUSTRATED by CHRIS DOWN

Celtic Tarot
Kristoffer Hughes and Chris Down

Journey with the Celtic gods, goddesses, and magical allies into a world of enchantment and inspiration. This is not just a deck of cards; it's a storehouse of ancient myth and magic. With symbols, icons, and motifs designed to express and transmit the wisdom of the Celtic mysteries, this deck plunges the reader into the depths of the subtle planes. Kit includes a 78-card deck and a 336-page full-color guidebook.

978-0-7387-4476-6   **$29.99**

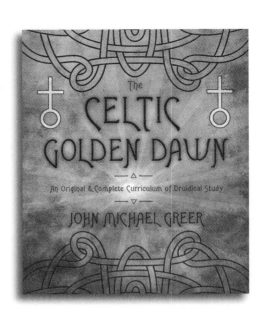

The

CELTIC
GOLDEN DAWN

—△—

An Original & Complete Curriculum of Druidical Study

—▽—

JOHN MICHAEL GREER

The Celtic Golden Dawn
An Original & Complete Curriculum of Druidical Study
JOHN MICHAEL GREER

A century ago, groups descending from the famed Hermetic Order of the Golden Dawn fused the occult lore of the Western magical tradition with the nature spirituality of the Druid Revival. They invoked Pagan Celtic powers instead of the Judeo-Christian names and symbols. Respected occult author and Grand Archdruid John Michael Greer has re-created a complete magical system based on the Celtic Golden Dawn traditions. This new book provides students with a complete curriculum of Druidical magic and occult wisdom, including training in ceremonial magic, meditation, pathworking, divination, geomancy, and herbal alchemy, allowing self-initiation into the three degrees of Ovate, Bard, and Druid. It features spectacular magical techniques for such things as invisibility, etheric shapeshifing, and conjuring spirits.

978-0-7387-3155-1, 384 pp., 7½ x 9⅛   **$21.99**

To order, call 1-877-NEW-WRLD or visit llewellyn.com
Prices subject to change without notice

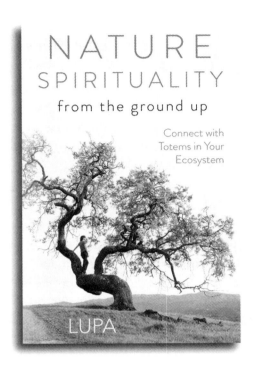

NATURE
SPIRITUALITY
from the ground up

Connect with
Totems in Your
Ecosystem

LUPA

Nature Spirituality from the Ground Up
Connect with Totems in Your Ecosystem
Lupa

Nature Spirituality from the Ground Up invites you to go beyond simply exploring the symbols of nature and encourages you to bury your hands in the earth and work with the real thing. This is a book on green spirituality that makes a difference, empowering you to connect with totems as a part of your spiritual life.

Uniquely approaching totems as beings we can give to, rather than take from, Lupa shows how orienting yourself this way deepens your spiritual connection to the earth and helps you rejoin the community of nature. And while most books on totems focus on animals, *Nature Spirituality from the Ground Up* helps you work with interconnected ecosystems of totems: plants, fungi, minerals, waterways, landforms, and more.

978-0-7387-4704-0, 288 pp., 5 ¼ x 8   **$16.99**

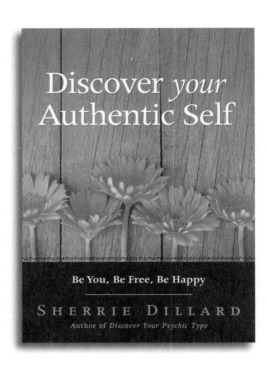

Discover *your* Authentic Self

Be You, Be Free, Be Happy

SHERRIE DILLARD

Author of *Discover Your Psychic Type*

Discover Your Authentic Self
Be You, Be Free, Be Happy
SHERRIE DILLARD

Embrace your authentic self and let your soul's light shine forth with guidance from 150 lessons meant to inspire, motivate, and teach. This empowering book helps you shed what is false and come to know, accept, and express your true self.

With essays to uplift and engage you through personal stories, meditations, exercises, affirmations, and question prompts, *Discover Your Authentic Self* shows you how to live according to your passions and purpose. Explore a range of topics for self-discovery, including intuition, spirit animals, recognizing personal abilities as related to archetypes, living your purpose, spirit essence and energy (chakras and auras), and more. With this remarkable book, you'll unlock your truth and set yourself free.

978-0-7387-4640-1, 360 pp., 5 x 7   **$16.99**

To order, call 1-877-NEW-WRLD or visit llewellyn.com
Prices subject to change without notice

DELLA TEMPLE

Tame Your Inner Critic

Find Peace & Contentment
to Live Your Life
on Purpose

Tame Your Inner Critic
Find Peace & Contentment to Live Your Life on Purpose
DELLA TEMPLE

Uncover the authentic you, control the critic within, and find the peace you need to live your life on purpose. Learn to silence the persistent chatter of your inner critic and replace it with the voice of your inner guidance, your spirit.

Tame Your Inner Critic takes you on a journey of self-discovery, exploring the energy of your thoughts and turning the negative into positive. Discover how to use your innate intuitive abilities to heal these energies and discard judgments and criticisms that have built up over the years. Find your true north—your own internal wisdom that is connected to the divine and gives you guidance. With specialized exercises and meditations, this book shows you how to banish negativity, improve your relationships, and realize new ways to share your gifts with the world around you.

978-0-7387-4395-0, 264 pp., 5 ¼ x 8   **$15.99**

Journey of Souls
Case Studies of Life Between Lives
MICHAEL NEWTON

Now considered a classic in the field, this remarkable book was the first to fully explore the mystery of life between lives. Journey of Souls presents the first-hand accounts of twenty-nine people placed in a "superconscious" state of awareness using Dr. Michael Newton's groundbreaking techniques. This unique approach allows Dr. Newton to reach his subjects' hidden memories of life in the spirit world after physical death. While in deep hypnosis, the subjects movingly describe what happened to them between lives. They reveal graphic details about what the spirit world is really like, where we go and what we do as souls, and why we come back in certain bodies.

978-1-56718-485-3, 288 pp., 6 x 9   **$17.99**

DJUNA WOJTON

KARMIC CHOICES

HOW MAKING THE RIGHT

DECISIONS CAN CREATE

ENDURING JOY

Karmic Choices
How Making the Right Decisions Can Create Enduring Joy
Djuna Wojton

Karmic Choices gives you the tools to get unstuck by designing an exciting, interesting, and productive life. With exercises, questionnaires, and Djuna Wojton's three-step karmic formula, this book will help you:
—Heal old issues and set new goals
—Go beyond self-imposed limitations
—Experience greater productivity
—Get support from friends, family, and professionals
—Create new strategies for lasting joy
—Take actions that positively impact the environment and the world

Release the blocks that keep you immobilized, and create a life you love. Develop your intuition and connect with your soul awareness. Open up to more satisfaction in your career, relationships, and in your self-expression. Djuna Wojton's law of karma brings a new perspective to working with the law of attraction to manifest the life you desire.

978-0-7387-3616-7, 312 pp., 5³⁄₁₆ x 8   **$16.99**

To order, call 1-877-NEW-WRLD or visit llewellyn.com
Prices subject to change without notice

"I believe what Kala writes about will be the science of the future. Intelligent consciousness, energy, and love are what life is about. So read, explore, and be educated."

—Bernie Siegel, MD, author of *Faith, Hope & Healing*

EXPERIENCING THE EVOLUTION
OF YOUR ENERGY BODY

The Awakened Aura

Kala Ambrose

The Awakened Aura
Experiencing the Evolution of Your Energy Body
Kala Ambrose

Humanity is entering a new era—we are evolving into super-powered beings of light. Our auric and etheric bodies are experiencing a transformational shift as new crystalline structures form within and around our auras. Kala Ambrose, a powerful wisdom teacher, intuitive, and oracle, teaches how to connect with your rapidly changing energy body to expand your awareness and capabilities on the physical, mental, emotional, and spiritual levels.

This book contains a wealth of practical exercises, diagrams, and instructions. Learn how to interpret and work with the auras of others, sense energy in animals, and sense and balance the energy in buildings and natural locations. Discover how energy cords attach in relationships, how to access the akashic records through the auric layers, how to use elemental energy to enhance your auric field, and much more.

978-0-7387-2759-2, 240 pp., 6 x 9   **$15.99**

MARGARET ANN LEMBO

CHAKRA
Awakening

TRANSFORM YOUR REALITY USING
CRYSTALS, COLOR, AROMATHERAPY &
THE POWER OF POSITIVE THOUGHT

Chakra Awakening

*Transform Your Reality Using Crystals, Color,
Aromatherapy & the Power of Positive Thought*

MARGARET ANN LEMBO

Bring balance, prosperity, joy, and overall wellness to your life. Use gemstones and crystals to tap into the amazing energy within you—the chakras.

This in-depth and practical guide demonstrates how to activate and balance the seven main chakras—energy centers that influence everything from migraines and fertility to communication and intuition. Perform simple techniques with gems, crystals, and other powerful tools to manifest any goal and create positive change in your physical, emotional, and spiritual wellbeing.

Chakra Awakening also features color photos and exercises for clearing negative energy, dispelling outdated belief systems, and identifying areas in your life that may be out of balance.

978-0-7387-1485-1, 264 pp., 6 x 9   **$19.95**